ANGEL VOICES

FROM THE

SPIRIT WORLD:

GLORY TO GOD WHO SENDS THEM.

ESSAYS TAKEN INDISCRIMINATELY FROM A LARGE AMOUNT WRITTEN UNDER ANGEL INFLUENCE

BY

JAMES LAWRENCE,

DIAL AND TRANSCRIBING MEDIUM

AND

REPUTED AUTHOR.

CLEVELAND, O:
NEVINS BROTHERS.
1874.

INTRODUCTION.

THEY who have attended the Spiritual meetings in Cleveland, remember a venerable man almost always present, of manners so *distingue* that the stranger never failed to point him out and ask his name. His bearing was erect and military; his hair and full beard of snowy whiteness; his mien dignified, urbane and courteous.

The frosts and storms, the sunshine and shadows of eighty-two years have been experienced by him. Yet, no one can see and converse with him without feeling that to grow old, like him, is to grow young.

His is the ripeness of the year prophesying spring; unlike that of the year the spring that is to come, is eternal. We feel the appropriateness of the departed ones coming to converse with one, who, after the years of a long and well-spent life, stands so near the threshold of the Great Beyond. Its light illuminates his soul with the dawn of the glorious day of eternal life.

He was attracted to the cause of Spiritualism in its infancy, more than twenty years ago, when it gave slight indications of the infinite power it was destined to wield, and when its acceptance brought only obloquy and reproach. He was not daunted.

by the frown of the populace, nor discouraged by failures. He investigated the subject thoroughly, became convinced of the Spiritual origin of the manifestations, and has ever since that day unflinchingly and consistently met the issue.

Commencing his investigation in a thoroughly skeptical state, he not only became convinced, but a medium for the Dial, through which instrument, I have received through him many communications, and as a writing medium through whose hand a vast amount has been written, on almost any subject mentionable connected with Spiritualism. For years he has given certain hours each day to this purpose, enjoying the highest pleasure in such communion. It has been with him a pastime, a season of sweet intercourse with those he loved and revered. He cultured their friendship and association, as he would if they were fellow mortals, yet yielded them the tacit reverence which their superior endowments called for.

When he says : "I desire to make my entire disavowal of the authorship of this book, having acted merely as an amanuensis to the spirit power, no one in the least acquainted with Mr. Lawrence will for a moment doubt his word. If he deceives, he is himself most of all deceived, for this communion has been to him for years the nurture of his life. They, who like myself, have been allowed the privilege of communicating through his mediumship with spirit friends, cannot doubt the correctness of their communications.

The authenticity of these essays, as referable to the sources they claim, is another matter, and undoubtedly will provoke criticism. The student of spiritual science, understanding the almost insurmountable difficulties in the way of the transposition of thought through media, and clothing it with fitting words, will not express surprise at imperfect results, but rather astonishment that even partial success crowns the effort.

His purposes have been honest, his efforts persevering, and his integrity without a shadow of doubt. One revelation alone through him will indelibly attach his name to the cause of Spiritualism. Through him, his guides first suggested the observance of the 31st day of March as the Anniversary of Modern Spiritualism. He presented the subject to the National Association, when that organization was vigorous and gave promise of a grand future. It was adopted unanimously by all Spiritualists, and will ever remain a marked day in their calendar, although the organization which accepted it has been numbered among the things that were.

Mr. Lawrence has nearly completed the task assigned to earthly life. Like a shock of ripened corn he awaits the hour he shall be garnered to the Spirit-sphere. His work is done, and well, and he has no fear or foreboding of the result. The pure and noble spirits with whom he has conversed these many years, will, he feels assured, welcome him to the immortal land. With his firm faith based on knowledge, death is but passing from one room to another, the laying aside the worn body as a faded garment, and the acceptance of a life freed from earthly trammels, of which it may be said, existence itself is a heavenly joy of which the insatiate senses never weary, and the purest aspirations of the soul are truly answered.

His spirit guides several years since urged this publication, but he, for various causes, has deferred its issue until the present. He now feels that this is the last important duty of his mortal life.

As some rugged pine, grand with the weight of its hoary years high on mountain summit, catches the last rays of the down going sun, and glows with prophesy of a coming day, so he reflects the light of the down-going years of mortal life, grandly prophesying the immortal future. He pauses, resting between the two worlds, physically in this, spiritually in the Beyond, and when his final work is done, will meet with joyous greeting from his spirit friends, who, by untiring effort have brought him thus far safely on his journey home.

Such we feel to be the ideal life—the fruit maturing on the parent stem—the labor of mortal life finished and done while here, and the spirit rounded and complete, in the fullness of years and ripeness of age, leaving the busy scenes of earth for the evergreen shores of continuous life.

HUDSON TUTTLE.

PREFACE.

In compliance with repeated injunctions from my Spirit Guides, I have prepared these essays for publication, and now present them to the public. Whatever of merit they possess belongs not to me, as I have only been from and through the organism conferred upon me by our great Creator, the instrument or medium used by the Higher intelligences of the Spheres above, to publish their thoughts and experiences—to show the interest they still have for this world and its denizens—and to proclaim the consoling and blessed truth to the vast legion of earth's mourners, that the spirits of their dear, departed ones are still hovering over and around them—laboring for their good—shielding them from danger—and guiding them by their influences from the teachings of superstition and degrading bigotry, into paths of truth and purity which lead to celestial bliss above, and enable them while here to attain a truer and nobler manhood and womanhood.

No higher ambition could stimulate me than to be able to avow myself the author of these essays. That I dare not do. Truth, which has been the pole star of my long life, demands me to disclaim that other than as a mere amanuensis of Ethereal Beings I have no share in this work of love to the human family. Yet, notwithstanding this disavowal of authorship, and in face of the declaration of my only relationship to these essays, I am prepared for disbelief, and, perhaps, censure from those, who, by educational prejudices, and warped sectarian principles, deny the possibility of such intimacy as I have enjoyed with the spirit world, and who question my right to differ from their convictions upon matters pertaining to the soul's welfare here and in the hereafter, thus proving:

> "The rarity,
> Of christian charity."

The truths of Spiritualism have been ridiculed, and sneered at, and treated as visionary; and believers in these truths have been too generally spoken of and denounced in language of the grossest character. These great principles deserve not such treatment, for their reality is as palpable to me as life itself, and I am as sure of their fruition hereafter, as I am that I must soon depart from this world. It is as an exponent of these truths this book is published. It was conceived in love—it is given in love by its celestial authors to you, and it is the earnest prayer of him who has been the privileged transcriber of their holy and Heavenly thoughts, that it may prove the instrument in God's hands of arousing a genuine spirit of earnest and honest investigation, and that these essays will receive a patient and candid perusal, that reason will be permitted to assert and exercise its sway untrammelled with bigotry, and unprejudiced by sectarian doctrines.

In conclusion, it is due to myself to state that I have no pecuniary interest to serve in this publication, as I am now and have been favored with sufficient for all my requirements;

neither have I any ambitious motive to gratify, as I am too near the grave, being over four-score years, to permit such feelings to exercise any influence upon me. Recommending this book of Essays to all investigators after truth, assuring them the Spiritual food they desire will here be found, that Angel help will be accorded those who, with singleness of heart, and sincerity of purpose, desire it.

As transcriber of this work I would express my regret at the necessity of curtailing the several essays from Jesus, St. Paul, Adam and others, owing to want of space. In my anxiety to show such spirits visit this sphere in common with all who are anxious to perform their allotted duty to God as His faithful servant, and to man as members of one universal brotherhood and sisterhood, acting in unison with each other for the benefit of all humanity,

I am, respectfully,

JAMES LAWRENCE.

ANGEL DEDICATION OF THIS BOOK.

TO YE, O Sons of earth, we come, greeting: Invisible to you, yet anxiously tendering our acquaintance, hoping it may in time ripen into friendship so firm and steadfast no doubts or fears can ever mar its force.

In confidence we come to thee, Oh, earthly ones, with full assurance, knowing the will of God, our Father, will be recognized by every grade of Nationality and clime, when in the fullness of time, the errors of the past will be but as by-gones, and so remain through all the endless cycles of eternity.

Friends, we come to you not in the spirit of disputation, but to present the facts contained within this volume, not in ostentatious mood, but in humility and truth, make proffer of it for investigation, courting a scrutiny such as the importance of the case demands.

No eulogy we crave, asking but justice for ourselves and total irresponsibility of authorship for our Medium, to whom we have incurred a heavy debt of gratitude as transcriber of these Essays under our promptings, meant to benefit mankind. A means appointed by the God of Nature, who, in times gone by, employed the pen of inspiration to make known to man His will, and claim a strict obedience to it, thus making manifest the glory of the Infinite. And here we ask, has that power become diminished? Is the law of inspiration less a law than formerly it was?

On such hypothesis we base our knowledge that all who once were dwellers on your earth can and do return to benefit humanity here, and in the grand hereafter. On such a subject proof is needed. Within this book it may be found. Regretting as we do, its incapacity to hold a larger portion of what our medium has transcribed; but as it is we would present it to a world needing knowledge of the hereafter, but lacking the desire to seek it.

Sent, as we are, to promulgate the glorious dispensation of Spiritualism, in fullest confidence that being of God it must prevail, requiring no commendation, but living in the hearts of all mankind, must generate the needed change, making this earth an almost Paradise in lieu of what it is at present. To this world we now would dedicate this Book of Angel Essays under the sanction of our Universal Father, God. AMEN.

SPIRIT INJUNCTIONS TO PUBLISH THIS VOLUME OF ESSAYS.

MY BROTHER : Often have I sought to come in holy rapport with thee, that I might reach thy inner soul and stir thee up to do a deed of duty to thy fellow-men, and justice to those invisibles whose efforts to improve mankind, through an organism well suited to their purpose, as a means by which a superstitious world might e'en be reached, and made more cognizant of Heaven and all its glorious realities; and while their efforts have been rendered almost useless by being withheld from public notice, what benefit have they been to those who needed them? Thy shelves are not the destiny of truths developed through thy organism under spirit promptings. A wider and more extended field of usefulness, we think, could soon be found by making such selections from the mass, that all mankind would bless the hand that penned them, and glorify the God who sent his holy angels to impart them.

My Brother, these are no idle words of flattering inducement to make the desired effort for their publication, but to energize thy soul to action in the matter, making it with thee a point of duty to thy God, the Angel World, and all humanity. Let nothing daunt thee in this glorious enterprize, but listen to thy angel friends who will aid thee in thy time of need, and give thee strength of body to accomplish a work of great importance to the world. But no delay must now occur. Time is passing swiftly. Thou art, even now, a wonder as regards thy health and strength, but for a wise and holy purpose, a larger share of vital magnetism has been allotted thee, on which thou hast depended, being to thy mentality what material food is to the physique, and for this glorious purpose hast thou drank from a fountain never dry, but always clear and pure as when it issued from a source from whence impurity can never come.

And now, My Brother, let me say to you, under all your difficulties and trials, through a longer life than usual, can you not trace a guiding hand stretched forth to recuperate your wasted strength, and give to tired nature its needed rest, so that with confidence and holy faith you might rely for aid when needed? and can you now so late in life become a doubter, and lose all faith in spirit power to carry on a work they have commenced successfully? Away! we say, with every doubt! Lose not the precious moment given thee to carry on a work most useful to mankind, for nations yet unborn, will rise and bless thy name as the reputed author of more truthful transcripts than ages have produced through human organism.

Now, but one word more: thy health is good, thy means are adequate, time thou'lt have to effect thy allotted work; angels and men will thank thee, and God, thy God, and the God of all humanity, will, in time, reward thee, for, as his servant, thou wilt have performed thy duty. AMEN.

ERRATA.

Page 84, line six, for "your altars" read "the altars."

Page 88, line twenty-two, for "leaving hopes" read "leaving tropes."

Page 92, line thirteen, "for which" read "on which."

Page 92, line thirteen, for "which depended" read "on which depended."

Page 109, sentence from line ten to line seventeen should read, "Such a theory might pass with the uncultivated intelligence of the times when Moses wrote, but in these days of research and analysis man's reasoning powers and clearness of perception denounce the statement as false and absurd, though ostensibly from the highest authority, even from God himself."

Page 123, line five, for "partly carried" read "partly earned."

Page 132, line two, for "Christly mortal" read "Christly model."

Page 139, line eight, for "Give us, we say," read "Give us, they say."

Page 242, line twelve, for "I almost forgot" read "I almost forget."

Page 238, lines eleven and twelve, for "horrors most foul" read "errors most foul."

Page 256, line seventeen, for "would enhance its truth" read "would not enhance its truth."

Page 266, line six, for "unirritated wounds" read "irritated wounds."

Page 267, line two, for "due monotony" read "dull monotony."

Page 274, line 18, for "furiously prepared" read "previously prepared."

Page 273, line fourteen, for "voilence is due" read "violence is due."

Page 274, line 12, for "modern share" read "moderate share."

Page 274, paragraph beginning line twenty, ending with line twenty-nine, should read, "But we would further observe we do not claim that indisposition is alone confined to those who are known as spiritual mediums. Far be it from us to limit to the comparatively few a world-wide privilege as yet unrecognized; for, although the men of this and other countries claim for themselves the ability to write and speak, elaborating subjects of the greatest interest to humanity, we are bold to say they know not how or why such thoughts are theirs."

Page 286, lines twelve and thirteen, for "may be sustained" read "may be enstained."

Page 286, line fourteen, for "tainted by" read "surrounded by."

Page 294, line four, for "seem to who comprehend" read "seem to comprehend."

Page 298, line nine, for "desires of which" read "desires which."

Page 301 line thirteen, for "should be" read "should not be."

Page 303, line three, for "privileges recorded" read "privileges accorded."

Page 309, line eleven, for "of divine" read "of the divine."

Page 368, line twenty-five, for "Is that a turth" read "Is that a truth?"

TABLE OF CONTENTS.

NATURE OF MY MISSION.

In your communications, you have often spoken of my mission. May I be permitted to inquire definitely, what is the nature of that mission?

Your inquiry involves so much that would, perhaps, seem enigmatical to your comprehension, that we should almost despair of succeeding in our attempt to explain. Nevertheless, with our accustomed desire to do so, we will make the attempt.

It is no uncommon thing for spirits, like human beings, to project more than they are in the ultimate able to accomplish. So has it been with us in your case, for in our anxiety to make you what we wished, we overlooked innumerable impediments in the way of success, which, with all our clairvoyant powers, lay so deeply imbedded in your nature, as to remain unnoticed by us; added to which, unsuitable connections and surroundings all combined, rendered our exertions abortive, as connected with our original purpose of developing you as a speaker, consequently an abandonment of that purpose became inevitable. Therefore, we endeavored to brighten thy perceptive faculties, so as to make thee a medium through whose organism we could write, and in this we have admirably succeeded, for thou art readily receptive of our promptings, so that our thoughts are transcribed by thee with an accuracy unsurpassed. This is, therefore, a portion of thy mission, and an important one it is, for although thy manuscripts may not, and indeed *are* not, appreciated as they deserve, yet the time will come when they will be sought, and the pure and divine inculcations they contain will effect much good amongst earth's inhabitants. But, perhaps, the most important part of your mission is one that is least comprehended by humanity, yet in the ultimate must be accepted as a boon incalculable to myriads whose condition is thus changed by and through your instrumentality in carrying out a great and mighty purpose, by which innumerable undeveloped spirits are relieved from a condition most deplorable, that of a settled conviction of their total unworthiness and inability to gravitate to a better and holier condition but through the exercise of that power vested in thee; in addition to which, thou hast also the power to exorcise evil spirits from the organisms of those who have become obscessed.

How many thousands have been relieved, and however unacceptable this may appear, to the finite mind, there are thousands upon thousands who now stand ready to hail thine entrance into the spheres as their benefactor and friend. Therefore, thou needs't not ask what is thy mission, for thou must see its vast and growing importance each day of thy existence. I admit all this, and yet sometimes, although the fact stares me in the face, and I receive daily expressions of gratitude quite as tangible to me (excepting sight) as any other transaction in life, yet the power conferred upon so unworthy an agent, excites occasional doubts in my mind, as to the reality. Yet I may as well ignore my own existence.

My husband, I am not at all surprised at this remark of yours, because although you are thus empowered to fulfill your duty, as it were, mechanically, yet those spirits being relieved thereby, fully establishes the reality ; though finite as you are, you see but with your finite vision, yet presently ethereal sight will be given you, and then your belief will be superseded by knowledge that there is indeed a reality in your mission to the glorifying of God, and the release of myriads from the cruel bondage of mental obscession, one of the greatest calamities to which humanity is subject. AMEN.

WHAT IS SPIRIT.

WHAT is Spirit *in* the form and *out?* God is a spirit, and who has ever seen him? To see God we must be like him in all things, and as that is beyond a possibility, no man has seen, or ever will see Him other than through his demonstrated works. In all things the creature is inferior to the Creator, and in nothing is it more apparent than when comparison is made. We are sometimes asked to describe a spirit—how can we do so and succeed?

A. How can man describe a thing he has not seen or ever will? Description says, it is invisible, and, being thus informed, why ask the question. Silly and absurd it must appear to such as often seem to think they have laid a trap for others. Much better would it be to say: I am not able while here on earth.

Q. Has spirit in the form the same ability to control man as it has when disembodied?

A. Spirit, whether in the form or not, may be deemed just the same, except, by being intensified, it becomes more capable of lifting or moving ponderable matter than in earth-life it is capable of doing. In all cases where such a feat is needed, increased numbers are enabled to effect that in which one or two must fail. To give you a living illustration of this fact, the minute living entity (the ant,) through aggregated help, performs wonders that have oft astounded philosophers and men of learning. Thus, in spirit-life, the law of combination almost without a limit, renders simple demonstrations daily given through physical mediums, who are oft denounced imposters. But let these opponents make trial for themselves, and, in justice to the mediums, honestly confess a failure, rather than persist in base denials of a truth they cannot comprehend.

Q. Is the same power to return to earth accorded to evil or wicked spirits as to others?

A. Assuredly it is, my son, a beautiful thought that God, with all his grand omnipotence, must thus be seen and known to be a just and righteous God. Are not his acts based upon this immutable law, Impartiality? The field of Nature lies open to the bad as well as good. The same unerring love pervades the whole; no undue obstacles are placed in the way of either; every traveller depends upon himself, or some guardian friend, to reach the goal he seeks. Thus is he left entirely free to act in such direction as he pleases, or, by attraction may be led.

Q. Do spirits when enfranchised from the body, carry with them the same proclivities into spirit-life as they had on earth?

A. Assuredly they do, and cling with great tenacity thereto; acting under a sad infatuation, that spirit-life presents a larger field for action, that in the sphere to which they gravitate legions of lewd and wicked souls, closely corresponding with themselves, will readily afford a more extended scope for sinful practice than when on earth they had been permitted to enjoy; thus, for a time, they are expectant, only awaiting opportunity, when, in bitter disappointment, they find *the desire* alone exists. The power is left behind on earth—a sphere more suited to them than the Heaven which might be theirs if sought in Spirit and in Truth. If such a thought exists within their natures, is it not strange they should prefer the noxious atmosphere there surrounding them, till their pent up passions become ascendant; driving them to almost madness by their heated force they rush in headlong haste to ventilate their o ercharged natures, by obcessing some poor embodied spirit with whom they can affinitize, and thus indulge an appetite of deep depravity, but which seems an act of mere imagination only, leaving the friend and ally the victim of a sad delusion.

Q. Can spirits in the second sphere, while probationers, of themselves acquire improvement?

A. To this we answer, they having gravitated to such a condition does not stultify a single effort they might make to change and improve themselves. The contrary would rather hasten such an effort, for often in their silent moments are they carried back in thought to times when spirit intuition reached them and almost persuaded them to accept their proffered blessings. Such reminiscences would brighten their dimmed capacities to think again, and thus in recognition does some angel answer such an aspiration as is then engendered and progression, hitherto retarded, is commenced anew, and heaven becomes again the goal of their ambition.

Q. Progression being so easily obtained, I would ask how it is that such myriads still remain inert and passive occupants of such a dismal place?

A. My son, to them it is not dismal in the main. Take, for example, the many thousands on your earth who congregate around your every sink of vice and infamy within your city, waiting but the secret shades of night to perpetrate the every crime that history records; seeking the dens of infamy in all their squalid, filthy state, preferring such to the broad green fields of nature, in all their loveliness, where they might breathe the pure invigorating atmosphere in which the human soul, if pure, might almost revel in the embryotic thought of heaven itself. It is *theirs* if they will take it, offered by some angel voice. But to the impure man or woman it is lost. In love and kindness is the offer made, but listlessly rejected. And so it is within the sphere we have named. Desire for change is seemingly outlived; the deadened soul cannot uprise from the lethargy of ages to claim that freedom which still might be its own for asking. No limit has there ever been presented for repentance, but unending time is theirs to fit themselves as aspirants for ethereal life.

Q. Are not angels sent as messengers to arouse such souls to action in the matter of removal from that state of wretchedness and misery supreme?

A. Men and women of your world endure more misery and wretchedness than is needed, in such condition as fate or destiny may have placed them, for such they are best fitted, and however gross their natures, assimilation gives enjoyment to them, much greater than could be realized by them in what the world calls respectable society. For such must be a failure; like oil and water they would separate; repulsion must ensue; disgust, abuse and almost violence would form the sequel, thus showing how needed adaptation seems to happiness. A host of Angels never could effect a change in such society till nature and art combined in time might reconstruct them, making them in form and comeliness more like their God and father as once they had been, but through perversion had become the very opposite of what they might have been. God, as their father and their friend, will so adapt them to a fit and glorious life-continuous, that those who had seen them in their low estate might then exclaim, a miracle is now performed. Is that a miracle, we ask, when God in grand omnipotence gives forth his mandate to create? Where exists the power that can contravene a single act of God's omnipotence? The puny voice of man may possibly be raised in ignorant opposition to his will, and transient, as it is, becomes the more ridiculous to those who witness the abortive effort. Hence, in everything is seen God and nature in harmony, and love working for the benefit of man, misery forming no part of God's behest respecting him.

Q. If in earth-life one spirit injures another, can it demand compensation?

A. Upon the broad, general question, perhaps not, but let me state a specialty; the one spirit gravitates to the second sphere, while the other reaches ethereal bliss.

Q. Please explain how such conpensation can be made?

A. You have now more clearly stated your question, which we answer by saying, God being omniscient, readily takes cognizance of every act of man or woman. Can it, therefore, matter whether the parties here concerned are *near* or *distant* from each other? A sin committed in the frozen regions of the north or in the torrid zone, it matters not, the crime is still as odious; no time or place can make it otherwise, and compensation must be made. And why, you perhaps may ask? Certainly not to gratify the injured or injurer, for they, perhaps, have forgotten the entire transaction; but the all-seeing eye of universal justice evokes from mouldy records an accusing entry, and, in an unexpected moment, utters a decree of compensation to the injured party. There's no escape; no *alibi* can there be proven. Time's recorded acts are better kept than in this lower world.

Q. I cannot yet feel satisfied. Supposing the aggressive party has reached a state of happiness, is such an one removed to a happiness of less degree?

A. My son, I admire your ingenuity in putting your question; therefore, shall endeavor to answer it understandingly. Ethereality, to men, seems so obscure that difficulties arise at every step in striving to elucidate a question so closely trenching upon the confines of *Ethereality* itself, that in sad amazement we are left in doubt and fear lest we should o'erstep the line of demarcation drawn by wisdom infinite. In this dilemma do we find ourselves. Not daring to advance, we will at once recede and decline response at present.

Q. Looking around and seeing nothing tangible to human sight connected with the future life, does it not follow that scepticism must be endured till such restrictions are abridged and seeming mysteries made more clear to man's perceptive faculties?

A. My son, experience responds at once to such a question, and yet not wholly so. Each day presents most clearly to the human mind that soon as the supply has ceased life becomes endangered. The motive power engendering life and action, calls loudly for repletion, which, if withheld beyond the proper time, the pulse beats slow, the eyes are dim and lusterless, the outstretched limbs are rigid, and the hue of death (at once) bespreads the admired features. A livid paleness, death like in its character, o'erspreads the countenance, the sunken, bleared, unconscious orbs of sight no longer do their bidding; a lingering, softened sigh, unconscious, as it seems, give tokens of departure. Where or whence has the former inmate fled? Perchance it lingers yet around its earthly friends. Ah! yes; in yonder flaky, misty cloudlet may be seen ensconced in deepest show of grief, the once director of that body, but e'en a moment earlier in living form a portion of the triune man or woman, as it might be. That spirit hovering there in token of respect for the clod of clay beneath its feet in humbled posture lays, showing the power of spirit over matter. O, what an ample lesson to the materialist. Can you explain the reason why that once beauteous form is now so motionless? Can you say why those once beauteous orbs of sight are so hermetically sealed? that mouth so closed that words of wisdom once uttered through those closed and silent lips are now no more in motion? those hands and feet remain inactive and unused? in fine, that noble form once divine, whilst spirit aided and directed it, lies now in utter helplessness?

Hast thou no magic art by which thou can'st restore depleted life and give it power and motion to describe surroundings? Can'st thou restore its reasoning powers to ask the why and wherefore of its now condition? Helpless, inert, and altogether useless, other than to replace a mass of matter, loaned by nature to make the earthly portion of the late living man? Am I not fairly entitled to a fair and candid response to these, my questions, evoked as they have been by sad perversion of the reasoning powers, as pertaining to a future and continuous life? Is divine and holy thought expunged from without thy nature, that doubts can so pervade thee as to infer this is the only life thou'lt ever enjoy? This, to many, is a sad, abbreviated life of suffering and perplexity. Where, I would ask, is that ambition many seem so boastful of? The creeping, crawling worm has more than thou can'st claim. True, its ambition is downward, but thither does its nature send it as better suited to its practice. Whilst men in moody helplessness will sit or stand in dark and gloomy attitude, thinking o'er the lank or meagre form they may assume, when all of hope has left them, that the term of mundane life may still continue. For withal this sad conviction of eternal death, this fact encircles thee with stronger wished-for life on earth. Poor, silly mortal, hast thou no common sense imparted to thee? If not, let that be the primary aspiration of thy soul; for coalesced, as soon it would be with reason, thy nature would be changed; the erratic views thou hast formed of future life would soon become engrafted in thy expectant soul, when once awakened to a sense of God's eternal mercy, for then the soul can rest in peace. It is a rightful claim, he has richly earned by strict obedience to his Father's laws. Oh, sinning mortal! such is thine by seeking; no angry, revengeful God will cut thee off from such inheritance, by plea of being sinfully and totally depraved! Under the latter charge, if true, thou mightst in wisdom make such selection as annihilation. But with such a God as Him we worship, no such desire or belief can possibly exist. Thou art a child of God, equally cared for by Him as the choicest saint on record. Thou needs't not ask a Savior beyond thyself. In thee is contained all the saving influences required to bring thee to that happy home thy loving friends have well prepared for thee, soon as thou art fitted to become its occupant. AMEN.

EARLY CONDITION OF MAN;

HIS PROGRESS INTO CIVILIZATION—THE PROMISED HAPPY BELATIONS BETWEEN MEN ON EARTH AND THE CELESTIAL SPIRITS.

To commence so unusual a subject, it may, perhaps, be necessary to go back to a period when all mankind were sunk in ignorance and superstition; having little distinct consciousness of the Great God of nature.

The only qualification known and recognized was simple muscular strength; and the individual possessing the most imposing share of this, assumed the right to govern, or, at least, control those around him. Mind and reason being as yet undeveloped, their functions were unknown.

Man, thus barbarous and unrestrained, carried out his cruel and savage proclivities. In such condition was he, at the time we speak of, that his wants were circumscribed to the absolute needs without which life could not exist. Little accountability had he to render to any other, unless physically stronger than himself, but ruled as sovereign over all he saw, for beyond that his knowledge did not extend.

In time, however, stragglers roamed as now, and became acquainted with others, and thus successive and increased communities were formed, but with little improvement in their form of government, if form it could be called. The individual ruled by brute force until a competitor appeared to dispute his power; more athletic in form, and perhaps a slight degree improved in intellect, which latter qualification he soon turned to account, and thus displaced the former bully.

There, then, was formed a nucleus around which was fostered the earliest germ of actual civilization.

From this crude commencement must we date man's grand advancement in the scale of universal progress. In gradual process, as his reason developed, he soon discovered needs he thought not of before; never dreaming, hitherto, that a single thing was wanting for his comfort which he did not possess. His wants were few, and, like the animal below him, he sought but natural shelter, where and how he could obtain it, showing, thereby, when his soul was uncultivated, how short a remove he was from the unthinking brute! Is it any wonder then, that from such a state of ignorance, the human mind developed so slowly as it did? Necessity, that potent law, was the only lever which lifted mind out of the miry pit of ignorance, and placed man's feet on better ground;

giving to him the needed confidence that eventually raised him from his savage condition. Necessity, his helpmate, developed his nature, and, by steady approaches, he more easily conquered the numerous difficulties at which he quailed before.

Thus, step by step, did man become capable of comprehending cause and effect. His reason was thus exercised, and as all of nature is improved by action, so did that important gift to man increase in volume and usefulness. But in proportion as his faculties improved, so did his needs increase. And were these needs imperative? the very term implies they were. Wants may possibly be put aside, but a need must be satisfied.

This is a faithful detail, speaking, as we are, of man's early condition; a constant lever was still at work to raise him from his low state to a higher, by engendering needs most absolute, and also necessary to the end designed.

Hence, constant changes were produced, well suited to the law of progress; each change effected showing vast improvement, rendering the past, as it were, almost useless, because unadapted to man's advanced circumstances, the natural result of change.

Here, then, is shown a depth of divine wisdom, unfathomable to the finite mind; the regular process of nature; cultivating the human soul, and preparing it, by almost imperceptible degrees, to reach eventually a state of celestial bliss. This fact should settle effectually those morbid, dreary theorists, who would cast doubts upon the *immortality* of the human soul.

Man in his most primitive state was the superior amongst animal creation, and to him alone was given the right to subordinate the great law of progress to his use, and for his final elevation; and whosoever cannot discern the presence of an immortal soul throughout this wonderful career, must be willfully, or morally, blind indeed.

Your present era bears conclusive evidence of the grand conception of a world raised from the chaotic mass to a beautiful symmetry, and which is being comprehended by a divinely imparted human intelligence. Who but the great Infinite could project a work of such stupendous magnificence? The answer must come spontaneously—none, none. Then, with such convictions, how can man forbear to worship such a being, so fully represented in His works, that all must feel His presence? Although no distinct form is visible to human ken, His divine influence and soothing goodness pervades and permeates the soul with a holy feeling of reverence and devotion to the power supremely exalted.

This divine influence is the talisman by which the souls of men have been directed in the past, *are* in the present, and *shall* be in the future—unchangable in principle, penetrating all things, and doing good to all creatures.

The question is often asked: Where, how, and when, is the completeness of this glorious era to be attained, which is so much alluded to? We answer; when the uncounted millions, now in darkness, shall have become awakened by their angel friends to a keen and clear perception of their own unworthiness—when they are made by angels' gentle chidings to feel the wrongs they have committed. When they become convinced that there is no God of vengeance to hurl them down to interminable torture, or brand them guilty through eternity, but instead of which, has sent His holy angels to portray His mercy, love and goodness, that a change may be effected within their guilty souls, whereby they may eschew those evil thoughts which have bound them as with adamantine chains to the unbelief of that which alone can soothe their sufferings, and heal their lacerated souls, by proving to them that a place of refuge is at hand which they can reach, and where they can doff their bespattered garments of sin and iniquity, and don that beauteous robe of righteousness and peace.

Keeping so close to a life on earth, strange as it may seem, is far better than launching out into the broad expanse of space, and so bewilder the finite mind in the vast, voluminous views surrounding us; therefore shall we still continue the subject we commenced, and which should ever be a study of deepest interest to man—The Rise and Progress of the Human Race.

This is in order to connect man's present with his future, and in so doing, we hope to show that progress and improvement is the grandest, noblest, and should be the sole motive of his pursuit; and the highest goal of all ambition should be a glorious immortality.

The dried up skeptic may ask, perhaps, what is this immortality of which you speak? From whence can man receive assurance that such can ever be his? Assertions may be made, but where is the proof? Define this immortality if you please. To which we answer: all these things, in the seeming difficulty of which, the negative mind appears to triumph, are easily proved, defined and comprehended where human reason is unperverted.

Immortality, then, is a condition of soul and spirit, entered upon after they are separated from the mortal coil. When restored to a state of consciousness, these co-existent entities commence ethereal life as co-workers in the grand plan and glorious efforts of the angel world, to complete the work of man's final redemption, and thus, by every means, prepare themselves and others for a never ending life; proceeding upwards and onwards in pursuit of knowledge and divine grace from the highest source attainable; to fulfill the behests of our Almighty God and Father, in imparting good and comfort to mankind, and thus rendering ourselves useful to the divine will; for, rest assured, the after life is not one of idleness, but of constant action, where each sustains his part in the duties of ethereal life.

The soul and spirit, elevated to light and freedom, goes out to do the Master's will, and whether in the blue ether, or on the mortal shores, it is equally imperative to do it well: when the halo of holy satisfaction may be seen radiating in every direction in token of a servant's duty well performed!

This, though a meager synopsis of immortality, is nearly as much as the finite mind could comprehend.

You ask for proof? You need no stronger proof than that within your own reach. If you can but control the opaque stubbornness of your own perverted will, and apply yourself to earnest investigation you shall soon discover that your atmosphere is populous with living, intelligent entities —lately mortals like yourselves, but now of sublimated and ethereal nature. These are striving with sweetest affection to obtain a confidence you should not refuse, for, be assured, a time will come when the close adherence of angel friends would be to you a treasure beyond all estimation.

Then say, ye ruthless advocates of dead theology, and of sterile skepticism alike, what more conclusive proofs of immortality do you require than these, which spirits bring you?

Ye, theologists, nothing convincing have you to base your hopes upon, that man lives again. You talk of a future state, but no positive knowledge have you of it, therefore, none can you impart to the enquiring millions who attend your churches. Those who seek these can find but baseless speculation, resting on shadowy inferences, but no clear conviction of a glorious immortality awaiting them as soon as death has burst asunder the bands of material life, so that the enfranchised soul can soar away above and beyond those steepled edifices, where priestly pride and arrogance dominates over all, where should be freedom from the accursed taint of ignorance and superstition.

Hence the millions who have listened for so many ages to unsound teachings, found their entrance barred to those celestial spheres, the right to enter which is theirs, but burthened as they are by creeds and dogmas, all the efforts they can make but prove abortive, and long before they become acquainted with the laws which govern Heaven, they find themselves involved in mental darkness, and surrounded by spirits of the same discordant views, dwelling in total unrest and inharmony, not seeking any other condition, but clinging to the same erratic notion of a fancied, universal Savior.

At present it would be worse than idle to expect reform amongst the myriads who, each day and hour, swell the unnumbered multitudes, seeking that which they never can find, and listlessly protracting a wretched existence, when, if a holier lesson had been taught them, it would have abridged, or even prevented their sufferings, and have led them by the silken cords of holy and divine love into the green pastures of a celestial home.

The means which shall be adopted to effect reform must be lasting, and not partial in its results —enduring as time itself, when all shall renounce sin and iniquity, when the angel hosts shall descend to your earth, and present themselves for recognition, as manifest, living beings, possessing all those elements of sympathy which form the basis of a community made happy by them.

Who, *then*, shall doubt the power of spirits to return again, and thus to be identified as those who have trod this earth before, proving the loving relations between themselves and those friends to whom they claim to be attracted? for of such is Heaven formed.

Those who have passed through tribulations and sufferings, and being thus prepared, are fitted for the higher spheres, when attracted, come again to earth, and seeking out the weary, and heavily laden, to comfort and console them, charging no tribute, but by solace and consolation plentifully supplied, giving them full assurance of a better, holier home.

My brother, would that we could impart to your mind a view of the glorious scenes surrounding us, which to some extent we have attempted, but failed to accomplish. The hosts of Heaven would then be unveiled, who glorify the power of Him whose rule is over all. AMEN.

DEATH A BENEFIT.

THE subject we propose to treat of, is one that appears betimes exhausted; and yet, each time we resume it, such varied phases present themselves for discussion, that we ever return with double zest to scan its merits through the medium of thought, which naturally demands expression. Hence, I come to you as the means of spreading broadcast that which I trust may benefit humanity at large. Few things in nature seems to call for admiration more than the fact that all mankind must die. Strange thought. Methinks, I hear you say, "Is death a pleasure we ought to be thankful for, much more admire?" Yes, my friend, it is even so, and as such will you view it ere long, be assured. When the soul is wearied of the things of earth, weighed down by care, pain and sorrow, chafed by an angry spirit to commit a wrong upon itself by uttering curses on its own existence, and tired nature sinks from very weariness, to whom will such a being, overwhelmed in wretchedness, apply for aid? To man he need not, for he has already appealed and found no succor; not a ray of hope has reached him that soon he may recover, and be again the man he once had been. All this he must endure without the slightest prospect of a change, by which he might perchance deduce some comfort to his soul, now merged in darkness quite appalling to his bewildered senses. Reflection aids him not, and why? Because his mind retains no recollection of a single effort he has ever made to store it with those truths, which angel minds have offered for his acceptance. Thus, in ignorance profound, he sits a morbid, thoughtless being, incapable of asking what he needs. Can such a creature, we ask, desire to have extended, or even continued, such a life? Yet, amidst all this wretchedness, to talk to him of death would so affright him, as to drive him to a frenzied state of terror, painful to behold. Strange contradiction must this seem to those who had heard those horrid imprecations previously invoked upon himself, and all things then surrounding him; but so it is with men whose lives have been misspent, as if no day of reckoning ever would come. To such a one, death may readily be deemed an unwelcome visitor; and so he ever would be, howsoever long his visit might be deferred. We can scarcely imagine the appalling dread pervading such a soul when summoned hence to meet, as he supposes, an angry, avenging God, as his teachers have ever shown him, and so misrepresented the great God of justice and benevolence! Think you, a doctrine such as this can make bad men better ones? We feel a deep assurance that no sinner can be reformed by such a faith. Who, but a fool, would sing songs of praise to such a God as this? One who would take from the wretched sinner all hope of being able to outwork his sinfulness, and seek, through mercy, that aid which angels strive so often to impart. Oh, monstrous iniquity! To so imbue the human mind as to wreck its mortal interests on the shoals of ignorance and superstition. Are there not sufficient of those amongst humanity who can rise superior to those awful teachings, by which mankind is driven to the lowest depths of degradation, rendering their condition, even whilst on earth, the most abject slavery conceivable? Did it stop here, it might be tolerated, for a time at least; but in the beyond, where happiness might be theirs, if not entrammeled by those damning dogmas, which weigh down the souls of men so low in the scale of self appreciation, that they dare not claim the promised joys they once had hoped for. These promises, based upon the delusions of their creed, have ever been a stumbling block in the way of mankind, who, but for this baneful influence, would have thrown aside the veil of ignorance, and become believers in a purer and holier docrine, than has ever before been tendered to man; and by which the prospects of a future life would have been more brilliant than a world of bigots can conceive.

Fain would we conceal these things, but truth demands it from us, that we uncover these acts of base and cruel men, who deem it worthy of their sacred calling to deceive their fellow mortals by sophistry and deception, when sober truth would answer the purpose much better, and they escape the obloquy attached to such a course of conduct, which must blast their own, and others' prospects of eternal life.

How, then, is such an evil to be remedied? Can man himself effect the necessary change? We know he cannot. If man cannot, who then shall be applied to? We answer: those whom you have hitherto treated with scorn and contumely—those holy spirits who have hovered around your dwellings, charged with such precious truths as would lead to the removal of those mischievous dogmas, that so heavily clog the souls of earth's children; and who are to-day so guided and directed by them, to the formation of a heaven, according to dogmatic notions, where the happiness of its occupants is increased and enhanced by the vivid consciousness of the unceasing tortures which their well-remembered earthly friends are now undergoing in the eternal hell of the damned!

How can a place be deemed a heaven where such dreadful contemplations are any portion of its enjoyments? And yet it seems best suited to the narrowed views of bigots, who are employed to scatter broadcast over your earth their poisonous doctrines of election, reprobation, and such like trash, persuading some with such hollow nonsense, an impartial God had chosen them above all others for a heaven He had specially prepared for them, while, with equal reason, He had consigned others to an eternal hell of burning torments. Can commen sense receive much longer such base absurdities, or suffer itself to be cajoled by men whose calling is founded on deception, whose statements are so inconsistent, that if in the ordinary affairs of human life others were made just as feasible, those who would make them would have their reputations emblazoned as habitually, unmitigated liars?

The time cannot be far distant when men will cease to tolerate false, unfounded teaching, and establish in its stead the immutable principles of integrity and justice.

[Recess taken here.]

In resuming the foregoing subject, we are led to think that a somewhat different course may be pursued.

While we are endeavoring to enlighten the minds of those who are seeking truth by means altogether useless, it seems a waste of time denouncing the system they are pursuing. We shall, therefore, turn our attention to show the advantages which must derive to those who investigate in search of the best doctrine, and what peculiar influences they should seek whereby they can be aided in their researches While the mind of man is perplexed with cares and anxieties, connected with worldly matters, he finds it difficult to so concentrate his powers of research in a direction that will prove most profitable. In order to meet this impediment, however, if the seeker be in earnest, a means is presented, which brings him to the turning point of advance, or retrograde—success or failure. It will not cost the investigator much, otherwise valuable, time, to faithfully seek and earnestly invoke the aid of his ever attendant spirits, and in proportion to the purity of his purpose, and the steadiness of his desire, will he find, within a reasonable time, that the difficulty is more than half surmounted; and that which previously appeared a stupendous work, becomes now more easy of accomplishment, and the knowledge and comprehension of truth his certain and happy reward. Here, then, is given to investigators an encouragement resting on facts, which are beyond mortal valuation. What can equal in value the information, if true, that here is a passage of communication open to human understanding with those beyond the grave, and that thousands upon thousands who,returning thence, are thus permitted to announce to an unbelieving world the joyful tidings that man certainly lives again in the untried future!

It certainly should be the all-absorbing thought, occupying the leisure hours of man, because it is the most important—whether a spirit can return to earth, and there communicate with those he had left behind, in utter doubt that they should ever meet again. But now all doubts must cease, and that which before was but a hope, has become a perfect knowledge. But to whom? the skeptic may interrogate. To which we answer: only to those who ask; to them this knowledge is imparted—a glorious piece of news to suffering humanity, and worthy the united peans of the Universe. All hail! we say, to that sweet angel voice, sent to announce this glorious news to man, doing more to elevate his moral condition than the entire efforts of the so-called Christian Church in nearly two thousand years of constant preaching. Oh, shame, shame to that establishment, with such a foundation as it had to build upon—even the inculcations of the blessed Nazarene, our elder brother, and our friend. Behold the issue—retrogression and all the evils of a baseless project, because of its perversion. But we said we would ignore denunciation, and so we shall.

To those whose minds are already opened to the light of Spiritualism, we shall now address ourselves. Can any thinking, reasoning person feel he is acting right, when having become convinced that Spiritualism is true, and yet withhold his public sanction of that truth? Why are there so many waverers and doubting souls, standing aloof in shivering form, fearful to avow sentiments forced upon their convictions, that there is surely something good in Spiritualism? They want an undefined something more, something to satisfy a morbid apprehension that there is not a bugaboo ensconced behind. The good is perceived so clearly, that, aside from scruples of timidity, they can discover nothing wrong or sinful; still they doubt, and there they may be found still doubting until the day of final accounting calls them to their senses.

Poor, poor feeble beings. Pity it is you cannot find some means by which your perceptive faculties might be brightened, to improve your spiritual condition, for certainly, ere long, the change called death, will overtake you, and then you will ask yourselves, each in anguish: "Why have I permitted those doubts and fears to dwarf my energy of soul, and to have rendered me incapable of trusting to the mercy of my God, who has sent His angels with the glad tidings to all men of an immortal life beyond the grave! Ah, me, am I yet too late to receive that aid so often proffered me, but which in ignorance I failed to receive? Come, then, ye sweet angelic beings, come and receive the sincere prayers of true repentance from my lips, and grant that instruction so much needed by me."

Think you, my brother, that such an appeal would be unheeded? We answer, no! but every angel within hearing, would arise and minister to his wants. Not only that, but to every human soul who would thus ask the boon. Are you not satisfied that Spiritualism can effect all this and more—much more; and if it can, must you not deplore the ignoraace and superstition prevailing in your community? It is painful to behold so many still clinging to useless creeds, which, false and unfounded, must eventually be despised by men, as they are now by angels. Priests will cling tenaciously, hoping to outlive the threatening aspect of affairs, and maintain their false position by accumulated lies and stolid perseverance, until the great and final change shall have taken place, and when the last blow is struck which shall level their priestly edifices in ruin irretrievable, this sound shall be heard throughout the universe of God: "I, thy God, who ruleth all things, am a Spirit, and must be worshiped in spirit and in truth." AMEN.

THE GREAT GULF BETWEEN THE MORTAL AND IMMORTAL WORLD.

OUR friend, we have called upon thee to write, in order to leave upon your record some thoughts which may possibly reach the convictions of others who may peruse these lines.

Your condition, at the present moment, renders you sufficiently receptive of our inspiration, because you have listened to the injunctions of those spirits who have long sought to bring you under suitable control.

We feel that every moment you are held under such influences should be used for the righteous purpose of instructing humanity through your organism.

Orthodoxy inculcates the notion, that the two worlds, of spirit and of matter, are separated by an impassable gulf, which renders the return of a disembodied spirit utterly impossible, and upon this hypothesis it assumes to prove, beyond any danger of denial, that Spiritualism is a myth. We avail ourselves of this opportunity to sift this matter, and show to these thoughtless sophists how very obtuse they are to all that is natural in the premises.

Spirit, they say, is intangible under all human conditions: we answer, it is not, but as completely tangible to your conceptions, under certain conditions, as aught else in nature; for although your finite senses cannot recognize spirit emanations, yet when your etherial nature becomes quickened by the soul's inspirations of spirit thought, then it is that things etherial become plain to your improved condition, and you must of necessity admit our proposition, that disembodied spirits become tangible to you, their existence thereafter a solved problem, and, to such minds, an established fact.

Now, we would ask, as soon as convinced of this, who can reconcile the theory of the great and impassable gulf? Orthodox belief is, that after death (as they call it), the good soul returns to God, who gave it.

If we ask where God exists, they say in heaven. Then we would ask how is the spirit on leaving its earthly tabernacle to pass this horrid gulf or barrier, and thus make its way to its plane of destination? Here seems a difficulty not easily removed, unless by the interposition of a special providence, such as the alleged passage of the Israelites across the Red Sea, or some other special act of favoritism, provided for the select few, but really to assist them out cf a labyrinth of absurdity, such as they fall into when attempting to disprove that spirits return to earth for the avowed purpose of becoming guides and directors to the loved ones of earth, who are heavily laden with divine and holy instructions to those who have been purified through trials and difficulties; to make them the recipients of immortal truths relating to man's condition in the eternal future.

Is there aught in this position that should startle and cause distrust? Is there aught, we would ask, that should affright the human mind, and give it a desire to discredit the assertion of millions, that this is incontrovertible truth?

If spirit lives (and that can be attested by such as are clairvoyant) is it at all strange or marvellous that the doings and sayings of those whom we have known on earth should again be made known to us, in order that the soul of man should be rejoiced and encouraged by the assurance that there is, after death, an eternal life, and that happiness can be realized by the substitution of virtue for vice in all our human conditions?

Beyond the grave those holy aspirations of the good will be gratified, which all men deem a grand desideratum, and which all hope for, though without any distinct base for such hope, but cling to the shadow without making the slightest effort to secure the substance. Their minds being all engrossed by worldly matters, the inevitable future forms no part of their untiring efforts. They are constantly seeking to secure worldly power and riches, the fleeting nature of which affords but a poor equivalent for what would be their unrestricted inheritance forever, if properly sought, and which is daily offered them without money and without price.

Oh, if men could but restrain their hungering after things that cannot supply the wants of the spirit, their souls would become the repository of that which they could feed upon without satiety. Each day and hour they would reap such etherial advantages as would bear the test of time, and prove to them a profitable and secure investment. AMEN.

THE NEEDS OF MAN.

THE very term implies something of too much consequence to be neglected; hence are we inclined to proffer a few thoughts in relation to it and suggested to us regarding it.

The needs of man—what are they, in the abstract sense? A need implies something special, arbitrary and necessary: want is a term often used to express a need, and used erroneously.

A desire to possess a thing does not make a need of it, because the will, if well applied, can readily remove the desire, but a need becomes imperative, and must be supplied, or suffering and disaster become the issue. This naturally involves the question—what are the needs of man? The ramifications of such a question seem so extensive as to render it difficult to follow successfully. It depends much upon the mental structure of the individual as to what he will most desire.

The person who is worldly seeks that which is most in accordance with his own—not very uncommon—views; and thus he doubtlessly supposes that what he wants he really needs. How many thousands upon thousands deceive themselves and others by this deceitful sophistry, trying to be satisfied by such a course of reasoning, that they are acting justly towards themselves and others, while seeking to gratify wants, the very artificial, foul offspring of covetousness. Such wants, when complied with, are often sure to rob others of actual needs, and become the sources of sore privation and sorrow to a brother or a sister, whose very forlorn condition and inability to resist may have been the inducement to commit the wrong. Is the worldling moved at the distress of his neighbor? We know he is not. Little cares he for the suffering of his fellow man—compassion forms no part of an organism where discontented, insatiate selfishness prevails. But, with a mental structure based on truth and righteousness, no such malign feeling can exist in the human breast. The sufferer's plaintive moans awaken his compassion, and selfishness finds no resting place in a soul of this kind. Love and mercy guard the portals against the entrance of lawless and unbridled passions, calling all the aspirations of a feeling nature into full activity.

Not so the worldly hypocrites who take refuge in the dogmas preached by a priesthood whose insatiate thirst of filthy lucre leads them to abjure the sufferers' claims morally and physically. Instead of leading them towards their God, they leave them powerless to help themselves by asking assistance from the spirit world. Bound as they are, by creedish discipline, they cannot pass the prescribed limits of such and such a church, and thus they become spiritually starved in the very sight of that food which would nourish and strengthen a soul thus tried and tempted.

My friends, this is the case with myriads at the present moment—multitudes in starving condition, because of the cruel bonds pressing, as it were, the life blood out of those numerous victims of falsehood and superstition! What then shall we deem the needs of those? With them it is not a mere want but a stern necessity that freedom should be theirs. To strip off their theological cataplasms, making their needs potent to their senses, and soon will they arrive at the true conclusions of what constitutes the real needs of man.

Here, then, shall we leave this subject, to be well considered by every lover of his fellow creatures; that when a real need is manifested, he may not only have the ability, but the desire also, to alleviate the sufferings of a needy neighbor—physically, morally and intellectually.

Then will sufferings measurably cease; the cause being removed, the disease will soon disappear, and man, having become less needy, must feel still more grateful for his improved condition. AMEN.

THEN AND NOW.

THE past is a theme for vast and profound contemplation. Whether taken as a warning or as a precedent, its importance is the same, and its usefulness to humanity is equally manifest. In all the conditions of the latter, there are such innumerable difficulties and dangers to be guarded against, that it requires an intimate knowledge of the past to guide and direct us in the present; particularly in our search after those antidotes necessary to eradicate from the human mind the baneful influences of by-gone times, and their garbled teachings.

No man, having lived in times remotely past, and returning now, with all his education, precisely as he then existed, could be fit for the times which are now.

The teachings of those days (then the law of progression) are for these utterly inapplicable and worse than useless. The mind of the man, filled with the knowledge taught in his own time, could not readily receive the advanced learning of the present era, so much at variance with his preconceived opinions and peculiar education. Principles remain the same, tangible and immortal; yet, truths never to be removed or destroyed may, by false elaboration, be so presented as to render them altogether incomprehensible to the mortal mind: not lost nor abrogated, but so changed, as to render man's attempts to improve himself by them as lost time, and a pervertion of those talents imparted to him from his Maker and his God.

Oh, friend, often when we reflect on the inutility of clinging, as with a death clutch, to those dark dogmas of the past, did we not understand the resisting disposition of the human heart, we should be truly astounded that the men of the Nineteenth Century continue so obtusely indifferent to the self evident principles of enlightened faith, presented to them free of cost, and, indeed, almost free from the trouble of research.

The happy tidings of manifest truths, which are of unlimited importance, should and would inspire the souls of men were they not clogged with material, worldly pursuits, and bound down, stunted by the inculcations of a dark, mystical theology.

The utility of deception, even as a moral check to licentiousness, has passed away; the excuse is not needed in the present age. The minds who needed this fictitious control, have gone into the eternal future, many of them to soon renounce the mystical teachings of bigoted priests, whilst others still hug to their souls the serpent sting of ignorance, suffering over and over their doubts, fears and uncertainty—restless in their condition, always expecting, but never realizing that rest which has been promised them.

We would say to earth's inhabitants: let the past be received as a warning, and although generation after generation has passed away, without salutary change in the unveilment of divine truths, even to the present age, the glorious advent of Spiritualism respects the past as a useful monitor, and in taking a retrospect, we accord all that may be deemed its due. You can draw in the future, from the mistakes of the past, the conscientious satisfaction of having acted from righteous motives, therein will you find your reward, and hence all regrets will cease.

We would now treat briefly upon the present era—upon this infant institution, scarcely fifteen years of growth, giving forth such mighty proofs of power and direct utility to man. Potent in its promises of the future, its suitable completeness and satisfying precocity. Every one of its propositions based upon natural reason, and seeking no other means of winning to its interests men, who, hungering for long years after soul nourishing food, which was unattainable beneath the altars of old theology—all *these* being husky, barren, and morally unpalatable.

Through spirit teaching, of the present era,

the soul becomes directed to that inexhaustible source of divine inspiration, which angels, holy spirits, are meting out to humanity those etherial inspirations, principles, elevating and invigorating to the attenuated spirits of those who have morally starved for want of spiritual food, until they have broken the bonds of church tyranny and cut loose from arbitrary and unsound creeds, presented hitherto as the guides of men, who, now ascertaining their established free condition, dare to stand forward and proclaim aloud, their entire and complete emancipation from all priestly domination.

Thus is the present age progressing; not by fire and sword, but by the mightier fire of man's unfettered reason. Glorious retribution is inaugurated, and thought is being freed from coercion, restraint and obscurity, undoubtedly for man's purification and happiness.

By the light of what we have thus far stated, we can now intelligibly recur to our premises: why not take the past as a precedent?—Every age has been but a step in advance, towards the eternal future, giving to the succeeding generation another step, upon which to establish a final institution, which shall bear upon it the experience of all that was good in the past, constituting a motive force of progression onward.

Perhaps we may again resume this subject, but for the present shall cease. AMEN.

PRINCIPLE.

In giving you this essay, we do so with a sincere desire to benefit humanity, by leaving on your record sentiments calculated to awaken in the souls of some a resolve to make principle the grand study of earth life; being that which will insure to them happiness in the great hereafter. Yes—principle shall be our theme, and in our efforts to elaborate it, we shall indulge in some remarks that may not please the multitude.

Oh, how little is this, that is termed principle, comprehended by mankind at large.

Not being led to its acquaintance at the dawn of reason, in their approximation to manhood they failed to recognize it, and in their declining years they are scarcely able to discern the odious void that produces mental malformation. Oh, what a dark, dismal condition for men, that through so long and important a period, they should thus ignore the true foundation of justice amongst their kind.

What, we ask, can be the result of such long studied baseness? Can there be any consistency remaining in such men, who are thus devoid of the great cardinal virtue which, alone, should be their guiding star in every transaction of earth life? Miserable misdoer—neglected and neglecting so long, thou art enclosed in the meshes of a sophistry which makes thee reckless of thy neighbor's rights.

Having no principle, thou hast no monitor to guide thy purposes: justice thou heedest not, unless it be thy worldly gain to practice it. Love thou hast not, because thou hast no principle whereon to base it. What thou wouldst call love, is but a matter merely material and mercenary.

That pure and holy love which draws two souls into close and happy appreciation of each other's virtues, being unselfish in its nature, cannot possess thee; thou hast no room for it. Mercy thou hast no conception of, because thy selfish nature ever inclines thee to grind the poor and enslave their minds by torturing their souls that thou mightest become enriched.

The perpetration of these villainies has disgraced humanity in thee, and brought it down below the level of the brute!

Oh, poor deluded wretch, that thus because thou hast lost sight of principle, hast wasted thy best days in deluding thyself. Poor mistaken man, thou hast deceived thyself through the days of thy youth and thy manhood, hoping that at the last moment of thy earthly existence, thou could'st gloss over the injustice of a life time. Thou wert destitute of principle, which might have been thine to guide thee through life had'st thou sought, or even accepted it; for, be assured, no partial hand has ever withheld it from thee. It was thine inheritance, but thou disdained to ask it.

Thy end of earth life being come, we would ask thee what are thy convictions, and at this moment, when thou must render an account of thy stewardship? Can thou stand erect amongst thy fellow men and assert thy fitness for that important change which now awaits thee? Can the retrospect of thy past life (devoid of principle in all thy social and public intercourse) prove more than that thou hast kept to thyself all that thy depraved imagination conceived to be good, and not an act of thine up to thy old age has borne the seal of principle. Thy neighbor's rights have never received thy attention or protection, but self—self was the only god thou hast worshiped!

Thus, then, hast thou passed a life useless to thee, and unjust towards thy fellow man. Of what profit is it to thee? No evidence can thou produce that thou wert ignorant, and plead thy error therefrom. No, for at every turn and inclination of thy useless life hast thou been entreated by holy spirits to listen to their teachings. Heedlessly hast thou rejected them, and preferring thy own perverted scheming for guidance, shunned that, which, if accepted, would render the closing hours of thy earthly life tranquil and serene, instead of being tortured as thou art with undying regrets, that disregard of principle has turned away the good thy Creator provided for thee, and His good angels offered thee in vain. Thy vitiated life now mars thy prospects, and will stay thy progress in the unseen future.

We feel that little more need be said here, upon this subject, unless to urge those who have the charge of educating youth, to make principle their highest study.

Without it every moral virtue becomes stunted, morbid and almost obliterated: while its effective inculcation illumines the pathway of youth to true manhood, and through receding age it gilds the downward road of life, finally ushering the untrammeled spirit into the mansions of the blest.

Oh, Glorious culmination! Hasten, we beseech thee, O, God, this happy sequel to the darkened struggles of earth life, and to thee we must give the glory. AMEN.

OBLIGATION OF DEITY TO MAN.

THE question propounded is somewhat singular, yet, to some extent, is it meet. In its abstract sense, it is assuredly true, for man, being a creation of Almighty God, naturally looks up to him for protection and support.

He, having ushered the creature into existence, and fully capable of surrounding him with all his needs, is, as his Creator, under the obligations to do as much for him—to use a mortal figure of comparison—as much as nature's laws demand that man should do for his own offspring. So that, in this sense, and by a parity of reasoning, your speaker's position was correct. And, however startling such an assertion may be, the angel world must and will endorse such, as true beyond all controversy.

On the other hand—of man's obligations to Deity, no sane man would attempt denial, because the natural relations of parent and child must naturally tend to bring about a condition where a susceptibility exists, secret in its combinations, but in its manifestations distinct and clear to every thinking mind, and nothing mysterious, but all plain as the noonday sun.

And as the rays of that luminary shed their genial influence over all created nature, so over every creature is imperceptibly shed the pure love and kindness from our common parent, God, striking down deep into our inmost souls, confirming and establishing the right we have to claim his fostering love and care of us, so long as we remain obedient to His laws. AMEN.

WHICH SHOULD BE THE HEAD OF THE FAMILY---MAN OR WOMAN?

QUESTION BY SPIRIT—Have you a desire that I, thy spirit wife, should give you a solution of this question, as it may possibly involve some matters not agreeable to yourself and others of your sex?

ANSWER BY MEDIUM—The truth must be told; it is that we seek.

SPIRIT—Then do I willingly undertake the task; and in doing so, I feel no small degree of pleasure, inasmuch as the question has remained so long an open one that very few persons, either in the embodied or disembodied state are willing to discuss it; but aided, as I feel I shall be, by the celestial light of higher spheres, I will attempt it.

Man, with all the elements of a strong, enduring physique, seems formed by nature to protect the more fragile form of woman, and in the pressure of adversity to possess endurance equal to the needs of both. The stalwart form of man seems better suited to perform the sterner duties he assumes; nor does he, in the hour of danger, flinch from fear if he be a real man in growth and in principle, to face the peril hovering near with fortitude and courage—ever ready to grapple with the evil imminent.

Thus does he show his fitness for the part in life, which nature has evidently destined him to perform.

If proof of this be wanted let us reverse the cases. Could woman's sensitive form endure the same rugged effects as that of man? Exceptions there are, but general rules establish law. Will she not, at the approach of danger, call on man to aid her, thus tacitly acknowledging his superiority as the head?

Were we to stop even here, we think we have shown his claim to headship as conclusive; but as some minds on this subject are so strongly biased we fain would give more lengthened views.

In all of nature's work a glorious equilibrium is ever being attained, and all things, by its unerring laws, are balanced and directed. The slightest disarrangement of its forces would cause such confusion as the human mind could not imagine; but this is scarcely possible amid the bright perfection of the wondrous works of God. God, who gives to every member of the human family, just such gifts as are best suited to the end designed.

Without this wise adaptation, what a world of terror yours would be for the residence of man!

The wild tornado would soon lose its distinctive character for destructiveness before the unwholesome blast from human discord! Pandemonium, as man conceives it, would be but gentleness compared to such a state!

Here, then, Almighty Power is seen displayed. With all of nature's laws withdrawn, your cup of misery would be full, and happiness forgotten. But to our subject. Man's fitness for the head we endorse; but how, or in what way such headship or ruling power is to be conducted, becomes the next and most important consideration.

Power is not always accompanied by wisdom, but when it is, the government is easy by comparison. Wisdom and discretion united can use power to best advantage, giving direction and effect to every effort for improvement, either in public or domestic government, and, guided thus, will always present the most marked contrast to that government which rests on its right by force of muscle, or other arbitrary means springing from selfishness, through man's perverted nature.

Tyranny, as a means of governing, brings in its train the baleful passions of the human breast; however strong in seeming, it is but weak and rotten, and, when stoutly opposed by the spirit of independence, fired by injured justice, it is but short-lived, being unsound and unnatural. But ah, the loathsome bloody trail it leaves rests darkly on the memory of those who have suffered by it.

Domestic happiness is often sorely obstructed by offensive tyranny, that, so oppressive in its influence, renders home a very hell! But we have dilated longer on this point than we had intended.

Take man according to nature's intent, pure and free from innate vice, the absence of partial intolerance and fuming hatreds, endowing him with the requisites of governing, not only in public, but particularly in his domestic relations, and woman in her natural condition, also, as man's true helpmate, equal to him in all of the intellectual character, and blest with those consoling gifts which form the gist of woman's power over man. Being dual in their nature, yet cohering by ties most sacred and divine, a joint and undissevered interest holding them by bonds which are indissoluble, if unperverted. And thus would we dispose of this matter in all honest sincerity. No desire for tyrannic rule should actuate any one, a harmonious condition should pervade the home; wisdom and forbearance directing, love and pure harmony must prevail, inducing relations so grand and beautiful that no head would be wanted in a demonstrated form, but in spirit the dual becomes a unit. AMEN.

BYE GONES.

To talk of things long gone, may, perhaps, appear unnecessary, if not absurd; and yet there is a usefulness in them, rarely comprehended by the masses—a utility, which if well applied, makes manifest much truth which no sophistry can prevent, or power control.

Principles founded on truth, emanate from God, and all humanity must, in time, accept them. Worlds on worlds are being created, and not a single orb as yet has wandered from its natural orbit.

With such a proof of God's unerring wisdom, who can challenge aught he does, and the sure fulfillment of its wise intent?

The tiny blade of grass, out-cropping from the earth, presents its green and beauteous blade as an emblem of sweet contentment, and reliance on that power which gives it the nourishment and growth it receives, without questioning whence it comes.

Is not this a beautiful example to man, to accept the life that is given him, with full reliance on the bountiful God by whom it is given? In all that is presented to him by the Deity, can man see a single thing unsuited to promote his happiness and ultimate prosperity, if not perverted by himself? Before him lies a vast expanse no eye can compass nor mind can measure, studded throughout with orbs of glory, whose rays pervade the entire universe, giving light, life and motion where and when they are needed. He who created them has wisely directed the course to be pursued; theretore, is all so well and providently fashioned, that no confusion can ensue, to mar the unerring purpose of God, their maker?

But now we purpose showing thee the negligence of man, who, instead of scrutinizing and investigating those essential truths offered to his comprehension, takes but little notice of their import until too late, and then expresses much regret for the now lost opportunity!

Thus is God's munificence overlooked, and at the important time when man's best interests demand the exertion of his mental attributes. Even a much worse state of things was seen in earlier times.

The laws of God or nature not being understood, men strove to make such gods as best subserved their interests, inciting confidence in what they themselves had formed, not knowing in their untutored ignorance, that they were but giving expression, in this rude way, to the innate reverence for incomprehensible Deity, which is inseparable from the heart of man. These gods were instinctive subordinates to One of purity and boundless magnificence, but of whom they knew little, and cared less, confined, as they were within their crude and narrow dogmas.

The gods which they themselves had made, paid much attention to their sacrificial offerings, and why? Simply because they had taken care to fashion them in such a manner as to impress upon the minds of their deluded followers, signs indicating approbation, or its opposite, while enslaving their dupes under dogmas of the most revolting character, yet who conld gainsay their truthfulness?

And are not men of the present day acting in accordance with the same deceitful usage of ages past, occupying the most valuable time in discussing creeds and dogmas which are daily growing obsolete and revolting to the sane and sensible members of the human family?

The numbers are increasing who recognize the baneful influence exercised by priests, who have the power to direct the multitude.

Such miserable perversions of God's holy servants are sad imposters, uncalled and unregarded by Him who seeks humility, but cannot find it within these hirelings, who vaunt their power to carry on the work of reformation amongst the children of the earth. AMEN.

THOMAS PAYNE ON THE CRUCIFIXION.

DID men and women contemplate the mischief they were doing when offering as a truth the Christly sacrifice on Calvary's Mount they would adopt a different course; because, concerning that event they cannot show a more truthful record, corrupt and base as it is, than that within the lids of that so-called Sacred Book, the Bible, concocted by a set of men devoid of truth and every God-like principle? Did they expect that coming generations would swallow such confounded lies as tend to mar their happiness—the mere utterance of which should blast the whole and stamp them as untrue? Every feature in the case can be perceived as false and blasphemous in a degree unparalleled, and worse than all the besetting sins said to be inherited by poor humanity.

Conceive, if possibly you can, an act of cruelty so rare as that of a father doing a deed like that described in Sacred Writ—recorded and by whom committed. Not a poor finite being denuded of his common sense and reason-abandoned in his nature, depraved from birth, a very monster, devoted to a demon, accursed of God and man; such a cruel being might be taunted with a crime like this and some consistency appear. But oh, horror! can man's imagination possibly conceive of blasphemy so abhorrent as that of attributing such an act as murdering, by slow degrees of torture, an only son, (for so says Sacred Writ) and who should dare to doubt its being the very written or spoken words of God himself, accusing himself of perpetrating an act atrocious beyond all things else recorded of depravity. Added words cannot enhance the damning character of such an act, and fain we would drop the subject, could we readily accept the apology, Christians, as they call themselves, make so often, couched in blandest terms, that God so loved the world that he gave up His only begotten son as a ransom for the sins of the world. Yes; that son in whom He was well pleased. Can you imagine common sense was still extant? that reason still existed? or could the twain have departed for a time, that riot and misrule might run a race, and thus, untiring in their efforts, yield pleasure boundless in its nature and fervent in its purpose, to an unrighteous people. Even every avenue through which Divine and holy influences could reach the souls of men seemed closed; and even Deity, bewildered as he must have been, bade Nature wield her power with treble force to announce to an astonished world a perpetrated act the supposititious fiends of hell would have blushed the blush of shame to be accused of, and yet sapient men, as oft they are called, and egotistically aver themselves to be, are constantly presenting to their so-called flocks, by-gone dogmas—now unfitted for the times in which you live, when superstitious bigotry is on the wane, and tyranny and freedom now at war, must fight it out unflinchingly, even to the bitter end; being a war of conquest to the right.

MY BROTHER: What means this hubbub in their churches? A sad unrest they are now experiencing; bitter, acrimonious feelings are expressed in words somewhat unseeming in appearance amongst men of godly habits, who preach so much to others about polite and friendly courtesy being a need in such society. Can such exist where harmony becomes a stranger, and stranger still, she must remain while common sense and reason are eschewed? Commensurate with that lack of prudence so essential to communities and peoples, I am not satisfied, but something might be added to what we have already said about Christ's Crucifixion. Convinced as you and others must be, the act was quite unneeded, but a work of supererogation answering a purpose cruel in its character, and altogether inefficient in its culminations; giving to the speculator a capital to work upon, by making dupes of such as they could influence to become acceptants of the creeds and dogmas they were peddling among the ignorant and superstitious, God had created for a better purpose, conceiving that a time may come when common sense and reason may return, and by proper application of their united power, bring to bear upon their senses a wise and holy influence that shall guide and direct man through the avenues of earth life to a brighter and more glorious land, where angel entities shall be companions of the wise and good of earth, imbuing their minds with things of holy and divine importance, thereby fitting them for a continued life of happiness and joy eternal in the Heavens. When all the united strength of angel power will work a change no mind can contemplate, a something no mortal mind has any conception of, being something invisibly kept, something altogether beyond his power to believe, till by experience, all wonder then shall cease, and to himwho, through a power entirely his own, doeth all things well, be all the glory. Can a being thus possessed of attributes sublime, with no competitor existing, commit a single error? Or need He give an account to any one? The world being His, and all therein, and all thereon contained, can aught occur unseen by angel sight, who, as watchers night and day, can readily report a fault, designed or accidental? And thus a check is often put and crime prevented. This is the supervision angels are appointed to, and faithfully they perform their several duties; and this is what the so-called modern Christians call a special Providence. What specialty is here evinced? A possibility of being successful while committing crime is all that gives encouragement to commit it, not suspecting angel entities totally unseen by them, are watching all their movements.

A sudden tremor seized the one engaged in lawless purposes; he listens for a moment; discovery he dreads, and instantly seeks safety where he can, leaving the coveted behind him, eliminating thanks to God for such especial Providence enacted in his favor. Thus the Pharisee is seen applying to himself a merit no one expected might have existed within his egotistic nature. Of this we need no multiplied reports, because each day and hour elicits proofs so unmistakable no one can err in recognizing.

Would we could say this is the only point on which we differ with so-called Christianity. A man that is good needs no agent to proclaim his worth and goodness; the faithful monitor within, gives proof sufficient. All is right, hence all is harmony and contentment without a show being made in pompous style to others. Was all the world so constituted peace would be familiar to you, and all inharmony and discontentment would flee your homes, being better fitted for your then improved condition, because the Almighty power that guides and governs this vast Universe becomes, as it were, your polar star, to guide you to that haven of eternal rest you would seek with fervent zeal. As the result of a power that's all-sufficient and absorbing to the achievement of all your God and Father desires you should attain to, Men often wonder and exclaim why is trouble and perplexity the lot of all existent on this earth. There seems but few exceptions. All are troubled, both good and bad, so far as you can see. Therefore there must be some underlying cause for what seems to us anomalous to wrong. Alas, poor, silly beings, are you speaking what you know, or rather what you think? Finite as you are, what know ye of the why and wherefore of such things? Are you able to comprehend the grand, important end of your Creator? Can you view the starry firmament and trace the planets moving in their several orbits? Are Nature's secrets all unveiled to you? Can you conceive the *modus operandi* of their transit? Are you given a power enabling you to scan immensity or describe the distance, density and calibre of certain planets you may be asked about? Therefore, if lacking such amount of knowledge, talk no longer about thy wisdom, but hide thy countenance in shame, and boast no longer of thy fitness to become a teacher of thy fellow-man. Canst thou deem thyself as worthy of a tithe of the bounties given thee by thy God in answer to those aspirations sent by thee in confidence they will be responded to? Could man, while dealing with his fellow-men be always true and faultless, a better state of things would be inaugurated. Then God's eternal truth would be the standard. All would choose as being the best and surest mode of gaining what the souls of men are seeking, yet rarely are they found, and fain we would ask why is it so? To this we answer, God's laws being unalterable and fixed, admit no deviation from them, but tracing back, the cause is soon discovered, which but few can realize till suffering and affliction becomes the Savior, showing them beyond all cavil that the straight and narrow path of right is the only one that can be traveled safely.

MY BROTHER: It is getting late. You need your rest, and I, by longer stay, shall infringe upon my prescribed time. Therefore, I say, Adieu. AMEN.

THOMAS PAYNE'S REPLY

TO THE EXCEPTIONS TAKEN BY MEMBERS OF THE YOUNG MEN'S CHRISTIAN ASSOCIATION.

QUESTION—What says Thomas Payne to the fact that the Religion of Christ, or Christianity, is the great power that is revolutionizing, civilizing, and enlightening the world?

REPLY—Deeming all things worthy of investigation and the closest scrutiny, I willingly undertake the task of showing the writer of the above question what an egregious error he is committing when he conceives the absurd idea that Christianity evolves a single thought confirmatory of what he states.

The first point we may admit as true, *i. e.*, its "revolutionizing effects," for that stands out in bold relief, admitting no denial. In fact, its very origin may be attributed to what its advocates call Christianity. Your friend may plume himself upon its popularity, but is that a proof of its superiority? We think no man of sense would rest his faith on such a frail foundation—a very mockery of security—being a vain and futile effort to spread its baneful and erratic teachings in a soil which soon must share its growth and thus prevent its spread, saving the expense and trouble of uprooting pernicious teachings contained within the several dogmas, creeds and formulas within your so-called sacred edifices. What makes them sacred, we would ask? Is it because men call them so? Whence arises that aroma, sacred in its character? Can ye rob your altars of your God, and steal from thence the coming incense as it soars in curling vapors to its destiny? Avaunt! We say there is nothing sacred in them all, unless we see some poor, stricken soul, bowed down with misery and wretchedness, on bended knees, with outstretched hands and tearful eyes, imploring mercy of his God for many sins committed, beseeching relief, a starving wife and child may need. Such a sight of commune with his God, gives to the place a moment's hue of sacredness.

Oh, poor, beguiled, and duped recipients of such trash as in those churches is doled out to ye! We fain must yield our sympathies. Hours of penitence and prayer ye may expend, and what result can ye expect? Each utterance of a truth brings with it a recompense all may recognize as being just, but statements made in falsehood's guise are soon discovered, and who can claim reward for such? The anxious look, and hectic flush of cheek, betokens an unrest no human mind can bear and live a life of happiness and comfort.

Who, we ask, with common sense and reason, could for a moment entertain thoughts so absurd that cannot yield a moment's satisfaction and become concentered in the mind, as of any value beyond its momentary appreciation. Better by far call some crude, unlearned being to avow there is naught of truth around those so-called sacred churches, as to imagine a building can be sacred where all is pompous show and vanity. Can that be sacred where the spirit cannot soar beyond the arched and ornamented roof? Can aught of beauty—adorning aisles and seats, add one iota to the sacred character of such a place? We think a man of common sense must answer, no; because if Reason be inquired of, denial she must give to such affirmative, as many make, that it "pleases our Divine Creator." Do you think your Heavenly Father can be moved to an appreciation of such trifles? Alas, with all your acumen of thought, crude and puerile they must be, to imagine that such gew-gaws could possibly attract One who, being omniscient, calls for what He wishes and obedience becomes the issue.

Does a man who cares about his character designedly commit a wrong? Announce the same to others, and then accuse another of doing the deed? Can you think such a man would be believed? Depend upon it, such a one, even though he were an angel, or an almost God, would not be credited, but scorned by the entire creation; it were better such an one had never been born, because the sin of lying would, and must, adhere to him with a tenacity all its own. But to the subject more closely:

Everything connected with Ethereal Life, demands by right of all the world, a truthful statement of its conditions, and this we deem the grandest point connected with the future life of man, dependent as he is, and must be, while on earth, on what the angel world imparts to him through such mediums as yourself, Gifted and adorned with truthfulness, the enlightened souls of men can rest assured that no deception can be apprehended, being under the control of spirits in whom (by constant intercourse,) they have the most perfect confidence, everything accepted by them, and transcribed for other's use, can be relied upon. Can aught be doubted, coming as it does, through such a channel? and even should it be, what renders such a doubt acceptable to those, who are well informed, and possessing intellect adequate to form correct conclusions? Ask no information from such men as carp at every truth presented, which agrees not with their own benighted views of what is wrong, or otherwise. And thus the world becomes misled by those who assume the right of thinking for their neighbors; and thus, while uselessly employed, forget their own condition, and careless, as it seems, float down the stream of time, unconscious as to what may be their destiny. Is not this the fate of thousands, who in stark inertness, while away their precious hours in almost imbecility?

Everything in nature teaches that each and every one possessing a constitution free from ailments, should be actively employed. A mind that is constituted as it should be, claims the uses best suited to its calibre. No matter what opposition it may meet with, all will be surmounted and every barrier removed, by angel power appended to its course of progress.

And now, my brother, to the subject proper, and particularly addressed to me, couched in terms almost triumphant. Your friend, the questioner, appears to be convinced that nothing can invalidate the assertion made, "That the Religion of Christ, or Christianity, is the great power that is revolutionizing, civilizing and enlightening the World." Certainly a question such as many so-called Christians may conceive unanswerable, and such, no doubt, your friend imagined you would find it. But let us test the truth of such imaginings, deceitful as they often are—mere echoes of the thoughts of such a dreamer, rather than sober, well-digested thoughts of a deep and solid thinker; one whose analyzing powers are also clear, who mixes naught that's fabulous with the stern realities of active life, but gives them to the world entirely free from hyperbole, nor aims to make it seem an effort for that occasion. They appear as a beautiful boat, or ship, gliding along the stream of life, as a something you cannot help admiring, well-fitted, as it seems, to perform its duty. Are you such an admirer of Nature's works as to suppose that man is destitute of a power or ability to copy Nature's works? and if his efforts fail, by what tribunal would you judge him other than by his own ambition? Appeal to that, and perhaps a second effort will be made—and a third if necessary. Can any one do more, I ask? Can angel effort always meet success? Can the serried hosts of Heaven accomplish greater feats than are commensurate with the power awarded them by the great I AM? A noble, glorious aspiration may ascend to God, to give them strength and power to accomplish all they have projected, and yet a failure may be theirs, and not by any neglect or inattention of their own, but a something analogous to discord among the subordinates of a force, capable (when united) of performing all they had projected. But leaving hopes and figures, we shall come down to solid facts, so unmistakable in their character and potent in their effect, no power can contravene them. Just here we shall notice the means, or power, (as they express it,) they will adopt to accomplish what they now avow is their intention.

Religion, as its adherents call it, and perchance by this asserted power, a conquest may be gained, but, to me, it seems a doubtful matter; therefore, let us analyze this pompous word of frequent use among those so-called christians, who boast continually of their Religion, as though it were a thing of special and superior growth and quality, we will submit it, accepting what good it may present, and rejecting all we cannot comprehend as truth; and with such an arrangment, who can murmur? To such a tribunal we are willing to submit.

But to religion: What are its component parts? Affixed to some unwholesome creed, or dogma, it may seem of value as a means of bringing under holy influence the many thousands, flocking as they do to yield their manhood to the guidance of some wily priest or priests desiring to control them, thwarting for a time the angel efforts to emancipate the dupes from thraldom most atrocious in its character, and thus enchain them to a theory they call religion. Better they should be without a religion than yield obedience to a cassocked tyrant, clothed in sacerdotal robes, mere emblems of hypocrisy and deep deception. Can any one conceive it possible that almost all the world should bow obediently to a power already on the wane—crumbling into almost nothingness, as the result of combined atrocities committed in the name and by the sanction of that power your friend refers to as so potently achieving the grand, important work of which he boasts, 'revolutionizing this world of yours?' Let us for a moment analyze the status of society in this enlightened period of the Nineteenth Century, only in its incipient state of revolution, when all your daily prints are teeming with murderous details, such as no other age has ever witnessed in times of so-called peace. Can war present a blacker catalogue of crime committed, evincing no cessation, but like the snow-ball in its transit, gathering fresh material to swell its bulk, and make a very marvel of it? Do you conceive the thing as possible that man can become any better by changing all the peaceful conditions of his nature, and at once launch into the very vortex of a revolution? Are such the means your sapient Christians would adopt to carry out your views of reformation? Herein you show your inefficiency, making manifest your total incompetence to carry out your favorite but fallacious project. Do you ever contemplate the injustice you are doing to humanity by disturbing and destroying the harmony and happiness of the world by agitating such a measure, the outworking of some fevered brain, incapable of quiet, tranquil thought, from which would emanate a better and wiser system, altogether void of strife and sad confusion, the sure concomittant of ill-digested plans, doing its work and then again undoing it; evoking laughter and derision instead of praise and approbation? Think of this ye aspirants for fame as advocates of modern Christianity! All hail to ye as paragons of sanctity and holiness, who seek to bear the palm of victory even to the very gates of Heaven, as martyrs in the cause of Christ's Religion! Was He the advocate of war, as revolution must imply? Was He belligerent in His views? The "Prince of Peace," as He was styled—a being meek and lowly in His nature could not, *would not* break the bonds of union between man and man, as revolution must imply.

MY BROTHER: You have chosen a term ill-suited to establish the truth of what you wish to to prove, and feeling we have answered this portion of your sapient question, we shall, as best we can, give some attention to your second.

"Civilizing the World!" Certainly a bold position you have aspired to claim; and while I must admire the ambition evolving such an aspiration, I think I see discretion somewhat lacking. Energy at all times, seems a need to those who are ambitious, because its very nature seems to crave the aid of others to confirm the right or wrong of measures they conceive as worthy their adoption. Being convinced, they cannot err by counseling with others. Can you not see in this a wise procedure? Does any prudent man attempt to raise a ponderous body beyond the strength he knows he is possessed of, because in doing so a failure must result, or else destruction to his health must be the issue? And here we would apply a simile we think is quite correct: You, as men connected with the church, desiring to become conspicuous among the members of that church, banding yourselves together as a sort of specialty, under rules and regulations seemingly devoid of fault or aught objectionable concerning those whose aspirations led them to conceive a special mission they had been appointed to, which depended, almost, man's salvation, and correspondent with such thought, another seemed connected, better suited to assist them in gaining popularity as reformers, doing as they imagined Jesus had done before—going from house to house, demanding of the inmates the privilege of asking God to bless and prosper them in all their lawful acts, claiming, as God's agents, to be the instruments by and through whom he dispensed such blessings as in time might teach them seemingly the result of the many fervent prayers they offered, by which God's purposes were surely changed, and their renown approved and trumpeted abroad. And is this the civilization you refer to? Is this your boasted power that must change the world and make it what you think it should be? A world of sin and wickedness, such as it is, would need a higher power than man can use to cleanse it from its base impurities, which tend to mar the purpose angels have in coming to its rescue—your fervent praying, notwithstanding. Prayer without work we know to be of no effect. Outspoken Pharasaic prayer is not attractive to the angels, having no standard value as compared with heartfelt adjuration, when the soul seems, as it were, lost in devotion and, for the moment, carried into the actual presence of its God, it feels the full glory of such commune. Is such prayer as this familiar to your senses? Do you realize the presence of your God? Do you feel those holy and divine impressions as tokens of approval from the highest spirit in the universe? If not, I advise ye to tamper not with the things ye are not fit to manage. Wait, and ask the assistance of those angelic beings who, even now, are striving to reach your inner souls to plant therein an inspiration better suited to the needs of those you would exhort to change their practices and lead a purer course of life. Such teachings they will better comprehend than murky dogmas can impart to them. Then you may in meekness and humility aver that you *have tried* to civilize your fellow-man. This we are ready to admit, but nothing farther.

Your third proposition we may soon dispose of because, without a proof, discussion is not needed. But, having some little time to spare, we think we cannot better spend it than in presenting some few thoughts instructive in their character. Enlightenment implies improvement, progress, etc. The mind, perchance, may need its aid in greater measure than the entire form of man, being, as it were, covered with an element which is accepted or rejected, as the case may be. If the former, every thought presented, if accordant with the attribute of reason, becomes a welcome denizen, and shows at every turn, deeper and still deeper thoughts eliminated, demonstrating this power, while acting closer and still closer in unison with all that is grand and beautiful in this vast universe of animated nature.

MY BROTHER: I would not willingly attempt to coerce any man into the acceptance of a thought he could not comprehend, permitting the conscience of every individual to dictate to him concerning what is right and what is wrong, as he is responsible alone to God for whatever consequence may arise by mistake, or otherwise. But, while we are convinced that every one who feels a principle at work within him, evoking another for which the soul of man has sought possession, such will be awarded to it. The world may carp at and ridicule all that appertains to Spiritualism; the ways of God may seem almost mysterious in the eyes of some, but to the enlightened ones of earth no mystery can be seen, and wonder-stricken do they seem, and are when men of science and philosophy avow eternal hatred to its principles; showing, as they do, a morbid and depraved condition, better fitted to insure a course of spoilation than an honest one.

But while we would prefer another plan, we are not bigoted enough to claim the adoption of our course when others are presented better calculated to improve man's status here, and in the coming future give him proof substantial that a God of love and mercy has not been unmindful of him. This is the enlightenment we would crave, being, as we know it is, the grandest, most glorious and noble attainment man can possibly aspire to. That being, based on truth, must cheer the soul with frequent glimpses of ethereal light, elevating the mind, enlightening the soul, giving happiness and contentment here, and a happy and celestial home in the summer land. AMEN.

AN ESSAY ON PAPER.

FEELING disposed to comply with your wishes, we resume the subject commenced last night, not that we expect to elaborate so as to instruct you, but you may possibly derive some amusement through a means but little anticipated.

Your object was more to show your wife the power a spirit could exercise over your mentality, by producing something you feel you could not produce unaided by such power.

Therefore are we anxious to convince her that a spirit, under right conditions, is capable of all you have represented. With these few remarks, we will commence our essay.

To elaborate an essay, based upon the above single word "Paper," seems almost absurd, but it is our province to try.

Paper, at the present period, has become an article of vast appreciation, from which one standpoint you may view it, whether as auxiliary to man's happiness, or otherwise.

Look at the condition of the man who requires a loan at the hands of another; does he think the lender would trust to him a sum of money without security in writing? We think a prudent man would hesitate to do so. You, and some others, might, under the influence of a strong psychological control, be led into such an unwary act, while the mass of mankind would avoid the risk. With the same desire to oblige his neighbor, think you a man, whose circumstances were limited, would dare take another's word without ample security?

Verily, a suspicious world is this of yours, and time, indeed, a change should be effected to improve its condition, and then your paper might be used for other purposes than keeping men honest, and checking the unholy practice of deception. Then might paper be applied to such a righteous end that man, while seeking knowledge from the bye gones, might find a record useful to him left on paper—seemingly a resurrected message from the imagined dead, detailing facts of wondrous import to the world at large, that might be deemed a legacy of value almost inestimable. But to continue thus our theme can be but a repetition of the numerous uses to which paper may be successfully applied.

To enumerate a few must we confine our effort in this essay.

Paper, as a means of perpetuating thought, is most invaluable. A thought, the most brilliant, committed to man's memory only, would soon lose its brilliancy and effect. Each mind that received it desirous of imparting to others the benefit thereof, in giving utterance, would vary, of necessity, and so change in circulation from the original; whereas, were it recorded and preserved on paper, no mutilating change could take place; years might roll on, but the record is still there, neither added to nor diminished, the faithful paper holds in freindly custody the gem submitted to its care.

Here, then, is paper useful; but does its usefulness stop here? Ah, no! The tender maiden in her fondest mood, casts upon its snowy surface glances of deep affection, and these are reciprocated in words of glowing fire from a soul of kindred love, expressed in written characters upon a pure white sheet of paper.

Thus, in mute, but loving tones, the soul's best affections are transmitted from hemisphere to hemisphere, thrilling every fibre of its nature, and pulsating through every artery and vein, making for a time, a paradise of earth. Need we limit our estimate of paper's value thus? Oh, no! Look from pleasure to business, and mark its untold value.

A general recipient of love, of hate, indeed, of every passion known to man; honest and dishonest acts recorded on its once pure white surface—all his virtues, all his vices emblazoned there immutably, making a study for a lifetime.

Without paper, what use would life's experience be? Memory would fail in reference to past events; no dependence could be attached to so uncertain means of proof; but paper, coalesced with ink, makes plain the matter, and puts beyond all doubt the facts presented, if faithfully recorded.

There are other uses to which we might refer you, and none more important than that after man has left this life, the written record of his will and purpose remains, by which the law of equity and justice is enforced, and the innocent and helpless become recipients of their legitimate right.

Then say not paper is a useless thing, but rather view it as a boon inestimable, and worthy of the highest gratitude to Him who thus directs His angel messengers to aid humanity in such discoveries as to render human life secure and happy. AMEN.

A LONG EXPERIENCE IN THE SECOND SPHERE.

PERSONAL NARRATIVE OF A SPIRIT WHO LIVED ON EARTH THIRTY THOUSAND YEARS AGO!—APPEARANCE OF THE EARTH AT THAT DISTANT PERIOD.

INTIMATION—A spirit from the outer spheres is now approaching who has had ages upon ages of experience in the second sphere. He will leave a transcript, depicting the feelings of those so long condemned to dark captivity. He will also leave you an older and more truthful record of the earth's existence than that of the Bible.

It would not be well, then, to miss this opportunity of exposing this ancient misteaching in regard to a matter of so much interest and importance.

PREFACE AND REFLECTIONS.

Age after age had thus rolled on, yet no power appeared to save us from the monotonous thraldom to which sin had made us victims.

Under this irksome weariness we desired and sought a means to relieve us of an existence seemingly accursed of God and man, which, with its unending tendency, was worse to bear than death, however manifold.

Oh, with what horrid imprecations have we often sought to ventilate our surging passions, and drive from memory's tablet the recollections of that life on earth which was spent in total violation of those laws that the good God had given to guide us in our earthly pilgrimage.

Such paroxysms drove us at times to the brink of mad despair, but whispers soft came to our ears, saying: "There is something still beyond this life of suffering thou yet mayest reach, whereby alleviation of thy woes may be effected; therefore, be not rash in what thou doest, but wait with becoming patience thine allotted time.

"This is a comfort granted thee by thy God, whose patience and justice are as limitless as space, for, in time, there will be sent thee a good and holy spirit, charged with mercy and compassion to the sinking and desponding soul, so, that at a time when least expected, thou wilt be redeemed and brought to fraternize with spirits in the spheres, who, like thyself, had wandered to and fro, in this darkened atmosphere, but are now revelling in the delights of heavenly happiness, freed from all impurities, and blessing the means so well adapted to their regeneration, and which has made them sensible of the benefits of pure justice, received from their father and their God.

"Without these merciful and controlling influences, think you, what an unbearable destiny would have been those almost countless ages of unmitigated sameness in woe and sorrow!

"The men of earth, now wallowing in luxury and pleasure, little dream of the change awaiting them, possessed, as they will be, with a goading consciousness of what they have lost by inattention to the warning voice of conscience, which is but the whisperings of guardian angels, who are anxious to arrest their downward course, and lift them to a higher and holier condition, which would fit them for a life of eternal bliss in the heavenly spheres."

My preface is somewhat long, but these sentiments flood my thoughts, as happy tokens of my gratitude for liberty so unexpected, that I can scarcely find a stopping place, and yet it is needful that I should, or else you cannot have my promised transcript, which I see, clairvoyantly, is your most ardent wish. Permit me a moment's respite before commencing my detail, which you shall have in candor and truthfulness.

After the preface I have given, I may perhaps be excused from commencing my narrative at the earlier stage of my existence. Suffice it then to say, that at the time I speak of, the earth was rude and rough in all its phases; indeed, all things remembered, it seemed but a vast desert, unfit to sustain the beings then upon its surface. I speak of the portions with which I was then acquainted. The vegetable world grew rank beyond conception; all growth was urged by the same gigantic effort to supply enough for the wants of animal creation, and man was cared for in a way mysterious to him, in his then condition. His mind, uncultivated as it was, improved each day by necessity; his wants, gradually developed, the reasoning faculties of his soul comprehended means to satisfy the cravings of his nature; messengers, invisible to him, were constantly around him, guiding and directing his movements, instructing him by kindly efforts to research amongst the supplies provided for his use.

With such assistance did he gradually discover the readiest means to supply his wants, and thus by slow degrees, through many generations, he improved, and with improvement he slowly advanced to a civilized condition.

QUESTION BY MEDIUM—Permit me to ask how long the world had then been occupied by man?

ANSWER—From all that can be gleaned, your earth appears to have been inhabited by mortals for millions of years, but that generation after generation passed into utter oblivion, leaving behind those links of population which continued the human race.

The dates of creation by the Bible record and chronology are merely mythical; statements of man's imagining, totally unworthy any confidence from thinking men.

QUESTION—Let me ask, how remote is the period you are speaking of, at the time of your advent, and what was the condition of man at that time?

ANSWER—The period about which you inquire cannot be less than thirty thousand years ago, and at that time the condition of man was rude and uncultivated, as must be supposed. It was a period of rapid resuscitation after a general exhaustion of population, and previous generations, for want of intelligent records, had been forgotten.

Shall I go further with the subject, or resume my former detail?

QUESTION—I wish you to feel entirely free to follow your own design, but would ask one question more: At the time of your existence, was there a means of education established?

ANSWER—The means were sparse indeed, but I perceive the point you desire to reach: Without education, how could I express myself as I do? To which I answer: The spheres abound in means of education, and to such a state of perfection has it attained that progress is very rapid, giving to the student all that is necessary to elevate a spirit's nature, and fit it for a celestial residence and progression.

MEDIUM—This induces another question: Have undeveloped spirits the same educational privileges? Assuredly they have, provided they will seek it; but it must be sought, or in darkness they remain, like those on earth whose souls are darkened and obscured by mysterious dogmas, which originated in the minds of base and sordid men.

At the time I speak of, men had very different classifications and attachments to what they have now. They were mostly attached in bands, some strong and numerous, with little idea of law or restriction, save that of arrogant tyranny, and with very loose notions of right or justice. It would be almost impossible to define such institutions to the present generation. To one of those bands, however, was I inducted, when a spirit came and warned me from it, showing conclusively that if I did not comply ruin, and destruction must overtake me.

The chief object of those wretches was the plunder of their neighbors, and to live without laboring. Through the spirit's warning, a change came over my views, and I withdrew at once, determined not to fraternize with such miscreants.

This so incensed the band that they sought my life by every means in their power, but ever and anon there came a whisper to me,—"Fear not, thou art protected by an unseen hand, therefore be encouraged, thy time of departure is not yet, but years thou hast in store for thee." After this the spirit left me, and never more returned.

I sought the new leader of that band, endeavoring to discover their motive in seeking the life of one who had never injured them and only tried to elevate them above the level of the brute creation.

They fiercely accused me of intended injury, which I successfully explained away—having no other motive than to bring my whole people to the best state of civilization then known.

QUESTION—Your words denote a rank as yet unexplained; you speak of your people? It was unintentionally spoken, yet such was my position; a chieftain high of rank and power, inferior to none around me; respected, I may say, as much as men of rank can be, but, alas! how few there are who wield that power as righteously as they might.

Their souls not being attuned to strict justice and benevolence, they deny it to those most in need—the poor and distressed of the human family. For myself, I failed to become the faithful steward I should have been, so that I sacrificed the poor man's interest on the altar of avarice, at whose shrine I finally became a constant worshipper.

Here, then, was the rock upon which my bark was foundered. Wallowing, as it were, in wealth, such as those times afforded, I had no ear for the cry of distress, but rather filched from my poor, helpless subjects, to fill my insatiate coffers. Ah, me it was ever so; at times, when gloating over my untold riches, did the piteous cry of the poor stricken victims of distress and penury come to me, but so callous had I become, that it never awakened any sympathy, and I tendered no aid to any.

Oh, my brother, an array of negative sins is seen but when added to crimes committed, a frightful catalogue appears, kept involuntarily by myself, written in words of fire on the tablets of my own heart—without power to deny, or explain, a single act of my guilty career of disobedience to the divine will.

But to return to the epitome of my earth-life; think you, was my condition there an enviable one? No, indeed. Nor was I alone in such condition.

Then, as now, the world though much less in numbers at that remote period, man had the same disposition as now; selfishness was the ruling vice. There is little, comparatively, of moral improvement perceptible; the baser passions of mankind, though restrained or screened, are still as rife, and man, for all his civilization, is but mortal still. Your strangling gibbets are in constant use, and your jails are full. Murder, lust and immorality, so boldly perpetrated and practised that at every turn you come in contact with the depraved, vicious sons and daughters of humanity.

This picture is not overdrawn—the myriad victims of pollution, and foul disease, who, in the form, became so loathsome, have prayed for death to release them from their state of irksome bondage, hoping by such change to cast aside the pains and penalties of sinful practices! And have they found it so? Alas, no; the change has not effected the expected cure, they have but changed locations—not conditions.

The undying worm is ever gnawing at their vitals, the fire still burns within their fevered souls until tired nature at length succumbs, when unconsciousness is in mercy granted to such guilty beings, to stay the ravages sin has made upon their over-exhausted natures.

Here is a picture that should be stereotyped on the human brain, as a warning against sin. If I could but take thee, oh child of earth, to the regions of space, I might show thee the myriads of suffering human souls, not writhing in torture in a lake of fire, but tortured by anguish indescribable, at the vivid remniscences of their past sinful lives!

I might show thee one who swayed a sceptre, and at whose word hecatombs of God's children have been sacrificed to please the tyrant, who with savage satisfaction witnessed the perpetration of such damned crimes, as to make the heart thrill with horror, that the unbridled passion of one man should be thus indulged by the sacrifice of so many!

MY BROTHER: I proposed giving you a transcript relative to the antiquity of this world of yours. Theology says a period of six thousand years only have transpired since creation first began. Such a theory might pass the uncultivated intelligence of the times when Moses wrote, but in these days of research and analysis, reasoning powers and clearness of powers of perception denounce the statement as false and absurd, though ostensibly from the highest authority, even from God himself.

The doctors who assert these things, do so in ignorance, or else they blaspheme against the living God. They, as teachers of the masses, are like unto the father, who, when asked by his child for bread, gave him a stone.

Geology presents to mankind at large, such convincing proofs that creation commenced long antecedent to the Bible account, that the human mind is forced to accept the evidence as entirely conclusive, and recognize science as superior to all the sophistry employed by theologians to deny or disprove the facts.

Man's energy, reason and research have piled

up testimony so voluminous and complete that all attempts to conceal the stupendous truth must fail. The earth, upon which you live and move, has been the habitation of the human race through ages almost uncountable—past and gone, far beyond the possibility of human reckoning.

Changes have followed changes, until further mutation seems impossible; but still, to angel vision, it is perfectly clear that others are at hand more important than any of the former.

Amongst all the creatures ever known on earth, man, only, is progressive. His immortal soul can never die, and hence, is ever struggling forward, aided by the great laws of nature, which none may transgress and escape without paying the penalty, be the same large or small. Nothing is forgiven, and nothing is compromised. Man runs his career of sin until satiety becomes a curse, sin grows hateful, pleasure turns to pain, and sweet into bitter; eventually, the wretched transgressor is entirely prostrated and helpless, surrounded with the constantly recurring and agonizing horror of gazing continually upon his conscious guilt.

Thus is sinful pleasure repaid in suffering by the law of uncompromising justice, and man's stubborn nature is utterly subjugated and humbled in proportion to his misdeeds.

Reaction is one of nature's fundamental laws

against evil. Man runs his sinful course until, overwhelmed by its enormity, he sinks hopelessly under the accumulation ; but in due time the merciful law of just retribution opens to him a means of escape, and when recuperation comes, his happiness is enhanced, for he feels unbounded gratitude to his Creator for that impartial rendering of justice which places him on perfect equality with all other regenerated spirits, no biased favors having been extended to him, or any one.

The Christian Bible, with its swaying uncertainties, and doctrines of partial favor, would teach otherwise ; but here is truth immaculate, presented to the grasp of human reason by one who has had bitter experience through untold ages of monotonous unrest.

To return to our original subject : all nature teems with evidence to disprove even the possibility of the Bible assertion that this world of yours was created in six days ; because, at best, nature works but slowly, and how could it be possible that a work of such stupendous magnitude could be effected in so short a space of time, even supposing a day meant an age, as some Bible apologists claim? Science steps in and tells you, by simplest facts, it can be no such thing ; ages upon ages have transpired, and yet no evidence have we that God or nature ever ceased to work.

This is truly shown by my own evidence,

through every change which has occurred in all the ages of the past which I have witnessed, and down to the present time, progression still continues. Yet your Bible states that God (being tired) stopped his work, and rested on the seventh day, though all the work was done by his mere word, or utterance of His almighty will!

What think you, O reasoning mortal, of a God so very human as this?—the Creator and Supreme Ruler of the seen and unseen universe, stopping to rest Himself as a tired human machine. Man must seek a more enlightened guide than this book, or than any of the doctrines founded thereon, before he can rest satisfied, or be convinced of a life hereafter and a happy immortality beyond the grave, which is really the bottom—the great, the one essential to human happiness?

When a soul feels thus assured, what can distress or dismay it? Yea, what can you conceive to compare with the unclouded consciousness of being immortal? Anxious doubts and fears always cling to and surround the Christian whose doctrines deal not in realities, but in hopes alone; quite unsatisfactory to the ardent spirit, whose aspirations are all heavenward, and in proportion to the force of his faith, his very being is paralyzed by the shuddering terrors of an eternal, ever-enduring hell, as if the errors of a purblind, incomplete, and almost evanescent mortality, could correspond with the intensity of unending torture.

The Christian finds no solid place whereon to base his expectations of a future life, but groping in the murky darkness of a twisted, contradictory creed, he finally leaves earth-life to find himself in another, a doubting, fearing, groping $pirit still.

I shall now allude to another phase of earth-life: the contentious disposition of the various religious sects, where each polemic assumes to be God's champion, specially delegated.

What kind of an insignificant God could he be, let me ask, for whom any of these mentally mutil ated creatures could act as proxy? Assuredly not the Supreme Ruler and Director of the universe. Whence proceed their quarrels and hatreds of each other? Is it that they deem God an eccentric partisan, and hence are prompted to abuse each other, through jealous feeling for the partial distribution of His gifts?

Let us terminate these thoughts, and try to soar beyond an atmosphere so dark and gloomy, to a brighter, happier realm where, light shines in upon the enlivened soul, giving zest to all its surroundings, and lifting it beyond the confines oi temporal influence to a higher and holier state, beyond the ken of mortals, where the enfranchised soul can best assert its rights and privileges, becoming the associate and complete equal of angels, bright and pure and holy. As regeneration proceeds, by which ethereal things are comprehended, the newly admitted soul assimilates with heavenly things, and heaven soon becomes the place of promised rest to those who have sought it in spirit and in truth.

The animus of human virtue is progression By natural law the soul seeks for ethereal knowledge, and based upon the solid principle of common sense, each earnest effort is rewarded by truth that yields to the children of earth returns more precious and comforting than all the mere worldly riches to be accumulated.

It is time to return to our original theme: the Bible's creation of your world. The power of God is infinite, and his wisdom omniscient, as all things in nature prove conclusively; and where, we would ask, is there a man enlightened by common sense, and whose reason is unwarped by prejudice, could accept that his God would require the creatures of His power to receive, as revelation from Him, a record so abounding in contradiction?

Where the baffled searcher fails to find, not only convincing truth, but, much less, consistency in the simple understanding of it.

Who can discover the mark of divine wisdom within the lids of this book? Its tendency is opposed to all that is liberal and just, giving erroneous bias to men's thoughts, and begetting complication, where a plain, ungarbled statement would fully answer every honest end designed. It must be productive of repugnance, the compelling of enlightened men to accept that which they cannot comprehend of their own reasoning powers, but have forced upon them the dictation of wily priests who, deeply versed in sophistry, delude their confiding listeners with solemn complications of mystical nonsense.

Remove this evil barrier, and half the work will have been accomplished, so that an epoch would follow to bless humanity, by giving such tutors as will reach the inner souls of men, with such enlightenment to their spiritual natures as the spirit world stands ever ready to impart, but in accordance with the divine law, must be sought. Ask, and you shall receive; we are ever ready to give you that which shall be lasting as time itself. AMEN.

THE CENTRAL POWER OF NATURE: GOD'S GOVERNMENT.

IS THE universal government of nature carried on by one grand central power, called God, without the intervention of others, supposed to exist?

The first effort we shall make is to prove that God's government being omniscient, admits of no other existent power equal to it, or in any way approximating, or independent of it. That in all of its ramifications, infinite wisdom can be traced, and nothing imperfect or defective can be detected.

Therefore, are we forced to the conclusion, that no assistance can be required, to carry out the magnificent plans of God's government.

Man may often imagine the possibility of improvement in many things connected therewith, until his vanity has even prompted him to experiment, so far as his finite mind is capable of analyzing nature's or God's works; when to his shame and confusion, he is invariably (unless insanity ensues) compelled to acknowledge his incompetency to even comprehend their vastness, much less offer an improvement upon the slightest and most unimportant work of creation.

Here then it is conclusively proven that the Almighty works by laws, the scope of which extends so far beyond the human understanding, that man, in his finite ignorance, cannot comprehend the *modus operandi* of a government so vast, and yet so minute in all its proportions, that the mind of man fails to discern, much less contemplate the extent of its glorious grandeur. Is he, then, (the creature) a fit reformer of those works belonging strictly, to the hands of the Creator? Oh, no. Let him quietly receive instructions from the angel world, where the agents and messengers from the great *center* are employod to receive and impart His holy and divine behests for the governing of those whom He has created, wherein they will they find great reward. The daily and hourly preparation going on within their own souls, would be fitting them to become, in their turn, promulgators of those divine truths, and by which they would advance to be agents and co-workers with the heavenly hosts, in the subordinate departments of God's Government.

Were it possible for the finite perception to take a microscopic view of the more elaborate arrangements for the conduct of this vast machine, no such question as the one we are now replying to could occur to either thought or reason. Each movement of nature's system, shows the complete adaptation of one portion to the other, securing beyond all contingencies approaching to failure of its intended purpose; so that every creature who has attempted to prove inconsistencies or imperfections in the laws of God and nature, either by theory or practical experiment, has been submerged in convictions of his own ignorance.

Mankind, in all ages of the world, has been much employed in theorizing; and oh, how many many brilliant intellects have been wrecked on the shoals of experiment, who, had they been properly directed, or had suffered themselves to listen to spirit teachings, might have become shining stars in the galaxy of human talent!

Thus has the world rolled in its orbit, carrying around in its diurnal motion, minds of such varied calibre, and dispositions of equally varied character, that in every direction you perceive the germ of intellect struggling, in its incipient condition, to rise above its surroundings, and soar into the regions of untold space in search of something it craves, but in earth-life never, never can reach.

This, however, is the elemental ambition of man which is ever expanding; and when in the direction of eternal wisdom, it seeks a closer affinity therewith, until at last a lifetime on earth has been expended, and the seeker finds himself far distant from perfection. Yet, in the renewed search after divine truth, never tiring, but, through the enlightening influence of spirit inculcations, seeing fresh and continuous beauties in the limitless garden of ethereal beauty, implanted in those spheres by infinite love and wisdom, for those who, through all time, will be apportioned to enjoy as a reward for a life well spent on earth.

Here, then, would seem to be the culmination of happiness to the spirit, which has now realized an entire suspension of the trials and perplexities of earth-life—but it is not so. Far beyond are other scenes still, of which, but a glimpse is given as a stimulus to progress, and by which, the awakened soul becomes animated and incited to greater exertions.

But this is rather digressing from our subject: Can this universal government be carried on by the one great central power? Oh, what a question to be asked by mortal man—one who has been created by that power, and whose perceptive faculties carry him so short a distance in his desires to know the eternal future. Is it not said that God is *infinite*—what, then, is the significance of this term? Can the puny mind of man grasp its wondrous import? Oh, no. Therefore let him be content to receive this teaching from the spheres. Infinity admits of no compeer—comparison fails, and man, under the conviction of his own nothingness, sinks abashed, but yet continues the constant, sedulously sought object of infinite compassion and holy love.

We say, then, cease to ask the idle question: "Is that great central power assisted in its government by aught of any distinct power?" for the ONE GRAND INFINITE, being, as the term implies, of itself beyond and above all things else, is capable of, and does carry on the divine government, and by such agencies as the elements of divine wisdom see fit by and through which nought but harmony exists, and one universal condition—perfect rule, pervades the created universe. AMEN.

FUTURE LIFE.

SOME SAY THAT THE DETAILS OF A FUTURE LIFE ARE TOO GOOD TO BE TRUE.

MY BROTHER: Whatever may be the opinions expressed as to a future state, each individual who contemplates it must feel desirous that the most favorable description rendered may be true, and merely express such doubts in order to excuse their own indifference about investigation. Too much engrossed with Mammon to devote a short period of their time to rational inquiry, they thus treat lightly the knowledge acquired by the industrious investigations of others.

Look around you and you will see just such individuals, generally, the most indefatigable in their attempts to obtain worldly riches, not always discriminating closely the right or wrong of their attempts; but to procure riches all their mental and physical energies are directed, never for one moment entertaining a thought that some exertion should be made in search of heavenly truths. Should you tell them the reward for all such efforts would be a manifold compensation for their labors, instantly would you hear in excuse:

"At some more convenient time we may make the much desired effort." Ah! say ye so, ye silly mortals? How know you the morrow will be thine, much less the years of coming time?

Thou little knowest how many of the teeming millions now existing may, within a brief period, be swept away all unprepared, and hast thou assurance of exemption? Perchance it may be so; but is thy chance more than one amongst the millions we have named? Canst thou not see that the vain and foolish expectation which thou art hugging to thy soul is but deceiving thee?

Arise, we say, from this untoward lethargy, and show thou art not spiritually dead to that which is in store for those who seek to find it.

All things in heaven demand research, and wilt thou stand in obtuse indolence, overwhelmed in the world's depravity, and see thy friends advance and pluck the very treasures so long proffered thee by thy guardian spirits, who have striven to break the barriers arrayed against thy progress?

Time is waning; and with unmeasured pace, Investigation is progressing, leaving thee and others like thee, a prey to discontent and misery, the sure concomitant of sad indifference.

We cannot see the slightest reason why the thought is entertained, that aught thy *Maker* has in mercy given thee can be deemed too good. To entertain a thought like this shows but distrust in His almighty goodness, therefore would we at once condemn its utterance as being unwise and almost blasphemous; for He who gives in love and mercy supplies in bounteous measure.

In all thy doings act in such a manner that thou canst feel thou hast partly carried God's bounteous gifts, not boastingly, but with manly mien accept the boon presented. No need within the presence of the holy angels thou shouldst utter plaintive statements of thine own depraved condition. Thy record will be seen, whether acknowledged or not. The All-seeing eye will be upon thee, and no subterfuge will then avail thee. The fiat will have then gone forth which stamps thee fit for heaven or not. AMEN.

SPIRIT COMMUNION.

ARE NOT THE DECLINING YEARS OF HUMANITY VITALIZED AND STRENGTHENED BY SPIRIT COMMUNION?

My Beloved Husband: This thought might have originated in the mind of your friend by contemplating your condition, and therefore does it gladden our hearts to perceive the fruit of our efforts to change and improve your condition, both physically and spiritually; for a proof like this is to us more potent and satisfactory than aught else could be adduced. Is it not said "By its fruit shall the tree be known." We therefore thank our God and Father for this result.

But, my husband, we must hasten to give our mature friend and brother some thoughts that will give him pleasure, combined with instruction, which he is ever seeking and therefore measurably prepared for. The motive power working within his soul is ever prompting his research in such direction as may evolve thoughts and ideas far beyond the material standard, resting upon his experience of the one, but looking forward with anxious expectation of something in the future; hence are all his aspirations upward and onward, leaving others far behind him groping, as it were, in material darkness, whilst *he* is soaring to the far beyond. And why, we ask, is this? Simply because his inner nature has been awakened somewhat precociously; for has it not been promised "he that seeks shall find," and is not every effort of his mind a seeking for the something his soul is ever yearning for? Is not every question he proposed but one of the many prayers he offers for enlightened wisdom? And if those prayers are uttered in full faith, shall they not be answered? Yes, my husband; the angel world are agents acting in the grand panorama of eternal life, doing their Master's will and preparing humans for their final transit. As such we are now acting, and earnestly beseeching the ability to proceed successfully.

The tide of human life at present seems setting in a new direction; even the derangement of all things mundane. A scene of anarchy and deep confusion seems ready to burst asunder its embryotic confines and spread broadcast among humanity the seeds of universal freedom, based, as it will be, upon the rock of truth immutable. Is man prepared for such a change? Can you, O man, declare it is so? Look around and see the terror-stricken countenances, pallid and care-worn; affrighted as they are, with even a shadow. How can they endure the real evil when presented? We are not fain to terrify with rumors quite unfounded, but through the sight clairvoyant are such scenes presented to us, and as a point of duty, are they given; and if no further good may come therefrom, the human mind can thus be urged to seek improvement in matters vitally involving his condition in the future.

My husband, I think I hear you ask what has this to do with your friend's question? To which I answer it will be our endeavor to connect the two subjects as rivals to each other, and however strange this may appear, you will even acknowledge it is true.

The question, seemingly, is somewhat special, but we claim the privilege of stepping somewhat beyond that specialty, in order to establish our position.

You ask if spirit commune tends to vitalize old age, to which we answer, only under right conditions. With some the effort would be useless. There must exist within the soul of man that with which the spirit or spirits can assimilate, the same as in earth-life, or what is termed friendship, in a degree either warm, enthusiastic or otherwise, as each soul is gifted and made recipient of such elements as are essential to the desired end. So it is in a spiritual sense. There must be either a natural or an acquired desire to be improved by spirit commune, which, when once perceived, unlocks, as it were, the element of love conjointly; and he who has the most of love within his soul, imparts thoughts so imperceptibly from that store of vital magnetism that strengthens and invigorates the declining physique of him who is seeking immortality at so late a period of existence. Here is seen a beautiful law of indemnity, though little noticed by humanity. Thousands upon thousands in the heterogeneous mass of beings closely congregated in your cities suffer most intensely from poverty, disease, and misery most dire. To such is oft accorded this vital magnetism, sometimes unsought, at others presented by some angel hand who has sought to awaken in the soul of some unfortunate, a hope of better things. It is this vital and sustaining influence that is thrown into his system, giving strength to all his weak resolves, and proving beyond all cavil, that there is a potent power at work behind the veil of human life, experienced but not recognized.

My beloved husband, may we not refer to you for testimonial of truth in this averment? Look back but two or three years; your experience clearly corroborated by others, all will tend to show that we, the appointed agents of your God, have placed within you the seeds of renovated health which, if withdrawn at present, would cause life's superstructure to fall at once, as if stricken by some plague token of destruction.

Here, then, the man who believes in spirit visits from the realms above, must take, as certain proof, that spirit commune can be so applied to mortal use that the decrepitude of old age can be veiled from mortal ken, and the individual so assisted, must in truth confess it is potent in its influence. It is also true, and to be expected, the skeptic may, and will, reject this statement. Well, let him do so; his statement to the contrary will not defeat our purpose in making known its efficacy in saving many a human being from the effects of pain and suffering incident to advanced years, and more particularly among those who, by imprudence or inattention to the laws of health, are made the victims of an accusing conscience. To these, particularly, is angel sympathy accorded, in testimony of expressed repentance. Here, then, is shown the healing power possessed by disembodied spirits who claim, not for themselves, a credit for the discovery of some unknown science which has thus enabled them to cure disease, for it is but a continued power, diffused throughout humanity, a sort of entailment from that pattern medium, our elder brother, Jesus. Yes, from him must have sprung that holy principle of universal love, at that time imparted, which, like the unused talent spoken of, was hidden, but which, under the inauguration of modern Spiritualism, has become exhumed, and is now with active energy proclaiming the glad tidings to humanity.

Shall we say more upon this most important subject, involving, as it does, the eternal interest of those who, through a long life, may have been persecuted and reviled because of their belief, as exhibited to erring humanity through ages past, in proclaiming God's eternal goodness to every human being, and in the sequel of a life of purity by the attractive influence of angel love, will be brought to enjoy eternal happiness?

My husband, the wonder ceases not with death, for as the mind becomes etherealized, new beauties constantly present themselves, showing the grandeur and magnificence within the spheres. Then would we conjure you to rest your hope on strict obedience to His laws; you will be rewarded more than adequate to your requirements, and to Him whose love is over all the world, we now commit you. AMEN.

THEY SAY I AM CRAZY OR INSANE.

My Son: The frequent charge that is daily uttered, such and such a one is insane, will soon have lost its force amongst those who have been so antagonistic to the doctrine you, and millions of the present day, esteem the best and noblest ever given to man.

But to our text: They call you crazy; and here we ask, does such avowal make you so? Are all your acts of sanity, before you became a medium, forgotten, and laid aside as nothing? Can vast improvement in your moral status prove insanity? Does integrity of dealing with your fellow-man add force to such a statement? Can the improved conception of your God be brought as proof against your sanity? Is the constant exercise of common sense a further proof you *are* insane? Can your disbelief of meaningless dogmas, often thrust upon you, afford sufficient proof of your insanity? Is it because your reason tells you the teachings of theology meet not the cravings of your soul—should sanction such a charge? Can your affirmation that spirits are your constant visitors, and hold with you those sweet communings that tend to purify your soul and make you feel an increasing nearness to your God; that makes you know Him as your father and your friend? Is this a crime for which they take from you your precious liberty, so dear to every thinking mind? Would those who claim that freedom is a glorious boon from God, on such absurd pretense, deprive a fellow-being of his God-given rights, by placing such a one in durance, making him insane in very deed?

But, ah! how little do they know the solace given by lips invisible, whom no bars or bolts can e'en exclude; but in defiance of all earthly espionage can pass unseen by mortal ken, the every barrier presented; for such avowal as we make through your organism, would they, did the law permit, confine your aged limbs and take from you the right to do our bidding. Sanctioned, as we are, by a power they cannot contravene, thus while under spirit guidance, your hand may wield your pen to advocate the glorious doctrine they, in ignorance, denounce; aye, in besotted ignorance; for while they claim to be the servants of the living God, (by his especial call,) as falsely stated, they know their own incompetence to fulfill the task assumed by them.

They may boast to a benighted world of their collegiate learning, they may search the ancient archives of the past and plume themselves upon their erudition, but where's the abode of Christ, their so-called leader? Are they not lacking the one important feature in their Christly mortal? Is His spirit with them in their costly edifices? Is it shed abroad amongst them like a beautiful aroma, making sweet its aisles, and by its fragrance giving tranquility and happiness to those who realize its presence?

With shame and terror must they admit the accusation just. And yet, while censuring others, are they not committing the crime of black ingratitude to Him they call their Savior, by professions of sincere belief in what He taught, without the practice of the sundry duties He enjoined upon them?

But, further on the subject of your craziness, the law of equity demands a proof direct of every charge that is brought. On what hypothesis do they attempt to substantiate this charge against you, the charge being personal? So shall be our defense. If difference of opinion be their data, we readily admit the fact, if this opinion be accepted. But to such a course we present our protest, and more particularly in this land of your adoption—this glorious, free America, the asylum of the persecuted of other climes. Should such a nation, blest with laws defending freedom, offer violence to free thought and free speech, in matters appertaining to the future life of all humanity? Where, we ask, is justice? Where is that God-like attribute which should give to all alike a true and righteous verdict? If sleep was ever sought by her, the present time she must have chosen, and left the present generation quite uncared for. But while reason holds her sway in mortal minds, some are still left to enter protest against its possibility.

Is there a being on your globe who would dare to take upon himself a responsibility half so great as theology assumes, in daring to assert a trinity of Gods, as rulers of this universe, and call on men and women of this time to accept their assertion as a truth, judging them by the meanest standard possible, and then denounce them as insane? Are such men, we ask, fit and proper persons to adjudge the sanity, or otherwise, of a single human being, nursed, as they have been, in ignorance and bigotry, their claim to learning, notwithstanding? Are they not superstitious and deluded when they speak to you? With all their boasted learning do they give a single proof it is useful to humanity? The very errors they charge on Spiritualists they daily perpetrate; presenting dogmas we, above, call meanignless? They ask you to believe and found your faith upon them; and because your knowledge, not belief, of a better doctrine creates disgust within your nature, they, not comprehending the facts presented, at once denounce you as insane.

Can such injustice be continued in the presence of a just and righteous God, whose every act toward humanity but proves Him good? Wherefore, while man continues inattentive to the monitor within him, the same unrighteous acts will still continue, and such conditions, baneful in their character, must prove a barrier to that improvement needed amongst the masses who, like sheep within a fold, wait but the movement of a leader to follow in the direction he may choose. And so it is amongst the various denominations in religion; they, like sheep, follow their *own* leader, however reckless he may be; believing, as they often do, the most outrageous falsehoods, if but uttered by some sacred, priestly lips. O, monstrous infatuation! fain would we ask its abjuration; that a better, holier doctrine might be substituted, more fraught with tolerance and spiritual beauty, so that angelic truths might be accepted as coming from the source of all truth. When unity of thought and action might direct the universe, when principle, opposed to fraud, might gain the victory, and many thus guided by it, would no longer wish to raise themselves upon the ruins of their brothers, but, hand in hand, they would tread the royal road of progress, supported on their march by Hope's extended finger, directing where the Eldorado lies—where love, happiness and truth, combined, would breathe the breath of amity and love. By such a combination all jealousy would cease, and justice claim acquittal for the accused insane. AMEN.

SPIRITUALISM.

WHAT DOES IT TEACH THAT MEN AND WOMEN ARE SO UNWILLING TO ACCEPT IT?

MY SON: With joyous feelings do we take upon ourselves the task of responding to your question. Eighteen hundred years have passed away, and half another century, since Christianity was first essayed on earth, and what has been the issue?

Based, as it is said to have been, on principles so pure that no possible objections could be raised against them—principles uttered by the lips of one whose purity and goodness could not be impeached; whose soul was filled with love for poor humanity. Many martyrs have suffered torment, far too horrible to name, while advocating the principles inculcated by the holy Nazarine. God and Nature seemed to smile upon the holy zeal thus manifested, and all went smoothly until dissention and persecution began among the masses, and those whose zeal had been most manifest, became the victims of the foulest hatred of the human soul. Too weak to stem the tide of persecution, they succumbed, and Christian worship was suspended.

Many efforts did they make at intervals to throw the yoke from off their shoulders, when, lo! a deliverer was sent, as if by magic power, to arrest the bloody scenes enacted among those professing Christianity. The spell was broken, and the long and cruel persecutions ceased, and once again was Christianity embraced with intervals of that unrest evoked by bigotry and superstition, and following on the years of time, Christianity became ascendant; its brief existence savored not of love and mercy, for unwise councils being preferred and practiced, human life was cheap, and victims fell in numbers on the shrine of mad ambition, to be thought more holy than their neighbors.

And is it at the present moment one whit better? Are not the same bitter, rancorous feelings still exhibited, the teachings of their Jesus torn to fragments and scattered to the winds of heaven, carrying in all directions the incipient seeds of discord, even as an embryo epidemic is carried from an infected region? Death and desolation soon must follow, and men be brought lower in the scale of being than before.

With such an element upon your earth, is it possible humanity can prosper and become the pure and holy beings they should be? As applicants for heavenly joys among the redeemed of earth, can they lay claim to aught that is promised to such as love the Lord and do His bidding when and where 'tis needed? for such should be the aspiration of every living entity who seeks to reach that home prepared by angel hands.

But let us to our subject: What does Spiritualism teach? To which we answer, all and everything the human soul can need, to fit it for the heaven prepared for it. Purity of heart has been the greatest want from generation to generation, till angel patience might seem almost exhausted; yet, untiring as they are, with energies renewed, they come again and again, if possible, to perfect what they have begun, giving to mortals lessons of vast importance to their welfare here on earth and in the distant future, more invaluable than man can possibly conceive; and if here on earth these can be deemed so valuable, how must they be esteemed as gems no time can peril or destroy? How, then, can man eschew such teachings that accord so clearly with his needs here and in the hereafter, where all is changed and quite unknown to mortals? Each thought engendered there will need confirming by an intuition from some loving angel near, and thus, by God's effulgent light, will each succeeding spirit wend its way through beauties far transcending all that earthly ingenuity can possibly devise.

But, "Is this all?" I think I hear the skeptic ask. Give me proof that God's holy spirits come to earth and demonstrate to mortals that immortality is theirs; that life beyond the grave is yours, and that error has led the human race and made them dupes to a deceptive influence; that truth is scarcely recognized, for all believe the devil reigns supreme over all such spirits as are thus employed by God as messengers to give a lie instead of truth to mortals. Give us, we say, the proof it is not so, and we will accept of all that Spiritualists lay claim to. Far more than life on earth is the assurance that in the eternal future, life and immortality surely will be ours.

God and Nature are ever working to accomplish all that man desires that is in accordance with the laws of universal justice. Thus, in all conditions, heaven must be sought for in spirit and in truth, and it will surely be obtained. AMEN.

WOMAN'S RIGHTS.

It is with considerable trepidation we undertake the task of elaborating a subject which has engaged the close attention of the civilized world, and well it may, for in it is involved questions upon which the weal or woe of nations and empires turn. Woman's rights! What does the agitation of this question imply? Nothing more or less than that she is entitled to rights and privileges which have been unjustly withheld from her. This naturally leads to the inquiry, "What are those rights which she claims, and man withholds?" he arrogating to himself a power which woman does not willingly recognize, but emphatically denounces as an assumption, and derogatory to the relative condition she holds to man. There then do they join issue. Let us see how far her claims are based upon justice and equity. We shall be compelled to go back into the past and inquire whether God or nature, in the formation of man sought to make him a perfect being at once, or whether he purposed leaving him gradually to unfold the elements within him, through the law of progression toward a state of high intellectual development which suit the conditions necessary to become a ruler and governor of all things connected with his mundane condition? This theory seems somewhat rational in its character, and one which we think we may safely take upon which to found our succeeding remarks. It is not our intention to draw any invidious comparison as between the sexes as regards intellectuality, because with the Creator, there is no respect of persons, but all are treated upon the same immutable principle of justice, therefore we must admit the equality of woman upon the intellectual plane of existence, whilst physically she is the weaker, and, consequently, the reliant portion of humanity, thereby awakening in man the affectionate elements of his nature, and demanding at his hands that personal protection her weakness requires when assailed by brute strength, which perchance might destroy her. It is then man calls into active motion that of which woman is comparatively destitute, thereby proclaiming man in that sense, better qualified to rule, for by a combination of equal intellectual powers with the superiority of physique, man seems best suited to rule, whilst woman, by her pliability of disposition, and comparative helplessness, becomes a fit co-worker with man in life's journey. This we present as the primary or created condition of man and woman previous to that of a perverted character, when both parties have seemed to step aside entirely from the line of domestic travel intended by their Creator, and have thus become contentious and discontented with their lot. Here, then, is the first commencement of a system which has been the curse of domestic happiness, where should be cradled elements which if not perverted and polluted by discontent, would fertilize the moral culture of man's destiny and preserve intact that harmonious condition which primarily surrounded humanity. We much fear the possibility of a return to this desired condition until men and women both, shall have drunk deep of tribulations and suffering the result of their own perverted doings. We may infer that God made man physically the superior of woman, that the excess of power should be for her protection, ruled and governed, by the affectional of his nature which as a natural sequence would demand a similar recognizance from her.

We shall now look at the condition of man under the influence of feelings antagonistic to right principles. He possessing power and losing sight of the divine arrangement, becomes aggressive in his nature, and, step by step, almost imperceptible to himself, advances beyond the limits prescribed by nature, and thus passes the Rubicon, destructive of that harmony which was intended by Almighty wisdom. Here, then, is the first invasion of woman's rights, and certainly a most important one as being the first, for we well know whatever may be the difficulties and struggles to avoid the first sinful attempt, when the barrier becomes once passed, the conscientious scruples soon subside, the door being opened, can seldom be closed, and a retrograde movement commenced. There then is the difficulty. After the antagonistic spirit has been aroused, each day and hour seems to increase its vigor and virulence, and each party commences to search out for allies to strengthen their position, which they each endeavor to define advantageously to themselves. Man asserts his power and demands submission thereto, which, had there been no aggression, would still have been, as before, quietly recognized, but not under the same guise; and why? because its objectional feature was hidden and covered up by woman's reciprocation, the affectional display in man for his protective influence thrown around her in the hour of apprehension and danger, but now she deems this fresh, and to her unnecessary intimation of power, an infringement of her rights. And thus all the dormant energies of her nature become alarmed, and at once she assumes the attitude of defense, often the result of vague fears of an imaginary evil, when if she had consulted her own reason, and followed implicitly its dictates, irrespective of injudicious advisers, how much of misery and discontent would have been avoided.

Now, then, we come to that which, perhaps to many, and more particularly to women, may be considered the most important portion of our essay, to describe what we consider the rights to which woman has an undoubted and inalienable claim, and which, in our endeavor to mete out impartial justice, would now present for a world's consideration, as being the best and most efficient means of setting at rest a question of vital importance to the world of humanity, because, as long as it is continued an open question, like an open wound, depletion of the vital principle must continue, therefore would we, agreeable to our promise, attempt to define the rights of woman in the pursuits of life on earth. Woman being equally the handiwork of infinite wisdom, equally gifted with reasoning powers, subject to the same progressive influences for the improvement of the race, must so far, be deemed man's equal and should in the presence of her God and the angelic hosts be recognized, claiming the right to rule through the affection and reasoning faculties of man, for it must be admitted as the result of close observation, that woman's perceptive faculties are in general superior to those of man, by which she comes to more rapid and often wiser conclusions than man. Indeed, she may be deemed the theorizer, while man is the elaborator of her theories; of course we speak of such matters as come within the sphere of her attainments.

Here, then, lies the secret of woman's power over man, a discreet exercise of which will remove barriers of the most stupendous magnitude, and to which man may be made to succumb and appear strictly obedient to woman's rule. This is all in obedience to the law of kindness, a law so little understood as oftentimes to make the heart grow cold. That the obtuseness of mankind should be so blind to their own interest as to abrogate the practice of a virtue that may be deemed the universal physician of nature, binding up the broken hearted, soothing the anguished soul by its mellifluous sounds, reaching deep down into man's inner nature, and by its divine influence arresting the vicious in their unhallowed pursuits, and rescuing the guilty from the perpetration of atrocities which would terminate fatally to their happiness here and hereafter. Now, if such are its holy influences in the broad and extended field of human intercourse, how strange it is that in the limited circle of a family it should be ignored and then still circumscribed in its influence on the man and wife, where too frequently it seems ignored or unknown. Oh, how many a useless outbreak might be saved, and that beautiful and harmonious condition be sustained, without which all the latent heart burnings of humanity are ever rife!

But to our subject, Woman's Rights: We have spoken of their equality, which we think will be readily admitted by every rational, individual as being a condition well calculated to preserve harmony in the married state. What, then, is the next right to be established or suggested? The right of consultation in all the important matters connected with their dual condition, for what is the interest of the one must, under right conditions of mind, be the interest of the other, by which process their contemplated enterprises may command success. This is an important matter because each party, possessing a certain portion of the wisdom element, subjects of great interest may be discussed and wiser deductions drawn from both than one, both being equally circumscribed by right principles. But we can imagine this question being asked, "Should these parties form opposite views, who, then, is to decide the question—which may not admit of prolix action?" We answer, under such a state of things, that both should yield a little, and by compromise, even if a failure should ensue, yet would they both bear an equal portion of the loss they might sustain of whatever character it might be, pecuniary or aught else, hence no discordant feelings would ensue and harmony still exist. We think it almost useless to go farther in defining Woman's Rights, conceiving our propositions embrace all the fundamental principles of right either man or woman could rationally desire! The preposterous attempts of women, who claim to be strong-minded, should meet with instant reprobation among all who claim the ability to judge correctly in the premises. The very thing which they brand as obnoxious in man, who claims the right to govern woman, would assuredly be the result of these wild and inappropriate requirements, for of necessity they must with the privileges also be constrained to accept a portion of the hardships to which man is subjected, and their own good sense, if not perverted, must confess to be altogether incompatible with their physical organization, therefore their position at once becomes untenable, because of its incompatibility to the laws of nature, which, whenever violated, at once recoils upon the individual who attempts to act in opposition to them.

There are many contingencies in the relative condition of man and woman in earth life which we have not noticed, because we think it better to abbreviate our essay than to increase its length without adding to its potency. As a remedial agent in checking the discontent of woman in regard to her own estimate of what are her relative and God-given rights, our effort has been to treat the matter with a view to conciliate both parties, by a close adherence to truthfulness, unbiased by any side issues, for the law of candor in all cases, regulates our conduct, irrespective of persons or circumstances, therefore are we led to hope that men and women both, may deduce from this essay some ray of divine light to guide them, promotive of happiness to themselves and as exemplars of truth to others, its ramifications may extend throughout society to God's glory and their own immortal condition. AMEN.

ANNIHILATION.

A THEME most horrible to contemplate, and one of which we shall treat but briefly, for two especial reasons. The first is the hideous aspect of the question, with the horror through which we must contemplate it; the next is the almost impossibility that men could unite in giving credence to it. Indeed, the thinking mind, however depraved, must revolt at such a notion, and no conviction could for an instant be entertained, much less indulged.

Man's natural instinct seems to shudder at the thought. To have been; to be; and eventually not to be—a profound and ghastly reflection!

Is it possible for the human mind, by the

utmost stretch of imagination, to conceive of human wretchedness more extreme than that which could elicit such a wish as is implied in that one word, *annihilation*, unless impelled by the wildest insanity? We are totally at a loss to understand how so repulsive an image could form in a mind unafflicted with extraneous malady, and find a word to convey the hateful idea, even from the most abandoned and forlorn wretch that ever existed!

Take from man all of that upon which he dotes with unmeasured fondness; remove far from him all that can stimulate his ambition; bring him down from the altitude of power and of grandeur; place him in abject poverty—nay, take from him even hope, and can he wish for annihilation? Oh, no! He will try to penetrate the dimmest, narrowest vistas of time for some inklings of a change, until in mercy he will assuredly receive some angel whisper that he shall again live in the untried future.

Let us, then, analyze this somewhat more closely, and ask the advocate of such a thought if there be aught in nature indicative of such a condition. Look throughout the vegetable world; the seed vegetates, the plant grows, matures and dies; but does the soul within the seed of that plant pass into nothingness? Does it not, in proper season, and under proper conditions, fructify and reproduce, and in time again become matured and die, thus showing that life continues; and as the soul of man becomes unconscious after death, as it is called, so like the seed, when it again germinates, is it restored to a conscious state, ready for the improving influence of divine and angel instructions.

Annihilation—dismal and disconsolate must be the feelings of that man who can contemplate such a terminus to earth-life. With our own convictions, we are compelled to assert our unbelief in any such mental condition, while man's reasoning powers remain intact; therefore would we pronounce it altogether the result of a mal-disposed, morbid imagination, to be deemed by all reasoning creatures merely a disease, which, thanks be to God, is not a very prevalent one. AMEN.

CHRISTMAS ADDRESS FROM MY SPIRIT WIFE.

CHRISTMAS—1869.

ONCE again, my beloved husband, am I permitted to address thee on the anniversary of a day when joy and gladness ever seemed the purpose of our assembled friends and relatives, who, at

Christmas, strove to cast all care aside and look but to the present for enjoyment. Many and many a time, with gratitude to God, have we assembled around the festive board, our children, relatives and friends, in joy and gladness, feeling no apprehension of the future, but using as best we could the moments given us in such a manner as to produce the greatest share of harmony and love, intuitively perceiving, although not actually demonstrated to us, that our reminiscences through eternity would be green and fresh, as beauteous gems of thoughts in after life.

And such we find them, for now we often dwell on them in fond delight; that those we love on earth can still enjoy the same. In all things appertaining to our life on earth, the same undying interest continues, and will, throughout the endless cycles of eternity. No forgetfulness of all that's good, but an entire oblivion of all that seems to us as sinful.

Think you, my husband, earthly scenes of virtuous practice can ever be forgotten? O, no! in Heaven they are as valued gems laid up in store to decorate the brow of he or she who has earned them—treasures which cannot be stolen, imperishable and valuable above all price.

But, my husband, more particularly would I now advert to thine own condition at the present time. Begirt with friends innumerable, if not of earth, a superabundance, yet above in the world of ether, whither thy steps are tending, wilt thou find host upon host whose love thou'lt realize as sterling, genuine love, unalloyed by prejudice or aught objectionable, not transient, but continuous through all the varied stages of ethereal life, will be administered in bounteous measure, but suited to the capacity given thee to enjoy it. Without hyperbole of thought or action thou wilt estimate the beauties of thy heavenly home, for with a mind attuned in that direction, thy thoughts will be governed by the law of adaptation. Thou wilt not tire or have undue aspirations before thou wert fitted to receive them. And herein lies the beauty of that heavenly condition. The sweet contentment thus engendered makes the meanest cottage a much happier home than a palatial mansion, however grand or magnificent its proportions.

Then with such a prospect, need we say to you, let all your thoughts be centered here, for here your treasures are. What worldly means you have, must be for those who'll have the power to use them. Thou hast nearly done with them. Loaned, as they have been to thee, with clear and honest conscience, canst thou make restitution of them with satisfactory account of how thou hast used them, and finally make rendition of them as destiny requires.

A thought has just occurred to me, that on such occasions as the present, a seeming inconsistency appears, in naming that which to some seems a solemn and frightful subject—death, seems somewhat incongruous; yet to you, my husband, is it not so. We mean by death, the final change which ushers into life immortal the enfranchised soul, and makes it what Almighty God intended it should be—the inheritor of happiness eternal. Hence, joy and gladness should be practiced by survivors on such occasion. Ethereal perception soon would show them what they call death with all its outward show of gloom, is but a glorious change—a new birth which should be celebrated with joyous, grateful feelings. And as ye rejoiced over the advent of your first-born, so will the angelic hosts sing hallelujahs when a fitted soul presents its claim to Heaven.

O, my husband, no tongue can speak, no pen can write of such a change, for, 'till experienced, conception cannot reach it. Above, beyond, around, all seems mythical to those whose minds are not ethereal.

And now, my husband, another Christmas is passing; enjoy it, I would say, as if it were your last; and yet another, and still another may be yours. Let not the loss of earthly existence trouble thee—thy mind should look beyond it. What value can it be to thee; its brilliancy has become dimmed to thee, comparatively. And yet thy sight responds to all that is beautiful in nature. The gist of former years has fled in strict proportion; as ethereal things have risen in thy esteem, terrestrial things have dwindled. As 'twas said, thou canst not serve God and Mammon, hence thou hast been prepared by angelic teachings, to become aspirant for that which seems more suited to thy nature, prepared, and still preparing for that better life, the Alpha and Omega of all who are unperverted and free to do their Master's will.

And here we close our subject, dear to us in all its several points, with a full conviction that time alone is needed to accomplish all we have projected, under wiser counsel than all that priestcraft could devise—that God's own truth with potency should rule and govern all things. When universal peace and harmony will be the basis upon which a government shall stand, immovable as the rocks of ages, permanent as time itself, and lasting through all eternity. AMEN.

BIBLE DISTRIBUTION CANVASSED.

HOW a man, possessing the experience of the writer of this article, in this enlightened age can, for a single moment, entertain the conviction that God, or what he calls Nature, could attempt to palm upon mankind a book containing more untruths than almost any other book extant, as the actual work of Deity, written under inspiration partly, and other portions directly imparted to such men as Moses, and others, to hand down as truth imparted to them by divine and holy inspirations, thereby making God a greater sinner than all history in the most barbarous times record.

Are these the proofs God gives that infinite wisdom governs all his acts? Would such a God be chosen, if choice were given to puny man, to rule and govern this vast universe? Forbid it Heaven! that such a God should ever wield a power so great. O, no! God and truth being, as it were, co-workers in one common cause, commit no errors. Enactments made by him bear the stamp of truth immutable; and, when read as such, become obeyed and held in duteous reverence by all who know the source from whence it sprang.

But to the subject—Is the Bible a God inspired work? To this we answer, No. Where, we would ask, can proof be shown it is? Take the entire volume; scan it carefully; give it every favorable interpretation you can; be lenient as you can in your research; and where is the infallibility so often claimed for it? Know ye a book containing such an amount of matter, interlarded as it is with inconsistencies and even falsehood, that would be for one instant tolerated by even liberal criticism?

No man of sense or learning, uninfluenced by some sinister entanglement, would dare to recommend it as a whole to form the basis on which to found a religious creed, unless God, or Nature, had provided means whereby its meaning might be made more clear to millions who have tried to comprehend its mysterious teachings, held as such by men who undertake a task they are not able to accomplish.

True, they may attempt it, but do they succeed? Has 1800 years' tuition produced a single proof the Bible is infallible? Age after age has come and gone, with little alteration made, but such as have been forced upon them by the power of outside pressure of truth and liberal sentiment. And as men's minds become enlightened—the blind fanaticism of bye-gone times will vanish, and truths, (not Bible truth) as some express themselves, but God's immortal truth, shall sway the minds of men and women to the extirpation of all that is doubtful and erroneous, not leaving a single error standing in the way of universal progress, thus bringing man into a more distinct relation with his God and the angel world. Until then, as time rolls on, this earth will be the scene of discord, strife, and all the base concomitants of ignorance and superstition. Hence, all that tends to bring the minds of men in closer rapport with their God, the higher and holier aspirations of their souls will rise to Him, and peace and happiness shall be the lot of all who love the truth, because it is such?

But once again we turn to Bible matter. God never created a single human being without imbuing him with a power adequate to shield him from all harm that might assail him where most weakness was exhibited, and that is where the passions demand restriction. Even when darkness reigned throughout your land, ferocious men attacked each other as if the hell that is spoken of had let loose legion upon legion of incarnate fiends to sweep your fair and beauteous lands with fell destruction.

Was it Bible influence that checked the mad career of horrid war? Did Bible teachings heal the wounds and bleeding sores of poor humanity upon the battle-field and in your hospitals, where groans and sighs were heard from morn till night? Did Bibles give the hungry food, or clothe the naked forms of your emaciated soldiers? Could Bibles give to man a blanket when it was needed to protect him in the hours of partial sleep? Of a Bible he might, perchance, have made a pillow, were it large enough. Would all the Bibles in your land, heaped high as Babel's Tower, have turned the tide of battle, and given victory to the right? We think no individual possessing common sense would answer otherwise than No.

With such conviction how should Bibles be appreciated? Give men solid truths, in language they can comprehend, and give the Bible where it is more needed. The money spent in publishing such stacks of Bibles, if judiciously expended, would supply with material comfort thousands upon thousands who, in misery, bewail incessantly their gaunt and squalid poverty. At home, surrounding you in all directions, may be seen what we have spoken of, misery and destitution left unnoticed by the strenuous advocates of Bible distributions.

Methinks I see a family in hungered state, almost starvation, presented with a Bible by some, perhaps good-intentioned person; the gaze of sheer astonishment brings paleness to the cheek; indignant flashes from the bleared and sunken eyes give rebuke and condemnation of the act. And do you marvel that such an act as this should stir the angry passions of a starving family?—better have taken as many loaves as the cost of that Bible would have paid for. The glow of gratitude engendered by such an act, would have been impressed upon the donor's soul through all eternity. Are not these truths no one can contradict? You are not satisfied with home consumption; but the heathen must be taught its value. Heaven and all its beauties God has shown through nature; not using His infallible productions for such a gracious purpose, preferring to apply it to some other use. And so conglomerate is it, that sapient men and women fail to comprehend its real meaning, and when found at fault, declare, although a statement, there is made, the meaning differs from what is there expressed. Is this proof the book is still infallible? We think a larger share of common sense, and less of mystery, would better suit the purpose. In nature, all things are simple as need be when the mind of a true investigator seeks the council of the wise and good, by which all mystery has vanished as the dew drop before the rising sun.

But little more we will say about this book of books, containing truths we willingly admit, but so covered up with vagaries and untruths, they are scarcely visible unless by microscopic scrutiny. And this we do not want as a means of teaching that which Nature gives gratuitously to all of every grade. Her book is always open, and written in a language known to all. Letters large enough for all, and being kept constantly before man's vision, he becomes familiar with the reading, nor wants a teacher other than some angel friend who, lingering near your earth, perceives your needs and readily supplies them. Then lay aside a book worn out, no longer useful as a means of teaching, but impressed with gratitude for whatever good it may have done. Speak of it as you would of an old friend whose companionship you have often sought to beguile some leisure moments, but never as a guide or counsellor; having no faith in such advice as he would give; and when life's journey seems about to terminate, look not to Bibles, priests, or deacons, for advice to guide you on your road to heaven, for hosts of angels will be there to give escort to the summer land. AMEN.

HOPE,

TO BE acceptable, must be founded upon something tangible, something man's reason must, or can grasp, otherwise? it is unsatisfactory or vague.

To hope—what is it? How shall we define it? A something incomprehensible; a mere shadow, without the substance; flitting, untenable, and void of interest; flattering, but uncertain; yet it is called the anchor of the soul. Strange misconception of its character. Better call it a seducer, offering blandishments where solid truth would better subserve the interests of humanity. O, how often has it flitted across the path of some would-be expectant soul, perverting its every movement, and inducing thoughts so adverse to its prosperity—a fallacious expectation of some fancied grandeur or renown, until disappointment, may ensue, and all of expectation thus is lost, sinking the soul in black despondency.

But still, there is a hope which seems to brighten as it grows within the human soul, under the fostering care of angel minds, so beautiful and steadfast, that all around it seems substantial and legitimate, being founded on certainty, so pronounced by angel lips, and thus enstamped with truth immutable.

On this the soul may dwell as firmly as upon the promise of its God; for, being thus promised, may be expected, and no failure can ensue. Thus substituting expectation for hope, thereby arousing the dormant soul to action, giving to it a fervent expectation of a serene and happy future in the Happy Summer Land. AMEN.

A GENERAL EXPIATION THROUGH JESUS.

WE ARE told that the only terms of salvation to be attained, are by and through the sacrifice of Jesus; if so, what will become of those who never heard His name?

This question, of necessity, involves another; therefore we shall proceed at once to show the fallacy of such a proposition.

There is no foundation whereon to base so vague an assertion. It can, at best, be viewed but as figurative—not positive. Let its advocates only consult their reason, and analyze each portion of the subject, giving common sense sufficient room to act in unison with reason, when suddenly, the position becomes untenable without a single prop to sustain its crumbling walls.

Man may attempt to prove the contrary, but such attempts must fail, because opposed to reason. To think a man like Jesus, endowed with all the virtues possible to mortal being, should thus be sacrificed to appease the wrath of God —His father! Can any thinking being imagine such a demand being made? and still farther, *in strict accordance with the attribute of mercy, wisdom and even-handed justice!*

Would a reasoning man, without actual knowledge of the fact, accuse an ordinary fellow-mortal of such atrocity? And yet it is our universal Father—God! who is thus maligned.

Justice, thou God-like attribute, thy sword, though keen and sharp as need be, must seem too dull to wreak vengeance on the heads of those who originated such calumnies! The meek and lowly Jesus never claimed the rank of a universal Savior; never sought equality with God, nor named himself as more than human. Yet, would those devotees to orthodoxy make Him God—the very

God—part and parcel of a trinity not comprehended by themselves, though offered as a fact not to be questioned by the masses—a truth indubitable! Whereas, a statement of such grand importance to humanity, demands of right, some proof to be adduced by which corrobaration may be had, and all of doubt removed, giving to man a system well authenticated by means indisputable.

We feel it is needless to offer more, having shown the improbability, or rather impossibility, of such a plan as that universal salvation could result from one man's death.

To charge such folly upon a God of infinite wisdom—to make a father sacrifice His only son; and even taking their own Bible testimony, copied into their ritual, a God, triune in His character, coming down to earth, assuming mortal form, offering Himself a sacrifice to appease His own wrath! Finally, on Calvary's cross renounces life, and leaves this stubborn world of humans without a guide or governor. So monstrous a concatenation of absurdities on which to found a faith, cannot be found on record, but itself.

While we look upon it as a fable, we must give its supporters credit for indomitable perseverance. Had they employed this in a better cause, success might ultimately have crowned their efforts; but as it is, disintegration has taken hold upon their system, and all the exertions they can make will be but useless, for men of the present era look for something better based than such theology.

The angel hosts no longer stand inert, doubtful as to their reception; the human soul is opening wide its portals to receive the immortal truths they bring to banish from the minds of all humanity the darkening influences of mystified theology, and substituting therefor a brighter, holier doctrine, which asks for no support, other than reason and common sense supplies.

And now, my brother, we will turn and take a review of the necessity of such a sacrifice: Will common sense exhibit to your view a single point on which to rest a reason why such a sacrifice was needed? A thousand arguments might be produced to prove it non-essential, without a single reason appearing to show why it should be enacted. Every person seeking safety comprehends some danger threatening him, and looks, accordingly, for the aid essential to his security. Nature prompts such desire; self-preservation being evidently a component in all living things; hence, would we infer that man, while seeking safety, or salvation, should strive to attain the most reliable means to fulfill the desired end. Can our untrammelled convictions accept as such the plan proposed in Jesus' crucifixion?

What a stretch of imagination, that a single death of a righteous individual should effect the entire salvation of all the myriads who have lived, now live, and are to live transiently upon this earth.

Enumerate, if you can, the numbers that have passed away; and those who are yet to come, and you may have an aggregate of folly and falsehood unparalleled! Hence it is, that looking from the various standpoints, nothing can you see but dark theology floundering in the midst of chaos, wishing to escape, but utterly incapable. With all their endeavors, through creeds and dogmas, aided by ignorance and superstition, no progress can they make towards emancipation from the bonds and shackles now confining them, and every struggle to be free but binds them tighter, causing moans and groans most sad to listen to.

From such a condition, how can they escape, we ask, but by rendition of every claim to truthfulness and total abjuration of a doctrine baseless in its structure, and quite unsuited to the wants of man.

On these grounds, we at once pronounce it unjust to humanity to promulgate a creed more fitted to suit the cravings of a fiend than those whose aspirations seek a pure and holier faith, who speak and act in accordance with the law of truth. With such a faith to guide, no one need err, and no danger being apprehended, no Savior will be needed; for then the law of individuality will be fully comprehended as being a standard well adapted to the use of man, showing him the natural boundaries and limits to be observed by him throughout his earthly pilgrimage.

What further shall we say to convince mankind that a holier, better place awaits the coming of those who have been able to steer their bark of life through sufferings and perplexities to the haven of eternal rest and happiness, not by or through the conditional influence of a crucified Savior, but by a close attention to the chart of conscience, aided by the angel hosts, and thus, in degree, making for themselves a valid claim to happiness in the Summer Land?

Again you ask: What will become of those who never heard of Jesus? to which we answer, man is never called upon by nature to do aught he is incapable of. As well might he be required to gain a seat in heaven without angelic aid, eventually accorded to him. But, while such aid is given, a man or woman asking it must know to whom they express their need, or still unnoticed they remain. Yet can anyone imagine such a God as ours would make man responsible for acts he is not guilty of? By every law of right a man is deemed as innocent till guilt is fixed upon him by testimony quite reliable. And here we cannot see the slightest taint can rest upon the soul whose every act is based on ignorance, the result of a condition only. But here it is altogether different. The crime allged is doubtful, dependent only on the statements of the few; while millions enter solemn protest against an asserted truth from priestly lips, intolerant in their utterance, and led by bigotry and superstition, to cast aside truth—aye, God's own truth—and cling to errors baneful to the interests of humanity. Therefore, rather would we be the unbelievers in such a doctrine, and chance the penalty attached thereto. AMEN.

UNKNOWN TONGUES.

YOU speak of Unknown Tongues—is it a mere fiction, or a reality? If the latter, are they unknown only to mortals in the form, and are they strictly languages understood in the spirit world, and spoken there?

My Brother: Your question is too long in words, and being so, we shall separate it somewhat.

First, you ask, Is it a fiction? to which we answer, No. Each utterance made by true and faithful mediums has its meaning, comprehended by the spirit giving it, and others also in the vast domain of spirit life; but ethereal life and mundane being opposites this cannot be described to mortal understanding; yet, the fact remains the same. Because it is not comprehended by the finite mind, shows no proof it is not so. Therefore, to deny its truthfulness, is neither wise or proper. Spirit life and action may be mysteries not understood by mortal minds. Not being prepared, they are not able to accept such statements, and thus the world denounces all as false.

But again we turn to scan the subject: "Are angels all conversant with these Unknown Tongues?" We answer: Those who, in earth-life, sought to acquire them may, in degree, succeed in attaining such knowledge; what number have succeeded, is of little moment; the principle or fact is just as well authenticated by a unit as by a multitude. The privilege belongs to all, though few may may seek the advantage. "Are they actual languages?" you ask. Why not? we ask. Can you imagine that God's gifts are frauds? To whom is He responsible that He should need to present a ficction? If designed at all, it is perfect and complete.

This is a fact beyond all cavil; therefore we answer your inquiry affirmatively; and if a power exists within the realm of mundane thought by which a medium can be made to speak in unknown tongues, it proves, conclusively, that God and Nature must have endorsed the fact as one approved by them.

Here, then, we fain would end this essay, somewhat scant of interest, beyond the fact that all which appertains to Spiritualism should have attention from the world of spirit life, where all is harmony and love divine. AMEN.

TO-MORROW.

MY BROTHER: Your question seemingly demands a reply which may answer the demand of society at large. Who, we would ask, among the myriads now existing, can claim the morrow as their own? As that they may, perchance, enjoy in health and vigor; looking forward in hope of many morrows being their own, and yet unmindful of the various intervening chances that a to-morrow may not be theirs. To the reflective mind, a subject such as this is all-important, as indicating a change they cannot comprehend. To such an one, it naturally occurs to ask himself, or others, whence came the necessity for such change? We are happy and contented here, therefore, we cannot see this change is needed.. Poor, self-deluded mortals, who gave thee a right to call in question a decree of God? Think you a God of wisdom and of love would ever decree a purpose which runs counter to the happiness of all mankind? Does Nature point out a single instance where this love does not predominate? in favor of the greatest good to man, whose recognition keeps not pace with the efforts of the angel world to benefit humanity? Is there naught in Nature's works denying these facts? We opine not; for in every direction may be seen the divine and holy efforts made to aid the sufferings of humanity.

To-morrow being our theme, we must turn attentively towards it, hoping to elaborate some thoughts connected with the future, of which the morrow forms a part, being as it were, one of the stepping-stones to the coming future. A close and still closer attention to it must show to the thinking mind that each day's sojourn here on earth but shows that within the human soul there is a something ever peering towards the future. The past has done its work, therefore is laid aside, almost as useless, until resurrected, to corroborate some present thought corresponding with the past, and thereby strengthening some resolve to commence and carry forward some new project on the morrow. With stern resolve man makes his preparation, conning over the chances of success, and at early dawn of the morrow he essays to carry out his purpose. Is he able to fulfill it? Some symptom of disease assails him; all his plans are frustrated, and he, himself, incapable of motion. It is just then his conscience is suddenly awakened to a sense of duties oft neglected, and errors still unatoned. The prospect of witnessing a morrow's dawn becomes more dark and gloomy. The pall of night falls over the earth, and naught but sad reflection seems to occupy his mind. Regretful melancholy takes hold upon him, and all the past of life arises in the distance; but each moment the panoramic view approaches closer and still closer on his vision, from which he strives to turn his gaze from scenes abhorrent to his nature. O, how he craves relief from any source, yet gains it not. He knows not where to make his supplications; all seems a blank to him, and in dread uncertainty he awaits the coming morrow. Alas! for him it will never, never come on earth. The tide of life is ebbing fast, despair almost has seized him, when lo! a whisper sweet he hears from a voice familiar to him, calling in tones of deep affection on the sufferer; still to hope for life, but not on earth. Oh, no; but to hope for that immortal life, far more desirable. Does he at once receive encouragement from such words? Ah, no; for worldly interests now crowd in upon his mind and check those new, but holy aspirations, just awakened, till a second and louder tone assures him of a home beyond the grave, when thus again he is drawn by the attractive power of divine love to lay aside earth's baubles and not desire to retain them until the morrow. Thus, is he in a better state to pass on the road of universal progress and realize the morrow in a better and holier sphere, where there is no morrow, but a never ending spirit life.

O, my brother, when humanity can realize this act, how readily will they renounce to-day, to-morrow, and the next, for that condition which, if properly prepared for, will give them happiness eternal. AMEN.

SIN AND ITS CONSEQUENCES.

TO DEFINE a subject almost undefinable may appear somewhat presumptuous, and in attempting it I may hazard a large amount of reputation, still I am encouraged to do so rather than lose the opportunity of my well intended purpose. Often we are led by certain impulses to attempt almost impossibilities, at least they seem so to the eye of those who have but little courage to experiment in things which appertain to ethereal, or heavenly matters. But to our subject:

All and everything which bears analogy to truth may be considered worthy of attention, because the same power that rules the one, governs alike the whole, but, being called by different names, and under different influences, may be mistaken, and hence the many errors oft committed, which tend to mystify and influence men and women to commit their best ethereal interests to the care of men who are totally unfit to do their thinking, or make a single move by which their road to Heaven might be smoothed and well prepared ; and while they are thus prostituting time and talent, their days are passing rapidly, never again to return and give them opportunity and ability to rescue from oblivion those precious hours, and by proper application benefit their fellowmen. And why is this occurring daily? Why are men so indolent that all the attempts they make but fail in carrying out a well-formed project, on which depends another's welfare ? A *something*, underlying all, may be discovered, and we think we even now perceive a leading cause which keeps the entire world in dark submissiveness to a blind and superstitious influence, totally unfit to raise up men and women capable of governing themselves aright, therefore, till change becomes a need, they cannot comprehend how God and Nature acts the tyrant, as it were, by their enforcement of each and every law extant. Kings and potentates are often tyrants from a conviction that they can be so with impunity. Not so with

God. A Being as pure and holy as He is cannot act subversive of His own created laws—as binding on Himself as others. A king, or legislative body making laws, and running counter to their spirit, could not expect obedience from others; and is it not so with God's eternal laws? And on this hypothesis we claim all deference should be paid to them, as being guides infallible to man in all his intercourse with his fellow-man.

And, keeping closely to our point, we feel no other influence should beset us than that which tends to purify our lives and make us cognizant that Heaven and all its beauties may be had by acting righteously and honestly in all things, not confined to things pecuniary, but to all and everything involving principle. Here lies the difficulty. Men too often limit their responsibility to the narrow standard of dollars and cents, or other currency, and thereby fail to reach a standard better suited to the end. Hence, passing by the substance and grasping at the shadow, find nothing left but vacuum, and consequently become dejected and forlorn, fall back on vice, and soon are lost within its vortex, never again to rise above or beyond a life of prostituted talent, till death has claimed them for his own and put a final stop to sinning; and here begins the change so needed to eradicate the evils of a lifetime. Perchance angel friends have watched them through their mad career of sinfulness, and often tried to check them, but all in vain. On and on they rushed till death o'ertook them. Think you those spirits have now deserted them? Oh, no! with tender care and assiduity they have watched them till the proper moment. Weighed down with sorrow and regret they count the many hours they have wasted in rounds of dissipation, and the numerous sins committed, property unwisely spent, and all the errors of a lifetime passing in review before them, their stubborn hearts begin to yield, their natures seem to feel the touch of holy sympathy; the germ of hidden value seeks an outlet for development and thus outworks itself, in beauteous form, to seek a brighter, higher sphere. Can a scene more grand and gorgeous than Heaven be presented to such minds, awakened as they have been from the grovelling haunts of vice and infamy? To a scene like this, my husband, a future more replete with grand sublimity can scarcely be conceived.

Little as men think of God and all His glorious attributes—there will come a time when, with an ethereal gaze of wonder and remorse, they'll take a retrospective glance and view the acts of sinfulness committed by them, contrasting their condition with what it might have been. The anguished tortures of minds that are so oppressed, must almost crush them. Still they will have to bear it. The undying worm of conscience, feeding on an attenuated mind would soon destroy it, but, in mercy, God has cared for such by sending messengers, well fitted for the task, to watch and guide them, at the fitting moment, into brighter paths than hitherto they have trod, to a more genial atmosphere, winning them into repentance of their past undutifulness to God's holy law, and thus by degrees, they waft them hence in improved conditions to seek a higher home.

My husband, can such a God be cruel or unmerciful? Impossible! and he who asserts He is knows nothing of Him, nor ever will in his unchanged condition; and with a hope that this essay may reach some erring soul whose views of God are based upon the errors of theology—may see and feel the need of change, we say AMEN.

COME TO JESUS.

SUCH an invitation seems delightful to an enthusiastic follower, as many oft believe themselves; but far the larger portion of mankind prefer declining it with all its promised blessings, and more often shrink apalled in expectation of the summons, and were it possible to get excused, would rack their brains to frame an apology for not being ready to accompany the unwelcome messenger. Why, we ask, are placards stuck in every public corner of your streets and stores, emblazoned o'er with gaudy colored letters, to attract the attention of unwilling devotees? May we so name them: certainly a paradox, and yet ironically expressed, conveys our meaning,—devotees in name, but in practice, wanting.

Of such, we are convinced, the largest portion of professing Christians may be found. And here fain would look to find the source from whence proceeds this effort to beguile the unwary and inexperienced of the race to accept their unmeaning dogmas. Outward show and ignorance seem, as it were, bosom friends—inseparable companions, almost patterns to the world in that direction. The interest of the one becomes the same to both. Not so in worldly friendships. Transient in their stay, self often interferes and breaks asunder the apparently strongest bonds of friendship.

But to our subject, Come to Jesus. Aye, come, we say. Come to him as to a friend who will answer with punctilious truthfulness such questions as a friend would put. Nay, start not back, my friend. No terror shouldst thou show toward Him thou hast named thy Savior; of such a one thou shouldst not be afraid. A Savior must be a friend, therefore fear but ill becomes thee to exhibit.

Come, then, and hold a closer counsel with Him. Can all the priests and deacons in His service perform a single act that will compare with what He suffered, and through that suffering saved a world from sin and misery?

Methinks I hear the answer given, it was but an act of retribution for the imprudent utterance of thoughts inimical to the laws under which I and others lived, and therefore, no benefit to a world other than as an example to prevent the repetition of the crime in others. Ten thousand others have experienced death in expiation of the self-same crime. I claim no merit for an act I could not contravene, and who could blame the authorities who took a life thus forfeited to appease a law I had thus transgressed? Then call not these men murderers who, acting as my judges, claimed the right of taking life under a law conceived by them as altogether sacred under their ancient Jewish code, thus making me a martyr in the truest sense. And not content with this claimed for me a position I never sought, or thought I I held, through all my checkered life on earth, uniting my name with that of Deity, thereby blaspheming a name too, too sacred to be coupled with a righteous character. But to associate with that holy name one to which a stain became attached by dying an ignominious death, seems altogether too absurd for acceptation by a world of humans.

Here, then, the error lies. A man becomes the victim of his own imprudence—power takes hold upon him, the law demands a sacrifice, 'tis made, and all the world exclaims a miracle is wrought, and with one united voice proclaim a Savior has been crucified to save the souls of all who lived in ages past, the present age and ages yet to come, from endless torture. But now, since liberal thought and speech have made their advent, their hell has burst its boundaries and wandered out of sight, no more to be the destiny of infants, countless as to numbers.

Think of this, ye advocates of theology! A God of mercy, forgetting, as he must, this attribute, to decree a law of such depravity that must shock a very fiend while contemplating such result, and yet approved and advocated by fiends in human shape, so void of all that constitutes the real man, will dare to stand and utter as a truth such damned libels on their Father, God.

We here must pause and wonder why such atrocious falsehoods can be tolerated by men whose calibre of intellect would warrant better expectations of them. Apparently wise and good in all things else, but in intolerance fanatical and bigoted, viewing all things through a perverted vision, making white almost black by sad distortion of their reasoning powers.

O, how many a bright and glorious intellect, capable of soaring to the highest altitude of intellectual grandeur, has sunk in blighted darkness, where no light can reach it to redeem it from a fate almost unmerited; but, being surrounded by unholy influences, can scarcely rise above the lowest grade of intellect, till awakened to a keener sense of self-unworthiness, by which repentance comes, and drives away the soul's worst enemy—superstition—aided by ignorance and bigotry, never again to take so deep a hold within the human soul, as to become repellant of the good which lies imbedded, where good and holy spirits delve to find it.

But when it is found, a jubilee is held, and angels cry aloud Eureka!

Thus, my brother, are we led to hope this cry of Come to Jesus may resound through every land, teaching there's a better meaning attached thereto than so-called Christians comprehend. And how oft we find a seeming folly become the avenue through which a wiser thought may enter, and good result where evil seems portending. Was man other than progressive, such utterance might be tolerated, but in the present age of great advancement, he claims the right of thought, and then a free expression of it, by which, if good and righteous in its nature, gains advocates, and thus receives assistance from the angel world, giving strength and moral force to all its influences, by which the crude and narrow notions of a world become expanded, so as to embrace a wider field for thought and action; by which society takes hold of every new and glorious enterprise which bears the genuine stamp of truth and usefulness, nor hesitates to put forth efforts almost superhuman to develop whatever beauties may be found by close investigation.

But once again we turn to Jesus. Meek and lowly as he is shown to be, he would not claim superiority of rank or e'en condition. His ambition reached no farther than to aid humanity and make it what it should be, and in doing so, showed the God within him, as others of his race had done before, and at the present day are doing. For every evidence of kindness to a fellow-being makes an almost God of man. And while we thus assert this fact, let no one say we are blasphemous, for hath not God Himself asserted a man who acts in mercy to his fellow-man and strives to aid him in adversity and suffering acts a god-like part, and thus by imitation becomes an almost God? And is he not in principle, and does not nature prove the fact? At every turn you see the effect of moral principle acting on the minds of men, leading them by the cords of love to aid their fellow-men by giving food and raiment where 'tis needed, lifting a fallen brother, or a frail and fallen sister from a state of degradation to a higher grade, where, freed from the frightful influence of sin and wickedness, a disordered intellect becomes brightened, the perceptive faculties more clear; in fine, the entire system reached and cleansed from that impurity which presses down the soul, and makes it truly inert and almost motionless.

My brother, time seems waning and your magnetism more depleted than it should be, wherefore we shall close our essay, hoping you may not deem your time misspent in thus transcribing thoughts so well intended, yet by some may still be unappreciated; but in time they will be sought, and if read attentively may reach the consciousness of some searcher after truth. This is all we look for, all we ask to make us feel our joint labor has not been in vain. AMEN.

THE BEAUTIFUL IN NATURE.

A MOST beautiful and glorious theme, embracing everything in nature and giving to the artist opportunities to copy every beautiful development as it comes fresh from the Almighty hand of God, the Universal Artist, and who, we ask, can imitate such mighty specimens of skill Divine? Who is able to portray the beauteous tints of an autumnal sky? Who can produce the gorgeous colors of the rainbow? Who can blend the beauteous tints of a rising or a setting sun in all its splendor? the blush of morning's dawn or the dim twilight's sweet expression? Not one of mortal kind. They may, and do attempt it, and in degree some may succeed. But in Nature's works there is a finish so complete as to baffle all the competition of a world.

My Brother, is there in all your midst one capable of portraying, with correctness, the human passions? Can Love, in all its redolence of beauty and holy fervor of affection, be portrayed by artist's pencil, pouring from lips ambrosial sweet murmurings of devotion to the object of her choice? Can the pencil touch those almost hidden thoughts so fitfully exhibited by some gentle maiden in her teens? It may often be attempted, but success is sparse. If adoration be the subject, is the artist capable of presenting all those glowing sympathies which deck the countenance of one whose soul seems centered in the heart of some long-cherished friend, whose inmost thoughts have been exchanged and cared for. Which should be prized for its intrinsic worth? Can such a countenance be faithfully portrayed? It may be attempted, but where's success?

Hatred may be next essayed. Where is the man of kindly temper, amiable and just in all his dealings with his fellow-man? Can he portray the angry passions of the man who hates? Can he present the glare of eyes so set and teeth so closely clenched, the hands so clasped in wrath and vengeful ire, and every muscle in a state of tension quite unnatural? Could he succeed? Ah, no. We might take of the passional and other subjects,—but one we will treat as being the greatest test of skill—Charity, with all the saddening circumstances surrounding her; the look of sad dejection, seemingly despairing, she looks with fondness on a sickly babe; unwelcome tears are starting from her wearied eyes, and every muscle, as it were, seems shrinking from further contact with a cold and cruel world. Her children cry for food. Alas, she has it not. Again, the tears fall more swiftly down her cheeks as she gently pats the little treasure, and gives a promise it shall have its needs supplied. Alas, no succor comes; the weary hours pass by, but no assistance. "Oh, God!" she cries, "where, where is help? Must these sinless beings starve, and I alone be left? Take them, I pray Thee, my Father and my God, or take us all, and show Thy love in doing so." Some listening angel hears her cry, and softly whispers, "Thy cry is heard, and I am here to help thee in thy need—yonder comes the help expected. Thy children must not, will not die for want of nourishment; be comforted, thy God is merciful; accept the gifts He sends, proffered by that man of humble mien. No pomp or show will he display, but thy needs he will attend to and supply." Not long they needed help, for he was there in time of need. With fond compassion did he ascertain their wants, and bountifully supplying them, took them to his home, and watched them as if belonging to him. And did they not? Was he not their brother and she his sister?

Shall we undertake another instance of the artist's inability to copy Nature, and succeed?—The ocean's angry waves whilst lashing into madness all around it, and strewing o'er a beach its sundry victims.

Who can well depict the fury of its foaming rage? The whitened foam and angry surge strikes terror to the boldest heart. To copy such a scene is far beyond the art of human skill. Can aught but God's own power upturn the mighty mountains which rise in grand succession one above another, making all beneath them dwarfs by close comparison; the verdant hills and beauteous glades beneath them seeming as a carpet sweetly o'ergrown with flowers of brightest hue and sweetest fragrance, giving to the scene transcendant beauty? To copy such a scene successfully, would plant a laurel wreath upon the brow of him whose genius had become excelsior. And, having pointed out a portion of the beautiful in Nature, let us ask a Father's acceptance of our gratitude for all the beauties given us by Nature's bounteous hand. AMEN.

SCRUTINY OF CHARACTER ESSENTIAL TO CONTINUOUS FRIENDSHIP.

THE subject I am about to treat, demands your utmost attention, and seeing you are prepared, I shall commence without further preface.

The natural conditions being rather indistinct to comprehend, there may be some little difficulties to remove before we can come at once to our subject.

Who, we ask, can scrutinize the human character sufficiently close to ascertain all its component parts, and thus come to correct conclusions as to what are its peculiar traits and mark them so unmistakably, that no error can be seen?

If there be so much obscurity, then, is it to be wondered at that mistakes are continually made in man's estimate of the character of his fellow-man? Hence, the frequent disruptions of the most apparently sincere and ardent friendships, often broken off by the most trivial causes, and why? Simply because one had mistook the elements of character in the other; hence, however good may have been the original motive, evil has been engendered, and without explanation, the holiest, most sacred friendships, have suddenly ceased, and both parties are made, in time, to regret most painfully the seemingly unnatural issue.

Now, my friend, have you not often witnessed just such sudden separations between those whose companionship had been valued by each other as beyond all things else?

This naturally brings me to the object of this essay—a desire to suggest some means by which the evil might be corrected; an evil that is decimating society, bringing death and desolation, through means sometimes most violent.

Look around you at the present hour, and have you not ample proof of how much misery and suffering ensue from misunderstandings, instigated by base and sordid motives?

Man but studies man to discover his weak points, and thereby gain an ascendancy over him, turning the defects he finds in his neighbor to his own sinister interests.

Let us reverse this picture and show the other side: Should a man study his neighbor to ascertain how much of good there is in him, perchance perceiving the bad also, and pushing aside the latter, that the good may expand and render him useful amongst those with whom he pursues his earthly course, would murder, theft, and so many other crimes, be so rife within your crowded cities? Would your green and fertile fields be soaked in blood, and so many homes made desolate by human sacrifice?

Oh, no! my friend,—till men are brought to scan each other's disposition from higher and holier motives, there cannot be those ties of brotherly love which alone can render the human, earthly existence, a happy one.

This being a state of probation, assuredly man is not fitting himself for an ethereal change, a change which calls for self abnegation toward his fellow-man.

A preparation suitable must be made for the final change from mortal to immortal life, if the seeker desires to enjoy it. Such motives would conduce to happiness here, and in the world above, celestial bliss. AMEN.

SUNDRY SPIRITUAL QUESTIONS.

QUESTION. Is the earthly condition of man triune?

ANSWER. Certainly, body, spirit and soul.

Q. Which is the superior or directing power?

A. The soul, of course.

Q. Why of course?

A. The soul is altogether above the spirit and body in earth life, being the purest and most ethereal in its nature, a part and portion of Deity itself, whilst the spirit and body act together as superior and inferior, the body being subject to the dictation or governance of the spirit, the soul, or God-principle, (remaining, so to speak,) passive or neutral, and making on great and important occasions suggestions as to the twain.

Q. What is the peculiar duty of the soul while united on earth with the body and spirit?

A. To act as supervisor in all that appertains to the spiritual or ethereal condition of man, giving him soul-energy, and directing the better impulses of its nature to seek all that is pure and holy as a preparation for eternal life.

Q. When is the soul supposed to take possession of the human form?

A. At the earliest period of conception it enters with the life-germ, and becomes part and parcel of the human form.

Q. Do you separate soul from spirit, or are they one?

A. After the soul has become possessed of the organism to which it has been attracted, a change occurs which seems almost miraculous and truly wonderful. The body, as it grows, by some mysterious process, engenders and throws off a most subtle element, which soon assumes a rapid growth, more so than any portion of the material body, and in proportion to its healthy state, a vigorous male or female child becomes the issue. This may seem a strange and marvelous position to assume, but not the less a true one, and in time must be accepted as such.

Q. Please give a more elaborate consideration of this subject.

A. Certainly I will.

Then listen. When the spirit becomes more powerful than the body, which takes but little time comparatively, owing to its ethereal nature, its rapid growth is truly wonderful, and being more subtle, soon acquires an ascendancy over the entire natural fabric, making it more its servant than its equal.

Q. How comes this spirit being a mere outgrowth from the material possessed of reasoning powers?

A. By the same law of progress which enables the first germ of life to assume the human form; the law of growth beginning with the seed and passing through the various changes of gestation, results in what it is—the full grown man or woman. Do you not see that order and regularity accompanies all of Nature's works? Designed, matured and finished, may be seen the handiwork of God in all things.

Q. Was that germ from which the spirit grew with such rapidity a co-existent occupant of the human embryo, and thus, during gestation, under soul-influence developed to the necessary standard?

A. My brother, you have asked and answered your own question. Some angel must have given you the intuition to have done so, and while you are thus supplied, you need but little other means to guide you in your search after ethereal truths.

Q. Are we to understand that at the birth of the child the spirit has sufficiently matured to become its guide under the soul's supervision?

A. Again, my brother, have you anticipated our answer; yet, we may be able to add some few items which may be instructive to you and others. A spirit being more sublimated than aught else in nature, draws around it most rapidly all those influences which tend to purify and enlighten the material portion of its nature. By such a powerful lever it is at once raised to a condition which places it side by side with its co-worker, the soul, who has quietly watched its rapid growth, and joyfully assisted it to rise above and beyond all the impediments lying in the way of its improvement. By this means a solid compact made between the soul and spirit, seems, as it were, to make another change more potently joyous than mortal mind can possibly conceive, and thus a life on earth may well be deemed a state of preparation for the ethereal realms.

Q. When the natural body becomes attenuated and almost unfit to contain the spirit and soul, do they both leave it at the same period of transition?

A. Your question partakes of something so near akin to etherealism as to make it somewhat difficult for us to find language suitable for response; indeed, we know not how to commence, yet we are not willing to pass it by unnoticed. The soul, so to speak, being the only part of man completely fitted for ethereal life, requires no kind of preparation, but is ever ready to respond to the call of death, which to it is but a change of condition—the mundane for the ethereal—therefore, being prepared, soars at once to the spheres celestial, and there awaits the coming of its counterpart, for such the spirit has become through a life on earth of long experience, paying due obedience to the laws of God, and thus fulfilling a destiny that could not be changed but through the law of retribution.

Q. The spirit, having quitted the body, does it seem unhappy? As in earth-life the death of a friend causes sorrow and regret, is it so with the spirit?

A. Here again we find the same difficulty arises — the want of language to convey our thoughts. The embodied spirit differs little from the disembodied; therefore, by analogy, you may well infer a spirit cannot show indifference at such a time; but why alone regret should trouble it we cannot see. The loss may be sustained, but, as in earth-life, the embodied spirit may oft change its dwelling, and regret may transiently be felt, but yet the house remains, and may again, if wanted, be used as heretofore. Not so the house of clay; no more can it be used as a fit receptacle for life. No, my brother, it has at last succumbed to that law of universal change to which all nature seems subservient. Thus, after the spirit has become sufficiently ethereal, another change comes over it, permeating every portion of its spirit nature, imbuing it with pure and holy love for the late co-occupant of that house of clay, now but a mouldering clod. The law of divine and holy love awakens the attractive power, and eventually the desired reunion takes place, more binding in its nature than can be conceived by mortal mind.

Q. Suppose the spirit has not lived its allotted period in earth-life, has it the same privileges in the land of spirits as one who has reached maturity?

A. My brother, you must not press us too closely in such direction, for the cause we have named. We can but generalize; and here we fain would ask your reason for such minute inquiry.

To this I answer, as one who is frequently questioned on this matter, 'tis better to be informed—no other motive have I. We must admire the motive and would strain a point to meet your wishes, but must defer response to future time. Will you excuse us?

Q. Is the reunion between soul-spirit for all eternity with but one individuality?

A. The condition thus assumed can be deemed no other than a unit. So perfect is the blending, the keenest sight could not perceive a difference. Speech, thought, expression and desire, all from one source emerging, makes that which was once the dual state a perfect unit. This, then, may be deemed a culmination of spirit happiness, coming by degrees to earth-life, even to the regions of eternal bliss. AMEN.

LEAD US NOT INTO TEMPTATION.

THE subject for consideration is one perhaps as little understood as any that is agitated. Lead us not into temptation! Was such a request made by one human being of another, it would imply so much of distrust as to almost amount to an accusation that such a person would act unjustly towards him. And if such would be the conclusion in the one case, what are we to conceive would be the enormity of asking Almighty wisdom and justice to desist from such an act? O, monstrous, almost blasphemy! uttered each Sabbath day in every orthodox church by millions, and even the little, lisping child is thus tutored.

We are truly at a loss to conceive how persons assuming to become the teachers of theology, have so long permitted such a request to be continued as a portion of that "*ne plus ultra*" (to them of prayer). Take from it that, and we admit its beauty and force; but whilst that is permitted to sully the remainder, we shall protest against it as being an unfit petition for adults, but more so for those whose minds are yet untainted by errors which must give them distorted views of Him towards whom their tender natures should be drawn as to a God of inexhaustible love.

WHAT IS SPIRITUALISM?

A. A DEEP philosophy based on fundamental laws, more binding in their nature than aught else in the created universe.

Q. Will you define the laws of which you speak?

A. A law of God demands implicit action in obeying it. A tardy movement shows unwillingness; hence is not acceptable to God, its author, and being so, is of non-effect.

Q. How shall we know it is so?

A. The human soul is sensitive at all times, and cannot act unlawfully without a consciousness thereof, needing no accuser, but listening to the monitor within, feels guilty of a misdemeanor.

Q. Can you describe more definitely what is meant by the term Spiritualism?

A. Certainly, we should have done so but for intervening questions asked. The word implies the profession of a doctrine based on ethereal or spirit life. *God is a spirit*, and as such must be worshipped or rather recognized as the grand authority by which we move and have existence here on earth, and to whom a world of human beings look for life eternal.

No eye has ever seen the great I AM. Humanity cannot conceive or think how grand the power he wields; space is filled with his immensity; worlds upon worlds are ushered into being at, his bidding each one ready to fulfill its destiny, God-directed as it is.

The doctrine or philosophy of Spiritualism embraces every science, reaching beyond the musty records of the past, delving deep beneath the surface of your earth and bringing forth such mighty proofs of wisdom infinite; whether displayed in every atom of the granite rock, imbedded deep almost beyond the ken of mortal, until encouraged to investigate he finds marks indelible that a creative power has been at work in forming geologic stratum on which to build a science most profound, giving ample data of the various periods of formation. Again, on looking to the starry heavens, the human intellect seems almost paralyzed at the sight of so much grandeur and magnificence.

Whether you contemplate their hight or brilliancy, the senses seems bewildered, and in deep humility man exclaims: "Lord, what am I!" But as a worm beneath thy feet. Have mercy, O, my God, have mercy on thy servant, and give me light to guide me!"

Q. How long has Spiritualism been known to man and recognized by him as a philosophy?

A. Such a question would rack the brain of a professed chronologist, and not being such, we must decline response other than by saying, from the earliest period after man's creation, death and burial, it has existed.

Q. Do you feel disposed to take the Bible record as proof that spirit power was early recognized?

A. No; because we antedate long previous to that time a power all spiritual in its nature—God, the presiding spirit of the universe—and that He existed singly in this universe we emphatically deny. With his creative power it could not be; therefore, to imagine Spiritualism a philosophy of modern growth is too absurd to contemplate.

Q. And yet, we find no record indisputable when first its advent might be recognized?

A. All that may be, and yet no proof recorded available to mortal vision. How many thousand things hitherto mysterious, or so-called, have been proved by science to be true, so simple in their nature, men wonder they have been so hidden or unrecognized.

Q. Has it not been so with Spiritualism? As knowledge comes, so ignorance departs. People express much surprise that a fact of such importance to humanity as Spiritualism, has been withheld from public acceptation; that so many hundred years have passed away and only so short a time since has it been given to the world. God being omnipotent could have blessed man with it earlier had he chosen.

My brother, your question seems too long, but we will divide it.

First, omnipotence at once decides the matter, being an answer in itself, evincing a power that cannot be contravened, or otherwise directed;

and he who questions such authority demeans himself irreverently towards one who claims a proper deference from all created nature. The one that feels aright toward God needs not to ask such questions, for knowing, *not believing* that man's deserts are but as nothing to the bounteous supply accorded to him; hence gratitude, common-sense and reason, all combined, might raise contentment in his soul for all the mercies given him. But, in conclusion, man, while merely mortal, has no power to scan the works of Deity. The finite falls so short of intellect, while conning o'er ethereal matters, that if a wise and prudent being, he will at once decline the effort, despairing of success. AMEN.

THE CHURCH OF THE SPIRIT.

A SUBJECT somewhat strange it may appear to those who do not comprehend it, yet one, we think, there will be but little difficulty in treating; therefore, we shall first explain, or give our views of what is meant by Church. The world at large conceives that all that is meant to be expressed, is a building or structure suited to the taste of those who desire to worship Deity, agreeable to their own conceived opinions, and in proportion as their ideas of Deity are exalted, or otherwise, so do they erect their edifice. The better educated portion of society naturaly are more refined, culture having improved their taste, and in proportion to that, their ideas of Deity became more exalted. Taste must be satisfied, hence the amount of cost is little thought of. Possessing means sufficent, with zeal excited, their vanity becomes inflated, thus a gorgeous structure soon is raised, satisfactory, perchance, to all but He, who is said to be the object of their worship.

But let us scan this matter somewhat closely. Has any one become acquainted with His views? Who has ever sought to know His peculiar taste in this direction?

Think you in all his works no better place can be discovered than that appointed by the inflated members of a so-called Christian church? We speak of them in such wise, because we cannot recognize them as true aud faithful followers of the meek and lowly Jesus. He never sought such a place to worship the great Spirit, in spirit and in truth; it matters little, then or now, where true worship is accorded. The meanest edifice is equally acceptable to the true and loving followers of the Nazarene. Aye! more grateful than a costly edifice from which the spirit is excluded. Here, then, we find the error practiced. The beauteous edifice may be erected; pomp and pageantry may be displayed; gorgeous pews and spacious aisles laid out; the utmost sanctity of mien may be essayed; elocution, grand almost beyond the power of mortals may be displayed, and yet there is something lacking. Machinery of the present day may appear complete and beautiful, yet without steam it is altogether useless. And so of all machinery; the motive power is needed; without it, no matter what its beauty, it still remains inert and motionless. The spirit there is needed—without it all is dead. But, with the spirit added, all goes well. Now let us pause a moment and make the application.

The steam engine as a piece of art demands the admiration of the people — engender steam, the thing's complete. With power unmeasured it cuts its way through the atmosphere, and like a well formed monster thus fulfills its destiny. Religonists ofttimes assume a boastful attitude, and vaunt their sanctity before a doubting world, but such assumption has its influence, nor bends in fit humility before its God, feeling a self-sufficiency most disgraceful, as its insincerity becomes more potent to the ken of all beholders.

As we have before shown, the edifice is raised, a pastor, fit, as is supposed, found to guide the erring on the way to heaven; with pomp and ceremony and priest ordained and every office fully filled ; the church is dedicated ; the organ's grand mellifluous swell ascends; the roof reverberates the sound ; devotion seems to swell the heart of every one, and yet there seems a lack of something needed. The chill of death pervades the inmates of that beauteous church. What can be the cause of such sensation spoken of, by every mouth, yet not understood by many of that assemblage of professing Christians? They know the want; for within their souls at home they feel the holy spirit working in them. But within this so-called or rather mis-called sacred structure, the spirit cannot enter—it is not the church it seeks.

The human soul must be the church of the spirit. Walls of stone have not been needed; within the human soul it finds a resting place. O! how many of our churches now are useless, occupying ground which might be better and more usefully applied. And now, we ask, what more is needed but to implore the so-called Christians of your time to cease erecting buildings for their worship of an unknown God? But with mien erect, as if you felt your claim was good, ask his entrance to the *only* church that is needed—the inner recesses of the human soul. *There* must and will be eventualy, the church, the Great Spirit, our God and father e'er will enter. May this be better comprehended, and then those edifices may be dispensed with, and with them the useless hordes of priestly pretenders to truth and sanctity may be dispensed with, and made to seek a maintenance by honest labor far more creditable than all their erratic precepts tendered to mankind. AMEN.

INTERROGATIONS ANSWERED BY MY SPIRIT WIFE.

Now, my husband, such questions as you may wish to ask about Heaven and hell, I am ready to answer as best I can.

QUESTION. First, I would ask, is Heaven an actual locality, such as a finite being can comprehend?

ANSWER. My husband, I have answered the same question before in the affirmative, and again repeat, *it is*.

Q. My object in asking it was to have it thus recorded.

A. Such we thought was your intention.

Q. Have you houses, palpable to you as such?

A. We have that which is such to us, affording all the comforts to be expected in a well arranged building.

Q. Shall I ask of what material they are

formed; do they in any way correspond with earthly dwellings?

A. The material used, you could not recognize, nor can I describe it to your finite mind. Description gives but little information where no comparison is.

Please ask your questions singly, to prevent confusion and facilitate description. You ask if they resemble yours, as buildings well intended, and subject to the law of progress. All yours can possess of comfort, ours under that law, must be better.

Q. Have you institutions there existing?

A. Certainly we have; you recognize the law of progress. Therefore would we ask, is not arrangement needed to give life and animation to this Law. System is as essential to encourage progress as material food is to your natural appetite.

Q. Are there workshops and artisans of every kind employed within them—actual workers?

A. Is Heaven and all its doings such a myth to you and others, that such a question ueed be asked? While your earth exists, to which we know no limit, will Heaven's workshops and artisans be needed. Life is but a continuance, and think you its employment ceases with the change called death? Oh, no! on, on, and on for evermore will the busy ring of industry be heard.

Q. Are amusements there existing ? Can you so describe them as to suit our finity ?

A. Gladly would we enter iuto close particulars, but remembering what we have often told you, the finite cannot comprehend the infinite. But this much we may inform you. The intellect of man's spiritual existence can always be amused. The arts and sciences of mundane life afford sufficient materials of amusing ; being intensified, the spirit mind can soar higher into its sublimity than in earth-life ; it is possible.

Q. Is Free Masonry an actual, positive institution in the spheres?

A. My husband, the same desire to have it recorded induces such a question. If there be aught of truth in such communications as are given you, you know it must be so. The invitations given to you to preside over two such institutions must be recognized as a positive fact existing.

Q, When spirit meets spirit in the spheres, what is the mode of communicating?

A. Symbolic means are used, just as useful in expressing wants or thoughts as words are to the inhabitant of earth. Indeed much more rapidly and correct is a want expressed, so clearly prepared is the symbol given.

Q. You speak of the locality of Heaven, which we can only recognize as having a foundation such as must be needed to support that which is placed upon it Is it so?

A My husband, let me refer you to that beautiful law of adaptation. All things in Heaven, as in earth, having been prepared by wisdom infinite agreeable to the law of adaptation, you must infer the foundation must be all that's needed.

Q. Are we to understand the spirit land is what we, when speaking of the earth, called Terra-firma, to you?

A. We cannot better answer your question than by saying spirit and matter are so unlike that we find it difficult to make a comparison of that which is ethereal, and that you have on earth but again, we repeat, to us it is as real as your earth is to you.

Q. How does a disembodied spirit appear in the spheres? Are they clothed with palpable garments?

A. All that we can give you upon this question is to say, that they are subject to the same wants named before, and provided with every thing that is needful, which, never having been seen by you, cannot be described before you pass away and become associated with such.

Q. Are the spheres innumerable?

A. Yes, no mind can calculate their number.

Q. And we may understand each sphere to be a separate locality; the higher in rotation being altogether unknown to the lower?

A. Your question is put so logically that we must express our admiration, and fain would answer it minutely; but the same difficulty again arises—finity and infinity.

Q. Are there spheres to which you have had no access?

A. My husband, your angel mother and myself are, as it were, upon the confines, working as we are, upward and onward, with becoming zeal and energy. Yet are we but learners in ethereal matters. Let not this dismay you, my beloved husband; compare, if possible, thy destiny to millions in the second sphere, who never yet have realized a hope of reaching to an altitude beyond this lower sphere.

Q. Will you describe the spheres below you?

A. Certainly; the first, or earth sphere, bordering close upon your earth, affording great facilities to worlding or earthly spirits to return and hold communion with such as they are attached to, by which they attain a grosser kind ot food than that which suits those less earthly in their nature. The second sphere becomes the abode of spirits so conglomerate in their nature, not exactly sinful, many of them, but each inhabitant thereof subject to probation, and when they are enlightened and prepared, an angel escort will lead them to a higher sphere.

The third, where light begins to dawn upon the

enfranchised soul, and, by degrees, a brighter and still brighter gleam they see, invigorating their drooping natures, acting like a panacea for all they have suffered during their probation, and when they are fitted for another change, there are good and holy spirits ready to direct them on their course, which, when once commenced, is ever onward and upward to still higher spheres; no stopping place, but ever rising to a higher, holier condition.

Q. After they have passed from the second sphere, how are they employed?

A. First in the pursuit of happiness, as it was intended man should do on earth, but perversion rendered that impossible. But in the third sphere perversion is not known; naught but love and harmony prevails. Each spirit following its highest aspirations, no idleness there is seen; that being a sphere of Love no inharmony can possibly exist; no coercion there is known, for willing hands and cheerful hearts are there enjoying those ethereal blessings well prepared by angel hands.

Q. How is angel or spirit-life sustained?

A. But little nourishment does a spirit need but *that* a God of wisdom has prepared, ethereal in its nature and thoroughly adapted to the end desired. Some spirits, being more gross than others, descend to the earth, and there imbibe the aroma rising from your viands, and thus replete their depleted systems.

Q. How is this nourishment partaken of by them?

A. To explain this matter demands a language quite ethereal in its character, because ethereal entities cannot be described to other than one gifted with ethereal sight, and clear perception; hence, all things ethereal must remain a mystery till man throws off the sensual and becomes etherealized and sublimated; then he can comprehend things of spirit-life.

Q. I would ask is the locality of Heaven near this planet?

A. We are aware you ask this question only to record it. We have before informed you, it is within your own atmosphere, not outside thereof, but immediately within it, forming a part and parcel of your globe, making a glorious home for spirits, who, by strict obedience to the laws of Nature have earned inheritance therein, and thereon.

Q. Will the teachings of theology, as at present given, lead a human being in safety to the Heaven you speak of?

A. We would in reply ask, would lightning feed and nourish any human being? As well might it be expected. Theology to lead a man to Heaven? Monstrous distortion of the reasoning power of man! As well might history record all Nature's madness as to suppose man's safety is enhanced one tittle in degree. At once reverse the matter, and thus come nearer to the truth. No soul was ever saved, or even comforted, after it had passed to the shores of immortality by recollecting all the promises proffered him by Priest or Deacon, that Christ, his Savior, would be there. Oh, no! in sad bewilderment and disappointment does he still adhere in ignorance to such promises, but finds no reality in all that has been given.

Q. Have you, or do you know any spirit who has seen Jesus?

A. But little trouble have we in answering this question. There may have been a man named Jesus, but that he was more a Christ than any other human being, then existing, we must deny. The word Christ, and truth, are synomymous, and may have been assumed by Jesus; but it is of little moment. The Christ, or truth principle, is becoming better understood, and will soon supersede the errors of theology, multiplying each day and hour, making more Christs than theology dare crucify, and then exalt them all as martyrs.

Q. Closely connected with Jesus, were the Apostles, and Judas Iscariot amongst the rest? Give me an opinion upon that statement.

A. These are mere matters of history, and have but little to do with man's eternal destiny. Each martyr, and even supposed martyrs, have had their admirers, and, hence, some notice may be taken of them. The Apostle, Judas Iscariot, may, like Jesus, have lived on earth, but we should accept his history as detailed, as a mere allegorical effort, to delineate treachery in its basest form, and thereby enhance, if possible, a deeper sympathy for the Jesus he is said to have betrayed.

Q. Will common sense accept the details of the Immaculate Conception, birth, etc., of the infant Jesus?

A. My husband, these questions to us and to the world at large, are of but little moment; yet we have an opinion upon this, as well as upon any others you may ask. God and Nature ever has and ever will be immutable, therefore, such a statement we believe to be a mere priestly fabrication to beguile the people. The law of Paternity or procreation, like all others of God's laws, change not for any special purpose. Men may, in darker times, have assumed they did, but now, in the nineteenth century, for a man to solemnly assert it as a fact, would but show his ignorance, because, to the perception of others, the evil is extensive and injurious. Such a child was born, it may be, but that nature stepped outside the law of strict virginity, no power in existence could ever convince me it was so.

Q. We hear persons speaking of the river of Death. Is it used as a mere figure of speech?

A. My husband, such expressions are frequently used in that sense, and that is one. The figure is intended to convey or express a line of demarcation between the mundane and the ethereal world.

Q. While in earth-life you must remember having read a work called Pilgrim's Progress. Do you ever see the author, or hear him and his work spoken of?

A. It is here in heaven, just the same as in earth-life, where men become eminent for some useful art, whilst others become equally notorious for some outrageous theory, or views expressed by them. So it is in the spheres; and Bunyan's Pilgrim's Progress is viewed as a tissue of extravagant untruths, unacceptable to all lovers of truth in its ungarbled state.

Q. Taking the aggregate of Potentates and Kings, may Royalty be deemed a passport to the higher spheres?

A. My husband, this question seems somewhat injudicious; being a kind of slur upon high and exalted personages who have at one time deemed themselves far too exalted to be supposed susceptible of a degradation almost beyond their powers of endurance, for self-sufficiency is the natural sequence of undue power permitted or conferred on any individual, and therefore when called upon to renounce the scepter and come down to sober consciousness, they are not able to forget a habit oft indulged in by them, but by assumption, act out scenes of deep atrocity based upon that sovereign power, as God-given to them in many cases, but falsely so, for if it was a gift of Deity, it must be given under law, and therefore might be held in spirit life, but no such case can be discovered ; all is left behind on earth where such trash legitimately belongs, but inflated as they are with earthly reminiscences they still retain the desire for power, but find it is gone from them forever. Thus they remain under such hallucinations inert and unconverted members of the second sphere.

Q. Do angels dwell in common?

A. They are, as in earth-life, scattered here and there, where most attracted, the same as in earth-life, a pleasant site attracts the man of wealth to build thereon, so in the spheres an angel is led to locate till change is needed.

Q. Have you varied landscapes, adorned with trees and flowers, undulating lands etc.

A. Your question embraces many points that must be answered *seriatum*. First, then, landscapes are as beautiful with us as ever such can possibly appear to you. Umbrageous shades, a soft and genial atmosphere, with sweet and gentle breezes, like the fanning of some zephyr sweet gently bending o'er you, a lovely cadence of some distant music gently swelling its beauteous strains, almost ravishing the senses, and steeping them in sweet forgetfulness of all but heaven and its glorious concomitants.

Q. Your second point is: "Have you undulating lands?"

A. In answer to your question, an aspiration so directed would waft you to a scene you seem to covet; such a one you soon would find, for by no limits are the spirits bound, but free to roam through the entire expanse of Nature's fields and groves in great variety.

Q. Leaving the supernal for a time, may I inquire whether its opposite, the infernal, exists as a locality?

A. Following up the general impression of mundane thought, we are forced to the conclusion that such a place is more essential than the happier state of heaven. The fear of hell becomes more potent as an agent used in governing mankind, and, therefore, sought and applied as a means of terrifying into such obedience as fear produces on the human mind, and many and many a stricken soul becomes obedient under such an influence, where love and keenest sense of duty e'en would fail.

Q. Will you give your views of hell, and how the term originated?

A. So far as I am capable I will try. An expression like this, you wish explained, is so familiar to the human ear that each and every individual in existence (or those who use the term) must, of necessity, form a vast variety of opinions as to what it means, but all, of every grade, invariably associate the name with tortures horrible to contemplate, and in proportion as they are ignorant and superstitious, so do its fires burn more fiercely, and all the added tortures of a distorted fancy seeking to impress the human mind with terrors far beyond reality, even if such a place existed of which no proof has e'er been given, other than the hell or torture by blackest crimes engendered in the human soul. A hotter hell no one need invent, for conscience, quickened as it always is by fear, stirs up within the soul a deep conviction of its own deserts in retribution for the many crimes committed. This we conceive to be the hottest hell you will ever find outside the brain of some fanatic priest whose trading capital is hell, from which he gains usurious interest, and so applies his vile-acquired gains as to bring a compound interest on which he hopes to found a fortune large enough to sway a world in such direction as he pleases.

You further ask me how such a term originated. To which I answer in all ages words being arbitrary in their character have, like all of man's requirements, originated in necessity; a want experienced had to be expressed, and thus has language been continually expanding coeval with the wants of society. Thus, as government progressed, a silent but effective agent seemed a need to aid the moral power of governing, a something suited to the superstitious element within the human soul, which, by excitement, could be made to reach the minds of the unenlightened masses, by presenting terrors beyond their power to comprehend, and, therefore, ten times more potent when once imbibed. What mind, trammeled as it would be under the rhetorical flourishes of some wily priest could long endure such mental anguish and not succumb? Such was the case in early days, when ignorance and superstition ruled as with a rod of iron the peoples of that day.

Q. How do you account for men of intellect and learning still clinging to such falsehoods?

A. Are men of learning always pure and honest? Are they not selfish beyond the proper limits? Could they be brought to think that larger gain from being honest would accrue, soon would they cast aside the hypocrite, which now best suits their purpose, place virtue at a higher premium than it now brings in currency, and they will be virtuous in appearance, only for the All-Seeing Eye of God, and angels too, can easily penetrate the flimsy veil they use to cloak their acts of dark hypocrisy.

Q. It often seems a stumbling block to the would-be investigator how such acts can prosper?

A. This all may be, and yet who has the right to impugn the acts of Deity? Some wise and righteous purpose underlies his every act, and finity can never reach the altitude of comprehension sufficient to scan his acts. Who can read the hearts of those whose outward show betokens happiness? A golden colored apple, with beauteous external, form and color, may within be all decay and rottenness, and so the human family by making outward show, deceive and cover up from public gaze its miserable condition; but above and all around are unseen hosts of spirit entities, watching and bewailing such a state of things.

Q. Is the promised benefit of death-bed repentance a fact to be relied on?

A. Again, my husband, your desire seems to be the record of a purpose well designed and much approved by us. If our opinion may be fairly estimated in answering such a question, we desire to be emphatic. No, we answer. As well might Nature sanction crime in its most atrocious form as to imagine such a sequel to a sinful life. The priestly prayers have no effect at such a moment, otherwise than to lull the mind into a dull and senseless state — that reason, conscience, thought, are stilled in transient quietude, uncognizant of all surroundings; and in this unconscious state, similar to that of being poisoned, the deluded soul passes away, and enters a country all unknown to it, and we, here leave him for the present, until some other time, we may again resume the subject.

Q. Dare we venture to inquire why a world of humans should be thus deceived by such vampires?

A. This question we are not capable of answering because it trenches on the privileges of Deity.

Q. For what is reason given us if we are not permitted its fullest exercise? Is it wrong to suppose Deity is in some degree responsible to His created family?

A. My husband, this is a bold and noble stand you now are taking, and one which requires judgment while you attempt its scrutiny. Yet is it correct and worthy of the most profound attention; not devoid of reverence, but demanding such in fullest measure. May I beg dismissal for the present, and when I come again this shall form a special subject.

[Spirit resumed.] According to my promise, I am here to redeem the same.

The subject being a grand and mighty one, demands of both implicit care, in my prompting and your transcribing. To attempt to describe God and all His holy and divine attributes would prove a futile effort, neither would it enhance His grandeur one iota, yet we may form but one conception, and thereby learn the obligations we are under to Him as our Father and our Friend, and in this condition to hold a council with Him, and thus bringing ourselves in close and holy rapport with Him, as with one who would sympathize with us and hear our plaints, and by the love He bears His children dry up their tears of anguish, and give them strength to battle with a world whose souls are so exhausted with a heavy weight of sin and iniquity as to render it almost impossible to make them fit to become inhabitants of a pure and holy atmosphere, where God and His holy angels dwell. And while we speak of God, clairvoyantly, perceiving you are somewhat inclined to inquire, how we apply this term to an influence that may be described as involving a set of principles, or attributes (as oft they are called). This we accept in the abstract only, because of the impossibility of addressing a single attribute when its holy influence is needed, causing a confusion ill-adapted to a government based on wisdom infinite.

CHRISTIANITY COMPARED WITH SPIRITUALISM.

MY HUSBAND, I have called upon you to write some few thoughts, which may, perhaps, to some extent benefit humanity. Can you imagine why mankind in general seem to think a Spiritualist almost unworthy to be recognized as truthful? We think there are many who, if they possessed the power, would even destroy them, root and branch. And why, I ask? Is there aught in Spiritualism that should cause the blush of shame to tinge the cheek of him who claims a right to think and act according as his conscience dictates, and is willing to accept the Spirit teachings, that there is one God, good and gracious in the treatment of His children! Is this a crime of which they accuse you, that should draw down upon your head the anathemas of men who profess to be exemplars to the world at large; and further, claim to be the followers of the one referred to as being a pure and holy medium and spiritual preceptor? Yes; from those pure and holy lips were ever falling truths ineffably divine, which if practiced by those who pretend to be his followers, but who in all directions fail to copy him, and then assume the right to censure those who are attempting to follow in his footsteps, by not only professing, but practicing each and every injunction to do right towards humanity in all their daily avocations and worldly intercourse, thus practically carrying out the several divine inculcations to the letter, by healing the sick and comforting the afflicted, imparting through divine and holy inspirations spiritual truths, denied by orthodoxy ; in fine, doingmuch that professors of Christianity neglect to do; thus showing that the professors of a despised belief are more the practical disciples of Jesus than those who expect, through pomp and pageantry, to conciliate the good will and friendship of him they call their Savior. Oh monstrous folly ! to think one whom they believe a God can be conciliated by earthly baubles and flimsy show, while the vital principle of good is little thought of, and, worse than all, becomes perverted. What, then, of success can they lay claim to? Do they suppose their God is blind or deaf, that cognizance he will never take of such hypocrisy in their worship, stripped as it is of all sincerity ; a mere mockery ; a shadow without the substance ?

Poor, inert souls, ye had better throw aside your tinselled trash, and look for something more substantial that will feed your hungry souls, so that you may not continue to hunger and thirst for that your misnamed Shepherds cannot supply you with, but of which they boast continually ; and yet with all their boasting, hunger frequently besets them. And fain you would wander from them to seek more wholesome nourishment. Their churches cannot give you the supply you want. Their salt has lost its savor, hence, decay and devastation are fast approaching. The spirit world has heard the dismal cry of Spiritual hunger, and in response thereto are daily bringing from the spheres supplies adequate to meet your wants. Are you willing to accept of this the bounty of your God, brought by angel hands to give you of that bread of life on which your souls depend for nourishment?

Then linger not, but break the barriers which a wily priestcraft may have thrown around you. Break! break those bonds with which they'll fetter every limb, and thus restrict your God-given liberty to seek that food that is more nourishing. We want you seeking; we come with gladness to the rescue, and hence the vengeance which is now aroused in opposition to our purpose. But need you quail before their efforts, impotent as they are, when met with an opposing force they cannot control—the force of righteousness supreme, which gives to men and women a right to keep intact their individuality, tempered and governed by reason, and further ordered by the angel hosts, the puny efforts of a reverend phalanx can never prevail, but, as the chaff before the wind, must scatter and be seen no more. How, then, would we say to ye, O mortal! God, your father and your friend, asks nothing more than strict obedience to his laws as that which is and ever must be acceptable to him whose impartial justice overshadows the entire universe. Let truth, virtue, law and justice be your guide, and all the united efforts of skepticism and ignorant bigotry will fall before you. God is with you to comfort and instruct you, therefore let your cry be ever Excelsior! Upward and onward be your motto. AMEN.

IS FOREKNOWLEDGE A GIFT TO MAN?

IN undertaking to respond to this question we feel a something like reluctance, as it requires but little ingenuity to show how sparse of interest the entire question seems within itself, when viewed as giving to man a power incompatible with his development, in any phase humanity can claim, as an inherent principle within his nature.

Foreknowledge! what, we ask, does it imply? A something so opposed to every principle of wisdom and eternal justice would be illy placed at man's disposal. Vain and presumptious as he is at present, had he prescience what limit could be placed upon him? Knowledge, like all things else must be restricted, or where would be progression?

In each condition man attains to, can he make greater progress under a conviction such attainment needs but little effort? By such impressions the mind becomes inert, and sometimes almost useless. A certain stimulus is needed to stir up man's mentality to action, and energize his soul to follow zealously the proper mode of seeking that he knows to be his right of close investigation. Can aught of doubt exist respecting such a maxim? We deem it quite impossible, and therefore claim it as legitimate. In all that appertains to man's ethereal condition, we feel confined within such narrrow limits, we would, from necessity, hesitate to utter thoughts which crowd upon us thick and fast. Yet silent are we kept from lack of language to impart it. Here, then, lies the difficulty. If men and women had foreknowledge, there would be no need of angel messengers to bring from Deity that they are commissioned to impart, or aught of that which calls them from their bright abodes, to bring such glorious tidings as they often do. Prescience, to self-opinionated men and women, would render useless all their efforts to improve humanity under the law of intuition. It has been said man was made but little lower than the angels; if so, the question must occur to every thinking mind, Do spirits lose that power by the change from mortal to continuous life, for no prescience or foreknowledge do they claim, but yield to Deity that privilege to them quite incomprehensible. In fact the supposition seems so thoroughly opposed to common sense, it cannot be indulged while reason still remains intact, within the human mind.

Does a skillful merchant make known his various projects, if better kept as secret until his plans are matured, and then, perchance, but in degree, or so far as he may trust them? All this seems necessary caution, but ah, how useless must it seem, if man is prescient, having foreknowledge of these secret plans. Is not the absurdity of such a theory manifest to the man that thinks and ponders o'er the acts of Deity? Such theory we deem an insult to the majesty of God. God and Nature both demand implicit recognition of every law enacted, but here a competition would arise between Deity and man as to which was best entitled to claim foreknowledge of the matter. In giving to man a power Omnipotence alone should wield, would be a folly such as a mind well balanced would not for a moment sanction. AMEN.

SHALL THE BIBLE BE USED IN PUBLIC SCHOOLS?

IN attempting to answer such a question, we feel assured a large proportion of mankind will be awakened to a lively interest in the matter, and whatever view *we* take, *we* must be censured.

This is altogether natural; therefore, being prepared, we shall endeavor to shape our course so as to prove, beyond all doubt, that we are sincere and candid in the matter.

Our first essay must be to ask the Bible advocates, what are the uses to which they will apply this book? and, secondly, when applied what will result from the experiment? and, in order to carry on the inquiry, we shall have to draw upon our own imagination, for such reasons as may be given by them; viewing it as holy and infallible, they hope to found a faith in strict accordance with their own, and thus increase the strength of each and every institution, professing orthodox opinions, without the slightest reference to those who claim an equal right to free thought and free expression of it.

Are those who differ from such views compelled to abide by such tyrannic acts? We answer, no; it were better far to let all sectarian views be banished from your public schools and leave the public mind untrammeled by the numerous and erratic dogmas offered, by which many a nation's green and fertile fields have reeked with human gore, and thus become the graves of nature's noblest sons, decimating families and making man the fell destroyer of his species.

Is not this a truth patent to the ken of all beholders, that war, pestilence and famine, have been engendered by this so-called religious education of the masses? We would advocate no such system, by and through which the bitterest wars have been commenced and carried on with more attrocities committed, than by any other means extant. That Bible, hallowed as it seems to be, by priests and bigots, but by millions viewed as vague and meaningless, by the people, apart from some few truths, scattered here and there, in sparseness, as sugar coated pills are given to render palatable a nauseous bolus, so is that Bible illumined, as it were, to hide the monstrosities contained within its lids, which we should deem altogether unfit to meet the eyes of youth—statements which would disgrace a publication deemed obscene.

On this would we base our objections, deeming them valid; for aught presented to the mind of youth that is not truly pure, should be objected to as dangerous to the best interests of humanity; for to them, as your successors, must you look, and as they are trained so will be the coming generations, and while you have the power to restrain the passions by withholding all contamination, 'tis your duty so to do. The present and the future loudly call upon you as parents or guardians so to do. The soil that is rich and new accelerates the growth of vegetation, and is it not so with youth, whose mind is thus imbued with knowledge, either right or wrong? All nature teems with the truth that weeds grow fast when unattended to, and is it not so with the yonng and tender minds committed to your care? How many a bright and glorious genius has sunk in dark oblivion, lacking care in rooting up the noxious weeds which have choked its highest aspirations. Hence, the necessity of guarding carefully the avenues of thought, and so directing it that no barriers may be raised to highly pure and moral inculcations on which depends its future destiny.

Admitting such to be the case, how essential does it seem to assume a censorship o'er the work of teaching those committed to your care, keeping a strict, judicious surveillance over each work presented; for by doing so you will make smooth the path of teaehers who, if well selected and properly restrained by rules and regulations, must succeed in imbuing the youthful mind with knowledge truly useful to humanity, free from prejudice and dogmatism so destructive to that harmony which should exist in every well regulated society.

By such a course of action, the countless blessings man is made recipient of would be appreciated, and anarchy and discord measurably removed. But while discontent and bickering still continues, sin and iniquity seems to flourish, and death and desolation rushes on and on the downward road to misery and destruction.

But, secondly, what is to be the expected benefit from its introduction? You, perhaps, will answer, an education, based on Bible truths, we hold to be essential. To this we answer, a truth presented to the human mind carries with it its own voucher, and requires no cassocked priest to recommend it to the acceptance of the pupil. By natural intuition does it make its own impression, and, therefore, needs no studied effort to impress it on the mind, and while kept separate from falsehood, runs no risk of being misconceived. Hence our objection to the introduction of the Bible, containing as it does some beauteous thoughts, which, if separate from the rest, would seem well adapted as a moral standard suited to the minds of youth. But mixed and interlarded with fable, and even falsehoods, our antagonism to its introduction grows each moment stronger as thought evolves conviction of its uselessness—a term by far too mild, while deprecating the act of introduction.

A public school, conglomerate as it must be of necessity, is no place for such a book. The human intellect demands something more advanced from which instruction may be drawn, without the fiction consequent upon such a laborious effort as the extracting knowledge from a source so mixed and vague; the mind of an adult would naturally tire of such a task. With such views as these, we cannot see that a single benefit can accrue from such appliance as a means of teaching.

We, perhaps, may almost be accused of atheism, because we would exclude the so-called sacred scriptures. What makes them sacred, we would ask, more than any other book containing truth? Does it become a greater truth because man sees fit to call it so? What proof can ye adduce inculcations there contained are God's own records? Ye have none; that ye must admit, other than those presented, being the concoction of some brainless priest, who, with unwonted zeal, has manifested proofs as baseless as the creed professed by him and millions of deluded followers.

But we must check this seeming outpouring of denial of the doctrine thus presented for the guidance of a deluded people.

Whilst we eschew religious dogmas and erratic creeds, we admit the grand and glorious power directing the movements of a universe as being incomprehensible to our finite minds; yet, permeating all things, making Himself known and seen through all creation. Let this self-same faith be made manifest in all your public schools; let it be written in golden letters on your walls, "There is one God; obey his laws and be happy." Herein would be religion ample for all man's needs, in an unperverted state. Parents or guardians have a perfect right to impress upon the tender minds of youth that which they conscientiously believe correct, and no one need complain; but as public teachers, paid by all of every religious denomination, ye are stepping widely from your path of duty the moment you attempt to clog the youthful mind; because that moment ye inviolate one of the most important laws of God—Charity, most beautiful in its character, but little practiced in your midst.

O, was this law better comprehended, this world might be an almost paradise; sin and iniquity would seek concealment, and all the brighter scenes of life would be enhanced and made to reach humanity in all the dark and dismal places which still remain unreached by the genial rays of sunlight to increase the happiness of poor humanity.

We hope the time is coming when ignorance and bigotry shall be removed, and man enfranchized from the incubus, may stand in presence of his God and the assembled hosts of heaven, ready to avow the unity and fatherhood of God, the maternity of nature and the brotherhood and sisterhood of all humanity. Then will resound from every portion of this universe, aye from centre to circumference, "Glory to God in the highest, peace and good will to all men."

My brother, to contemplate such a result seems to stir up every faculty of the human soul to increased action. Let us pray the author of all good that all schism may cease; that one universal belief in God's supremacy may enter the heart of every living being, to the entire seclusion of all that is dark and mystified, so that all errors may cease, and truth, aye, God's own truth, may prevail and man be benefitted thereby.

With deference we offer the foregoing thoughts, hoping that they may be received in all kindness, as they are now presented, for whether salutary in their influence or not, *we* have the consciousness of having performed our duty. AMEN.

MY SISTER'S ADDRESS FROM THE SPIRIT LAND.

MY BELOVED BROTHER, to whom I am bound by stronger ties than natural affection; yes, by the bonds of holy and divine love—engendered in my soul by the many efforts you have made to render me capable of becoming the recipient of angel teachings. But, alas! no efforts could succeed, while every avenue to my inner soul was barred against their entrance by prejudice so strong that nothing short of force could break asunder bonds that chained me down to dogmas most revolting to the enfranchised soul. Often have I thought whilst pondering o'er the many proofs you have sought to give me that Spiritualism was true, poor, poor, misguided soul you must be to accept a doctrine based on mere delusion. O, how many, many prayers I have offered for your safety, imagining every time you wrote me on the subject your final doom would soon be sealed, and heaven be lost to you for ever more, never for one moment dreaming heaven was the place it is. Theology assumes it is the ultimate of happiness to those who seek and claim it as their own.

My brother, oft have I thought when dwelling on the subject that it seemed so strange to me, that you, who never seemed to be religiously inclined, should, all at once, become enthusiastic and a perfect devotee to that I could not comprehend as possible. To talk of holding constant commune with your spirit friends, appeared to me a perfect myth ; hence, in ignorance and superstition I denounced it folly and even false ; but since my advent into spirit life an awakened state of consciousness has clearly shown me the error I committed and the injustice shown toward you, my brother ; a miserable return for all your kindness. Will you forgive me, brother mine, for thus rejecting every attempt you made to bring about a changed condition which would have been a boon to me, indeed ? but bigoted and superstitious as I was, my heart was steeled to all of spirit power ; hence my inattention to your statements.

It is needless to enter into a minute detail of my unconscious state in passing to the spheres, to you 'tis not unknown — at least, the theory. Suffice it then to say, all was strange and unfamiliar to my sight. At every turn the busy din of industry was seen and heard, and thus without an effort of my own, was I at once ushered into a place of harmony and love—fit place of rest for every way-worn pilgrim from a land of inharmony and misrule, both in the domestic and public circles.

O, my brother, when I reflect upon the time I lost on earth, when listening to the miserable teachings of a long life, I am truly ashamed, and wonder why with intellect sufficient I could not see the errors of that doctrine, which now appear to me so void of truth that but a little time it will take to remove the veil of darkness used to cover its deceptive influences, and give to those who seek it under angel guidance, a brighter and more glorious faith.

But to my detail. Unconscious as I have been so long, I scarce could recognize the beauties of the place, nor who was there to greet me but my own sweet Julia. O, my brother, to her I owe a debt of love and gratitude unbounded, for soothing and consoling me in my bewilderment. She might be deemed my savior.

But while my mind was on the stretch of

expectation, a beauteous spirit came towards me, and with anxious scrutiny peered into my face, desirous of recognizing me as some one known to her. She suddenly embraced me, and, smiling lovingly, exclaimed, "Thou art, indeed, his sister! come, come, thou dear one, and dwell with us within these realms of bliss; we've wrung thee from the hands of those who would have still withheld thee from us, and sunk thy soul in black despair; but we have watched thee carefully years long past, hoping, before thy transit from earth-life, to have changed thee from those erratic views by education fixed, almost beyond our power to remove; thy brother's efforts failing, we soon perceived 'twas useless to continue longer, knowing time alone would e'en assist us in our design to shield thee from the priestly meshes of deception."

Thus have we at last the innate gratification of meeting thee here, where sorrow cannot come, and where thy untrammelled nature may act its part in common with the unnumbered hosts of spirits, who through earthly trials and vexations have become bright and shining lights.

Really, my beloved brother, it seems so strange to be able once again to commune with you, that all which has transpired since my death (as it is called) seems but a dream; and yet so real is it to my spirit senses as to make a reality of that which gives me so much pleasure and delight; that, with all the obstacles removed, I can now look forward to a joyful reunion with you in the celestial spheres.

My brother, whilst enjoying to a great extent these proffered blessings, am I wont to dwell upon the untoward condition of a beloved sister and daughters two, whose souls are so environed by the self-same odious dogmas lately advocated by myself, the soul at once recoils in pure disgust that they are thus exposed to dangers and perplexities, so overwhelming in their nature as to mar their prospects in the Summer Land. O, could I but come in rapport with our beloved Eliza, such glowing thoughts of heaven I'd then impart that no longer would she hold adherence to a doctrine so destructive to the best interests of humanity, that all the powers of angel effort scarcely proves sufficient to arrest the evil. Thus am I ever striving to affect a change which, once produced, would show her where the treasure lies—not in the musty dogmas of the past which, long ere this, should have been consigned to the dead past, but to the living present should be as things that were but now are not.

But, my brother, modern Spiritualism presents a code of laws supremely beautiful in all their phases, but in no phase more completely so than their simplicity and truthfulness. O, could your world but imbibe this thought and act upon it, how readily they would throw aside those baneful teachings which have deadened the souls best aspirations, teaching it reliance upon all that is doubtful and pertinaciously objecting to all that is truthful and instructive.

But while I am thus dilating upon these matters, I am somewhat forgetful of the object of this my first visit to you, my brother, whose sympathetic nature draws me more closely towards you than is usual by those ties of closer affiliation —our twinship—which now seems more clearly demonstrated than in earth-life where a different atmosphere encompassed us, rendering us as it were, repugnant to each other, owing to our surroundings—mine, dark and almost fanatical, yours, my brother, brighter and still brighter under the divine and holy influence of spirit teaching, leading you upward and onward to the royal road of eternal progression.

Strange as it may appear, up to the latest hour of my conscious state in earth-life, the same uncompromising doubts of spirit power and presence, still adhered to me. And why, I often ask myself? But because I had become so saturated with priestly teachings that no room was there to accept instruction from the angel world. Thus did I pass away, ignorant as I was of all ethereal things. Long, long unconscious was I, as you have been informed by Julia. You know the rest by my brief description given. At present I must leave, but soon will come again when called for by you, my brother. Till then, I say adieu.

COMMUNICATION FROM SAINT PAUL.

My Brother, no mortal or immortal ever longed for your commiseration more than I do. Nothing would induce me thus to urge my claim on your immediate attention than the fear I entertain lest something may interfere with an arrangement I have sought to make for centuries past, by which I might unfold to human ken horrors most foul and noxious in their import. Oh, with what eagerness I sought you on hearing you were gifted with the power of transcribing spirit-thoughts without hyperbole, or slightest variation from the truth as prompted by them. Jesus, my friend and brother, made this known to me; in eulogistic terms he spoke of thee as being a very marvel in transcribing angel thoughts, and such I have already found thee. No inaccuracies appear, but plain ungarbled statements given.

In that I do rejoice; for, at the present time sincerity and honesty of purpose dwells not in the heart of man. The times in which I lived on earth, were bad enough; corruption in its basest form had fastened on the minds of men, unfitting them as teachers of the good, but thoroughly initiated in all that men's imperfect status might aspire to. Can you imagine a man like Jesus could approve such things in his day and generation? In token of his abhorrence did he not rebuke them in a way peculiarly his own, and never yet improved upon by others who came after? a way no one but he, the God-imbued, a holy character, sent as a seeming speciality to check the mad career of men, who, being ignorant, knew not the risk they ran in trampling on the laws he enacted for their benefit, and save them from the penalties attached thereto. No threats of vengeance passed those sacred lips; no hasty steps were ever taken by him; but calm, deliberate action marked his every movement. Meek, but majestic, was his mien; awing the rebellious by a look, and giving to the afflicted some words of comfort commensurate with their needs; not in pompous mood, but as one who had the power to accomplish all he promised. And was not such a course majestic in its character?

But is it needed I should attempt to eulogize a character I can scarcely comprehend? one, who in comparison with this world, has not a single compeer, and, in Heaven, no one will seek a competition? But here I find myself at fault. I have no language suited to describe his glorious and celestial nature; free, almost as God himself from imperfection, and thus was he the chosen messenger to impart the glad tidings of continuous life to those who would seek it in spirit and in truth, with trumpet voice endorsed by all the angelic hosts of Heaven.

My Brother, with deep regret, I leave this grand and noble martyr to the cause of truth, who, in renouncing life upon the cross, seemed, as it were, to seal the act as just in retribution of the crime alleged against him, making himself almost a God, when he exclaimed: "I and my Father are one." And was he not then, as ever since that day of expiation? Were not his utterances but further proof of the oneness spoken of—truth, that coming from the Father and accepted by the Son, a seeming unison of thought and action, not comprehended by the masses, but true in principle. If aught can be more clear and comprehensible, I ask the doubter to avow it, for aught that he presents but proves conclusively, no man can controvert. Language is sometimes so perverted as to render common sense but a mere jargon of words. Just as the inspiration of the so-called sophist must appear to those who use their common sense and reason in adjudging sentences and chapters conglomerate and absurd as pretentious efforts to produce a work of inspiration; but not being genuine it is like the floundering of a fanatic while endeavoring to explain a theory without a foundation. With oft repeated ahem and much of hesitation, at length subsides, and is not seen again. And if it were needed we might add much more in words and yet not add one tittle to the truth.

Nothing can be more ungrateful to an observant mind, than undue repetition of a thought, however beautiful it may be, because seemingly out of place, without companionship or voucher for the act being proper. Pray, my brother, excuse these brief digressions; they seem to me like pictures in a book, illustrating what is there described; or like keys which open passages of seeming difficulty to comprehend, ostracising thought and making clear its meaning. Look at Nature; like a meandering stream keeps on its course in tranquil, quiet measure; in seeming rippling pleasure wends its way in search of such companionship best suited to its destiny. The meeting seems to be a joyous one; the ripple of the one blending with the new found streams, seems like the inter-twining of two loving souls in sweet affection's bonds. With close adherance do they cling together, for all their hopes of happiness seem, as it were, dependant on that union continuing intact through a life on earth, even to its natural terminus.

If Heaven is in such condition reached, think

you we shall need a Savior there, crucified, to appease the wrath of an offending God? Monstrous supposition that, to imagine a God supremely wise and merciful could e'er be wrathful and vindictive, apparently with less of self-control to guide him than poor, puny man. Avaunt! we say. Such a thought is too absurd, too great a compromise of God's eternal majesty, and every phase appears to partake of blasphemy. Retributive justice must o'ertake the authors of such a calumny.

But I find while thus I am moralizing, I almost forgot the purpose of my visit, being, as I said before, to unfold the errors of the past, by giving a truthful detail of events that then occurred; a record garbled in its character, concocted by untruthful men who sought to aggregate the bad, letting virtue and integrity remain unnoticed and unprotected.

My Brother, which would be your choice; to accept my detail of events, consecutive in its course, or adopt the interrogatory plan?

My reverend friend, methinks your detail would be interesting unless a question may possibly be asked. Such a wise decision I will accept, and in furtherance of such avowal, first I will speak of inspiration, it being an element or gift of grand importance to humanity, both embodied and disembodied in its nature, as it were, joining together the two worlds in one solid bond of glorious intercourse, bridging that gulf of separation so much talked of by imaginative christians who sapiently believe the same road which leads from earth to heaven, unless removed, or perhaps destroyed, must admit of a return to those who, finding such a privilege existing, by natural instinct try the retracing of their steps to visit earth and seek communion with their friends, and there impart to them the fact of a continuous life beyond this vale of tears and suffering, as many think it, but of which in fitting place we may again revert to. If common sense and reason play their parts in truthfulness, they must endorse the fact that the road to heaven is still an open one, their so-called avowal to the contrary notwithstanding.

Are ye not told in heaven there is no coercion used; its occupants are under no restraint; the door is left ajar for those who wish to leave, whilst those who seek an entrance must knock—not loud, but meaningly, and wait admittance while their right is fully tested by examination of the needed record asked of them?

With such precautions, heaven is a place that many seek, but few, comparatively, gain admission to; but not from any other cause than carelessness and ignorance on the part of those who have not listened to the angel voices speaking to them in tones of love and tenderness, beseeching them to share the wiser, better plan which leads to peace and happiness in the Summer Land ; where dwells those beauteous spirit forms in love and happiness supreme. Yes ; had they listened to their loving words and wise injunctions all of misery would cease, and happiness celestial theirs.

In this no mystery can be seen ; the simple law of truth to guide them ; angel hands outstretched to lead, and heaven's best light to make their path a clear and pleasant one. Why should they falter on the road, or, perchance, prefer some other one, adorned by artificial means to mislead the unwary doubter, looking to the surface without a knowledge of the many pitfalls overspread by means concocted to deceive? We here would ask, is such the path a man of wisdom would make choice of? Oh, no. His path would be the great highway of nature, where slight obstructions may be met—seemingly, at first, impassable, but, seeking aid that is ever ready, are soon removed, and in peace the traveler pursues his journey pleased and satisfied, no retrogression does he contemplate.

My brother, is not this a sermon quite as good as many an aristocratic congregation listen to? At all events, more truth is therein contained than in the costly edifices of your several towns and cities—mere monuments of human pride, more numerous than they'll admit. If candor was an element amongst the infatuated of these churches, we would not complain; but of that they seem entirely bereft within their narrowed souls for that to dwell in; and should it by mistake obtrude its presence, a shriek of terror would be heard indicative of deep distress—the sure concomitant of fright, and wildest apprehension some calamity was then impending. Can it be supposed an element like this of pure and holy parentage could feel at home with such associates? We deem it quite impossible. No congeniality exists while assimulation is the absentee; a combination of the twain may aid the one, and give a stimulus to both to lay aside the prejudice of early education, and by much forbearance practiced by them, better and more righteous feelings may be engendered in their minds, subversive of the many wrongs committed by non-observance of the Law of candor, much to be regretted under their new and changed condition.

Think of this ye trained deceivers, for transient must be your triumph. Scanned and scrutinized by eyes invisible to you, eyes that never blink in sunshine's glare, or fail to see in midnight darkness what the sons and daughters of humanity are doing; reporting *that* they see both good and bad to such as are appointed to make the record.

Many are impressed with the idea that crime can be committed, and in secresy be kept, because in darkness it may have been committed. Poor,

poor, mistaken souls. Awake! I say, to comprehension of the truth; let reason do her part, and common sense assist her; let them think the matter over what truth there is in such avowal. Men are not all as Gods, knowing good from evil, embracing the one and casting aside the other, or being altogether without temptation could glide along through life apparently in happiness and joy, nothing annoying or distressing them; no affliction of the physique, but under conscious throbbings of the tortured soul, a hotter hell need not be sought. And yet the so-called christian of the past and present here denounces that fancied hell as insufficient to accomplish what a malignant, furious God would doom His creatures to experience, and that experience unending in effect. And here we would expose a fallacy magnifying a law which, when carried out, becomes an entire nullity, a very mockery of law or justice.

Law, to be effective, must be just. Its tendency should be reform. We ask can cruelty, unswerving, implacable and interminable, produce the desired result? Who, we ask, will answer otherwise than No? Voices doubly vociferated will rise in deprecation of so base a supposition.

My Brother, if heaven and earth could be consolidated, its intercourse might be increased; the wants of one, by interchange of holy sentiment in all things appertaining to the one or other, must excite more interest in ethereal matters, because, at present, they are seemingly a myth to those who, from indifference and stark inertness, feel as if heaven and earth are separated by a gulf so wide and deep, 'tis thought impassable.

In and under such condition, men become but little interested, and thus neglect a most important duty; for from whatever standpoint you may view it, your every day of life presents such grand and glorious reasons for investigating.

Does a prudent, careful man purchase estate without seeking counsel of his friend, unless by long acquaintance that friendship had been tried and found to be reliable, would his advice be followed if time he had to inspect the same himself, yet being satisfied that all is quite correct, eventually, a purchase he may make?

And if all this caution seems a need in worldly matters, how measurably beyond all cavil should man investigate the truth of modern Spiritualism, which has no parallel in beauty, grandeur, truthfulness and glory; the very acme of eternal wisdom! the all and in all of science and philosophy. No novel thoughts are proferred here. From earliest times it has been known, accepted, and like a treasured jewel in times of danger, secreted as best it could be, to save it from the vandal hands outstretched to harm, or perhaps, destroy it.

But in every time of danger menacing it, there

were those attentive angel watchers ready to enshrine it within some place of safety, far beyond the reach of ruffian violence, till days of darkened ignorance have passed away, and then in modest but effective mood, sought the accomplishment of a plan concocted in the angel world—having for its purpose the inauguration of a brighter, holier, grander inspiration, as it were, reaching beyond the grovelling thoughts of men who live but to enjoy the luxuries of mundane life without even thinking of the future; looking no further than life's terminus on earth. AMEN.

AND THERE SHALL BE NO MORE DEATH.

MY HUSBAND, your friend who prepared this question for solution is one of those minds which has become, as it were, insatiate for truth, and spares no time or opportunity to obtain it. Oh, how we delight in responding to such, even when our difficulties seem almost insurmountable, for they deserve our utmost efforts, and freely we accord them.

Our answer might be brief—a mere "No;" but we think the subject will bear a further elaboration, and the mere negation might prove unsatisfactory; therefore, permit me to use your organism for a brief period. To define death, as it is called, would be almost impossible, because it could be but a detail of one's own individual experience, which, perhaps, would not prove very clearly the question. Therefore, we shall omit the description, and proceed at once to describe its use and end.

The *entree* of animated existence shows most potently that birth and death are existent institutions in the divine economy of supply and demand. The former is as essential to the people of your world as the latter, as a means of disposing of a worn-out or diseased population, a means, peculiar in its character, almost incomprehensible to the human ken; but yet in all its various bearings so efficient as to fulfill the design of him who created all things.

Why, you may perhaps ask, the necessity? Could not infinite wisdom have devised means which would have been less dreadful to human susceptibility; something that would have been less terrible in contemplation; something that could be looked at less dreadful?

Looking at men as they are at present constituted, these questions might be rightly asked as showing the result of bigoted and superstitious teachings, which tend to veil and obscure the beauties of the institution called Death; and from them our diseased imaginings make death the very culmination of mental suffering.

Is this a truth, or shall we view it as a mere excresence from the soul of bigotry, acting upon the human mind like caustic when applied to a wound upon the human body? Is there aught of reason in such teachings, we would ask? Aught that can assimilate with truth, and being so, is it not neccessary every effort should be put forth to check evil so world-wide that the soul of man seems for ages to have been submerged in misconception of living truths, that they seem to prefer the erratic dogmas of a worn-out and decayed theology, which darkens and mystifies one of the grandest and most sublime institutions known.

Conceive, if you can, your earth at the present moment, destitute of a means to answer an inevitable end. Generation after generation in quick succession are born, live a time in beauteous youthhood, manhood's prime is then enjoyed; old age even, if health is still continued, brings with it that which abbreviates its former pleasures and enjoyments; decrepitude and *ennui* follow in the train. What is mundane life to such a one? Has he, or she not measurably lost the attractive principle which bound him and others together in the bonds of well tried friendship? True, there are somewhat isolated cases where continuance of those ties exist, and yet they are not common ; but when abrogated, is not death or removal deemed a boon to suffering humanity.

Is it not evident that wisdom has directed all things appertaining to humanity ? Life's limit is a wise enactment, even was death its ultimate ; but when viewed as it is, a mere change of conditions, suited to the high and mighty purpose of translating the human soul to more bright and beautiful condition, it seems as if an eternity could not suffice to express man's undying gratitude for such a boon.

If any man was inclined to grant a favor, one unusual in its character, think you the warmest feelings of his soul would not be fired, and all his energies aroused to manifest his high appreciation of the gift ? And if a mere material gift demands such recognition, how should this gift ethereal be valued ?

No power within the human soul would be commensurate with the demand existing. Surely, then, he who can contemplate the grandeur of such an act of goodness should never tire in the exhibition of his gratitude.

But, my husband, how few there are who are willing to investigate this most important feature in the divine economy. Many thousands at the present time erroneously accept the teachings of theology that death must be esteemed a penalty, inflicted on humanity for the disobedience of our fabled parents, a folly only equalled by some other acts, so chronicled as sacred, in their birth and origin. Here, then, we see the folly of attaching much importance to preconceived opinion so long pre-dated, and call the same infallible.

Where, we ask, is that safeguard given to man to save him from illusions detrimental to his present and future prospects, that reason which, if untrammeled by superstition, will be his surest guide, acting as it should in close connection with the teachings of your guardian spirits, who clairvoyantly note the workings of that reason which being well directed, is ever faithful to its trust.

But, my husband, to the text more closely: "And there shall be no more Death."

The glorious promise there announced strikes upon the ear of humanity, as does the cooling breeze directed to the way-worn traveler whose nature seems almost exhausted, and therefore at once becomes receptive of its refreshing influence throughout his system. It is then and there his grateful soul in silent mood transmits his liveliest tones of gratitude to God the donor.

What, we would inquire, did the ejaculation of that sentiment mean? No more death? Verily, we may find it difficult to meet the objections of the skeptic that it is too much a mystery to be solved. Amongst them, it may be so, but we are all wont to show that no mystery surrounds it; that all things connected with it can be rationally accounted for. The man who finds the holy and divine influence of truth coursing through his nature, feels within his soul that after passing the transition state he will enter upon a life of eternal perpetuity. His intuition tells him so. His very inmost soul responds with holy gratitude to the assurance he thus receives from those who under their divine impression utter thoughts which sink deep down into man's inmost nature.

Are ye not told by angel lips that there is an immortal state beyond the grave? and if it be immortal, how can death again occur; and if the immortal or continued life be true, reason at once rejects the idea of Death as quite illogical and altogether false.

We quarrel not with those who are thus scripturally infatuated as to believe a matter called inspired, which stands rejected by our reason.

We have no other guide by which to separate the truth from error; therefore, whatever bigotry and superstition may present as a creed to thinking men and women for their endorsement, think awhile before ye accept, and we feel a settled confidence that thy reason will evolve objections, based upon the law of justice, which demands the utterance of truth beyond all the sophistry of modern Christianity. Therefore, we say to ye, as children of one common parent—God—waver not in your acceptation of all angel truths, for be assured the same benign power that has given you strength of mind and body to accomplish your destiny here on earth, will not forsake you now, neither at the time you are called upon to recognize the call Death will make upon you. Be assured it will be his last and final one, for then will he be swallowed up in victory over every sinful passion that has measurably made needful that so much dreaded ordeal, which has been instituted as a means by which the preparation necessary might be effected, and the redeemed soul of humanity becomes a sinless applicant at the door of heaven.

My husband, this subject might be carried to an indefinite length, but we feel the mind imbued with Spiritualism and free from undue prejudice, must coincide with us that agreeable to the law of supply and demand another death cannot be needed; therefore, acting upon this hypothesis there will be none. AMEN.

WHAT IS WORSHIP; AND WHAT ITS OBJECT?

The above question calls upon us for marked attention, as indeed do all connected with the act and purpose as above propounded; and in treating it, it perhaps were well to explain our views upon the first and main point presented—Worship, by which you will better comprehend its object. The term, itself, presents a compound nature, somewhat complex, made up of many parts and portions of elements essential to the end designed. First is implied approval, admiration, deep and holy appreciation of the character considered, a something near akin to the highest human conception of perfection; a concentration of all the purest sentiments the human mind is capable of realizing, in fine, a condensed mass of infinite purity and God-like wisdom that alone should be the ideal fit for man to worship. And if he is capable of realizing such an object for his adoration, let him do so. You then ask the object of so doing, to which we answer, self, and nothing else. He seeks, as best he can, an issue pleasurable to himself; no other motive has he than, as he supposes, to conciliate that God, or power (call it what you will), whom he imagines he has offended by an act, or acts, called sinful by some priest, who claims to know God's will, and thus in angry tones denounces acts pronounced by him offensive to his God. At this, the terror-stricken sinner falls upon his knees, and worships, as he thinks, a God of vengeance and malignity, and, as such, proceeds to flatter and offer praises to him, seemingly, as if addressed a being like himself; returns well satisfied; the object of his worship has been obtained—the forgiveness of his sins. Thus, is his selfish nature satisfied, until a repetition of the act brings him to the same condition, seeking each time the same ordeal; here, then, is the object of worship in the main. But the exception may be shown in the spontaneous out-gushing aspirations of the soul to Him he knows only as a God of Mercy and of Love, thus ventilating his soul, o'er charged with a deep and lasting sense of what his God has done for him. This may be termed soul-worship; no selfishness is here; the mere acknowledgement of bounteous blessings, constantly presented, not a word of flattery or praise, but a continual welling-up from the lowest depths of his inner soul. We might dilate upon this subject to a greater length, but elaboration would enhance its truth; it must be felt before it is understood.

CAUSE AND EFFECT, AS GENERALLY UN-UNDERSTOOD AND ACCCEPTED—IS IT A PROPER EXPRESSION?

My Friend, in order to meet the contingincies of human thought, and comprehension, we shall be compelled to go far back of the present time, when the minds of men were far less cultivated than now, when everything presented for elucidation was submitted, not to the reasoning faculties, but more frequently the passional, so that the rash impulses became the grand motive power which guided and directed them in almost all their deductions; hence, the difficulty in discovering whence these impulses came, and the direction they might take. Almost every man in the Universe is the victim, to some extent, of the passional elements within him, which will readily account for the various imperfections in his resolves. Reason is seldom or ever consulted, hence every act is impulsive, destitute of a base upon which to work out life's problem. With such a want of system, how is it possible the result can be correct, or satisfactory? for every effort that is made, renew them often as you will, partakes but of the same imperfect element, and must produce but a similar effect. Herein, we propose showing these imperfect efforts to produce a result, which has failed, but shows conclusively to our minds that such impulse, or imperfections, are the cause, and failure the effect. Again: suppose we admit the proposition that no cause exists and, consequently, no effect can be produced. Look into Nature's works and there behold the most potent proof that there must be a cause to produce a result. Take the acorn, perfect in every particular, let one be selected with the utmost care, and laid aside as a cherished thing—the production of infinity, put it away so carefully, that nothing can harm it. Spring, summer and harvest, aye, and winter, too, have all passed by. Look at your acorn; is it altered in appearance since last you handled it? Oh, no, it has been kept dry, and no rude blast of wind has passed over it. You lay it by, determined once again to try its condition. You select for your experiment one equally perfect, but of last years' growth. Instead of treating it as tenderly as you did the first, at a proper time you plant it in the earth, with no particular care, for now, it is where nature's laws prescribed it should be. In proper season, a tiny spear of living growth is seen peering into life, with slow but certain progress; no failure now, and why? Because iu the one case you have obeyed the law of nature, and placed the acorn where nature intended it should be in order to bring into action the life principle of that embryo oak; there, then, you have one illustration of cause in the following of nature's law: the cause, and the growing oak; the result, rendering, according to our view, a very proper mode of expressing a principle which cannot be gainsaid. In these times of experimental research, you must expect to find adventurers, who, for the sake of notoriety, will ever be ready to substitute what they call "new theories," which are, after all, in the general, mere carpings at the old. A mere denial without a difference, with this exception, that the former has reason's base to work upon, while the other is a mere phantom of the excited brain of a would-be philosopher. AMEN.

RESURRECTION.

AFTER THE HUMAN BODY BECOMES A CORPSE, WHAT WILL ITS CREATOR DO TO RESTORE THE SCATTERED FRAGMENTS AND PREPARE THEM FOR A RESURRECTION?

To convince mankind a Resurrection is not needed we are aware is a task of some difficulty, because, so impressed, has it been, upon the human mind, that to remove it may be deemed an almost hopeless task, yet are we willing to essay its accomplishment, because, while reason holds its sway, there still is hope; therefore, to renounce an effort which may benefit mankind is altogether wrong, and shows a craven spirit which should never be displayed by those who claim to be the messengers of a God, whose love for all humanity has sent us as purveyors of all that can enlighten man in his researches after living truth, and by such means all that is false may be removed, leaving the perceptive faculties clear and unencumbered by the erratic teachings of a priesthood, base in falsehood and in purpose, too. Upon this we found our theme. Strange as it may appear to some, it is no less true, as shown by offering such a thought as that contained in all their several rituals, that after death comes the resurrection; when the last trump shall sound, each material body shall throw off the shroud, and once again appear as sensient beings, capable of recognizing and being recognized by former friends and relatives. Yes, resurrected from the silent tomb many have occupied for ages past and gone, even far back beyond the earliest records, known, there and then, to give account of deeds done in the body, and recorded in a book kept by some angel, or, perhaps, archangel, in the far off Heaven; a book, forsooth, methinks however large, could not contain a record such as would accrue for sins committed through the various ages past and gone. The damning traits of crime, as there described, would make the angels blush, and God express a keen regret he had ever created man. But within the so-called Sacred Book, have they striven to show the right Deity has claimed to call on all the dead to awaken from the sleep of death, even down into the dark regions of the damned, to be exhumed from endless torture, and once again to breathe the cooler atmosphere of *somewhere*, to be again judged and again condemned to endless torture with numerous recruits, for such a horrible condition. Avaunt, we say, ye cruel priests; stir not without the limits of your so-called sacred edifices, but wait, with patience, your allotted doom, for soon you will find your level among those deluded victims you have been the foul instruments of bringing to such conditions that must affright your guilty souls on becoming companions of those you have so basely misled. Are you not aware that he who attempts to deal with his fellow-man in such wise must soon experience that reaction which, sooner or later, will recoil upon his own devoted head? And, think you such a fate will not be yours, if truth there be in what you have taught? If God demands a resurrection, you, of all men, must dread it most, bemired, as you are, with foul and nauseous dogmas; no respite can you claim, for all in heaven would rise and clamor for your condemnation, as being a just and righteous retribution for hypocrisy and deception practised by you. But further would we say, a God of love and mercy, never could feel compunctions at such a terminus of evil doings. When the soul of man becomes thus hardened, by undue punishment, no effort can be made to bring it into such condition as to render Heaven a place well suited to contain such spirits, whose souls being permeated with all of hate and vengeance, must rebel and seek some better place wherein to vent their rage and maledictions on those whose cruel misteachings had brought them to a condition so deplorable. But I have somewhat wandered from my subject. A God whose vengeance could be thus employed, must feel within himself a strong desire to show his power, and drive to desperation, those, who under better teachings, might have aspired to something holier and higher in the spheres. Thus punishment and suffering might do its work, and man's inherent right to immortality be recognized at once, and, with a soul regenerated, would seek a haven of rest and pure tranquility. But while this is doing, the very atmosphere he breathes becomes polluted by the stench of myriads of suffering souls, burning through all eternity, in endless torments, cruel beyond the conception of a fiend, and this for a finite crime, committed by souls incapable of being otherwise, while under the guidance of a deceptive priesthood. But I see, my Brother, you are all impatient to be told what God or Nature will invent to gather up the scattered fragments and prepare them for the promised resurrection. Strange conception, this, I think I hear you say, and one which at all times seems must have a tendency to abrogate those laws which govern the entire Universe; for, when the laws which govern heaven, are better known and understood, a better state of things must soon appear, and man, himself, seeing the necessity of obedience to them, will at once become so, thereby aiding and abbetting the angel efforts to accomplish the grand and important work of man's redemption. Thus, as time rolls on, all things will change, and man's opinion must keep pace, so that all must feel a Resurrection is not needed, and thus will Deity be saved the trouble of seeking out the fragmentary portions of decayed humanity, than which a sillier proposition could not be entertained, or one that should be summarily expunged from all the records in creation, by which a stumbling block would be removed, and better, holier sentiments imbibed, which soon would bring about a change most salutary. But while there are so many obstacles continually presented , there must be anarchy prevailing. There are various opinions as to the anticipated Resurrection, whether it can be effected by and through such agencies as are now appointed; for after man has become a disembodied spirit, and laid aside the mortal coil as useless, (indeed, to which he has no claim, no longer being his, and indeed, no longer capable of recognizing the various atoms once forming an integral whole), how can they be gathered up and made to affinitize together, each atom having formed fresh combinations, separated by wind or wave, connecting themselves with other atoms, *ad infinitum*, altogether beyond the ken of mortal or immortal beings? What agent could be successfully employed to aggregate these atoms, scattered throughout the universe of men?—a limb or portion of a body here, and yonder, other members of the human frame, distorted and deranged in form, some mutilated and disfigured so as to baffle the most acute observer. Is there, we would ask, the slightest probability of a recognition? Then we would ask, why resurrect a mass conglomerate, as it would be, unsuited to the end designed. Would He, whose wisdom is infinite, adopt a course so utterly useless as to call upon the dead, to arise from their solemn resting-places to become the mocked of all beholders. Could Wisdom infinite adopt a course so reckless and absurd? We never can accept the thought; therefore shall infer no such effort will be made by him whose wisdom can never be doubted. Therefore, no preparation need be attempted, other than that the soul requires to fit it for immortal life; to give ethereal instruction to the acceptant soul, and thus in time, lead it onward in the path of eternal progress to the higher spheres. Thus, my Brother, will man become purified ftom all sin, and rendered fit to ascend to the home of the celestial good. AMEN.

CHARITY.

DEFINED BY MARY, QUEEN OF SCOTS.

MY BELOVED SON, feeling desirous of treating this question, given upon the broadest scale of usefulness I am capable, a term so comprehensive must draw quite heavily upon the intellect to reach the many avenues of human receptivity. A stock however large will soon exhaust itself, unless repleted by some power adequate to the task imposed, and such conviction now I feel; therefore, shall call upon some sister angels to impart such thoughts as are adapted to the end designed.

Charity, though seemingly a simple theme when first considered, yet as its complicated influences are felt and realized by the contemplative mind, evolve such holy thoughts and bright ideas, flooding, as it were, the human soul, hour by hour and day by day, with more of God and all of his glorious attributes, by which the latent love within man's soul is stirred to deeds of Charity, more grand and noble in their character than all the glittering pageants of the past or present time. The soul that feels this genial influence needs no prompting to do right, but nobly proffers what it hath. Thus, in time of suffering, the needy are supplied, and pain is thus alleviated.

Many and many a stricken soul while writhing under pain of mind, and body too, has learned to bless the hand of Charity, not alone by having food presented, but when a kind and quiet word is spoken, some lacerated hearts respond to words that fall like oil upon unirritated wounds, producing for a time, and perhaps for ever, a tranquility of mind so unexpected as to swell the heart almost to bursting, overloaded as it is by gratitude overwhelming.

Yes, my Son, this, this is the work true God-like Charity performs. The mere alms-giving or supply of food, though always good, reaches not to the depth of the inner soul's sorrows, whose deeply seated power spread throughout the entire system, clouding, as it were, the brightest scenes of human life. These have to be reached. Will what the world calls Charity exhume them from their hiding place and heal them too? Oh, no. Charity cannot, of itself, perform a task of such importance, and sympathy is what is needed when it could go out and seek a soul with which it can assimulate. There a cord of divine and holy sympathy is touched; the life principle is again awakened, and that which before seemed almost dead, has become a renovated entity, self-recognized and warmed into active life as one prepared to reciprocate the aid received.

O, my Son, could the world but witness such a

scene of resuscitation from deadened lethargy to active sentient life, methinks the due monotony of earth-life would change, and slothfulness no longer curse your borders. The busy din of industry would soon be heard, increased with force and energy of purpose. The dull, inactive life they had passed would soon disgust them, and once again they would be what God had made them —active, useful members of society, ready and willing to bear their alloted portion of a burthen all must bear. Whatever condition they may fill they cannot find exemption from those worldly cares, the sure concomitants of wealth as well as poverty. But Charity being our theme, we must stop digressions and keep more closely to our subject.

The varied phases Charity assumes would take more time to name and then explain than your readers might willingly devote, therefore, shall we notice them but briefly. Hence, people speak of Charity as a sylogism, being more frequently practiced from sinister motives than any generous impulse; arising spontaneously from a soul imbued with tender sympathy for another's woes, not confining that sympathy to the mere act of feeding the hungry and clothing the naked, but to reach down deep into the inner soul's recesses; to discover the deep-seated cause of anguish oft exhibited in tearful gushes or spasmodic throes;

betraying the internal struggle to conceal them. Here in such condition Charity is more often needed. The soothing touch of sympathy bestowed in words of kindly import has often dried those tears and made the sufferer's heart beat quicker in response to such. We ask, can time and talent find better use? We think it cannot. The holy sympathy of kind compassion carries with it a potent power no one can tell or recognize. unless it has been felt. 'Tis the soul becomes attuned to Charity in imitation of its God who, by angel hands is ever scattering His several bounties o'er your land in measure suited to the needs of man.

But the Charity of which we speak is that which can alone be given by angels in the form and out. Nay, start not, my Son, 'tis even so. It is not always needful that a disembodied spirit or angel must perform a service so sublime and God-like, for men and women angels have you in your midst, performing all those holy rites attributed to us alone. Oh, no. In heaven there are no brighter angels than on earth we often see administering to the wants of some poor stricken mistaught soul, who needs a higher, holier sympathy than priest or deacon can impart.

To do our Master's will is no small task. O, 'tis indeed a glorious one, and Charity in all its purity is the channel through which we act in doing so. To heal the sorrowing soul, to make the sickly well, to succor all distress is what our mission calls upon us to perform, and will not man assist us? will he not withdraw the power that guards his fancied treasure and give the angels access to it? Will he not accompany us to the haunts of wretchedness and woe, and witness there the glassy eye of some poor death-doomed mortal, gazing, as it were, on vacancy, quite unconscious of its own surroundings? Yonder, a mother importuned by her hungry children for food she has no power to give, the parched and haggard features of the whole bespeaking wants so gaunt and wretched in its aspect—thither would I take the miser, for there would he witness scenes which should stir within his frigid soul the pent-up fires of compassion to assist distress.

But ah! he looks around him to escape the horrors of the scene, in dreaded apprehension such a fate may possibly be his. He makes an effort to depart, when he reels and falls a corpse upon the floor, nor stirs a single muscle of his form. Reaction there took place. The sight he had witnessed caused a struggle—'twas Avarice and Charity—'twas fatal to the former, and leaving the untold wealth to be distributed in Charity, fit retribution of the wrong practiced and intended by this counterfeit of man.

Again we note another phase of Charity, but sparsely noticed by the many. Oft slander's tongue is busy meddling with the character of some poor, unoffending being, stealing from such a one the only thing of value he possessed, with anxious care for years and years he has watched it as a mother would her darling son; has sought to hide it from the gaze of insolent cupidity, when all at once a rumor floats upon the air conveying calumny and suspicion of a crime committed. No charge direct is made, but hints of dark suspicion gather round the victim making almost a certainty of mere surmise.

My Son, is this a case unfrequent in your midst, slandering innocence and goodness where'er its slimy tongue and fetid breath can find an aperture?

Who, we ask, at such a time stands forth a champion of the right? Who dare investigate the merits of the case and bring to light the infamy of such malignant conduct? Methinks but few, if any, except an earthly angel such as we have named, perchance, may come by accident, or by some angel led towards the spot, from very sympathy becomes a helpmeet in his time of need; vindicating a righteous cause, and thus by exercising Charity has saved the character and perhaps the life of a human being, almost a victim to the basest crime humanity can dread.

And now, my Son, 'tis better I should close this essay, perhaps too long already, and yet but half elaborated as the subject should be yet enough to prove that Charity ramifies through all space seeking advocates to dispense its blessings and make it better known as God-like in its nature. AMEN.

INSPIRATION.

MY FRIEND, the moment the above subject crossed your mind, it seemed to me you and I became immediately in rapport; therefore, did I claim a right to occupy your time with some thoughts upon it. Inspiration—a word expressing much more than the masses of mankind can comprehend; indeed to speak of it to some is but to excite their ridicule and incur the shaft of bitter sarcasm. O, how often do we witness their attempts to insult the majesty of Him who has thus provided means by which the erring condition of mankind may be improved, and his God-given intellect turned to some account, in being made the recipient of angel thoughts for impartation to humanity at large, and thus fit him for a residence in the beautiful hereafter.

Would that the tide of humanity were more willing to accept the inspiration tendered them from the angel world. O, what an improved condition would it soon assume; when all things heavenly became the subject that should give a bias to man's actions and thus a change so vitalizing would ensue, that men and women soon would show the influence surrounding them enlarging and purifying their intellectual and physical conditions.

But while the several senses are mute and unobservant, how can angel thoughts be recognized? Can the blind see, or the deaf hear? Well might it be said by the great Teacher, you have eyes, but you see not; ye have ears, but ye hear not; thus teaching, or rather attempting to, a lesson which, had they understood or accepted, would have been to the suffering generations that have passed into and out of existence since that period, an advantage to them incalculable.

But to the subject, Inspiration. To define it so as to be understood, we may find it somewhat difficult, but it is a matter of too much importance not to be attempted.

The mind of man, being somewhat complex in its character, must be well and closely studied before a spirit becomes enabled to grasp it with sufficient force to hold it under such control as to abstract its attention from all things else, and to keep it fixed within the folds of that control which gives it power over the entire organism, so that it becomes, as it were, a second part of the individual himself, subjecting its co-worker to act and speak precisely the words and ideas given through the organism of the medium controlled, who, whatever may be his or her own previously formed views upon the subject, has lost the power to devise sentiments differing widely from those with which such medium has been inspired to utter. But this is only in extreme cases, because, in selecting our mediums, we endeavor, in order to be successful, to select those whose opinions are not in direct opposition to those we deem correct and truthful. Therefore, it is but seldom much voilence is done to the feelings of speakers.

When a medium has been brought into a suitable condition to be used as a means of imparting our thoughts, there seems, as it were, an element surrounding him from which he draws a supply of that vital magnetism essential to quicken his intellectual powers and make him readily receptive of such promptings as the controlling spirit sees fit to impart, or such as the surroundings appear to need. Upon the closest spirit scrutiny in this direction, much of success or failure will depend; and here, we would observe, the greatest danger is to be apprehended; and spirits, inexperienced as they are at their advent into spirit life, oft mistake their own discriminative powers and involve the medium in a labyrinth of difficulties for which he or she becomes answerable to an earthly audience; yet among the spirits is there a chord of sympathy excited, which ultimately becomes beneficial to such mediums who, having sufficient strength of mind, placidly and courageously breast the storm of ignorant skeptics, unknowing as they are of the underlying cause or causes of such apparent failure, sneer and jeer at the sufferers in lieu of kindly sympathy; unconscious, as they seem to be, that in such a failure lies a potent proof of truthfulness. Think you, a man or woman having even a modern share of ambition would fail, where by the exercise of his or her own will power, success might be attained? We conceive no opposition can be presented to such argument, for naught but mulish obstinacy would advocate a doubt of spirit power over the minds of those who are furiously prepared to be deceptive, and being so, are what is termed as being inspired.

But, we would further observe, we do not claim that Inspiration is alone conferred to those who are known as spiritual mediums. Far be it from us to limit the comparatively few a world-wide privilege, although still unrecognized; for although the men of this and other countries claim for themselves the ability to write and speak such thoughts elaborate in subjects of the greatest interest to humanity. We are bold to say they know not how or why such thoughts are theirs.

Let them look back at by-gone times and see whether a more remote and distant generation has not uttered the same idea, and giving them the means of compiling book after book with variations and sometimes disfigurements altogether perversive and destructive, so that a principle, however clear, becomes delusive, rather than instructive. But was this the main consideration, fain would we excuse it; but, in addition to the former, we have still another reason to assign. Why are these writers inspired whose thoughts appear to rise above the mental calibre of men and women who are known to speak and act at variance with what they are inspired to write. We think a spring that sends forth pure and limpid water must be clear and pure itself; and when we see an author's name attached to works containing thoughts of high and holy character, whose acts and thoughts in all of life's career partake of lust and infamy supreme, and carried out in all their daily intercourse, whence, we would ask, come these pure and beauteous gems of thought? Certainly not from the mind of such a source as would pollute a world of beings whose souls were pure as alabaster and white as snow. No, indeed, my friend; such are not the ideas elaborated by such ephemera. They are emanations from those pure and holy beings who claim but slight affinity with such.

And yet the minds of such are thus impressed, because they have within them aspirations that may in time become imbued and made available as true and holy mediums, with powers beyond the common lot of human spirits; and whether in this world of humanity, or in the world to come, it matters little; because, being thus prepared, their work is half accomplished, and they made fit to control the mind of others in the form.

Think you, such minds will long remain inert after they have thrown off the mortal coil and ascertain the nature of the prize for which they'll then contend? Aided, as they then will be by the good and great of those who have passed away, they'll cast aside all obstacle to that ethereal improvement so essential to make them wise and pure preceptors of a mundane sphere.

My friend, I perceive a doubt assails your mind, as to the possibility of such views being placed in such position as to make them pure and holy as they should be, because you think a spirit must he *prepared* before it leaves the mundane sphere to act its part as the preceptor we have named. But it is not so; although it were better it should be. Yet an eternity of time is given to accomplish a work of vast importance to a world of humans for which assistance is most readily accorded; therefore, no one need despair, for each one has a destiny to accomplish separate and apart from every other individual. For each must act agreeably to his or her own impulses, whether right or wrong, and thus experience becomes the safest monitor to guide them whither they should steer their bark to find that haven of eternal rest the soul so yearns for.

Here, then, you see that everything in human life but tends to bring the soul into such condition that all affliction and distress to which mankind is subject, but purifies it and makes it ready to become recipient of that element we call Inspiration. AMEN.

MORALITY DEFINED.

A THEME so grand and beautiful I have much pleasure in attempting to define, it being like the commencement of a pleasant journey—the more you contemplate it, the more pleasure you receive. And who can con this theme without a glow of holy satisfaction that such a principle exists within the realms of mundane thought, whereby a state of things may be inaugurated that should thrill the human soul with gratitude unbounded, and raise it to the highest pitch of ecstacy? That man, with all his imperfections, can be brought to think aright by exercising all his faculties, guided and directed by such a standard? for without morality, life would be like the storm-tossed ocean beating on a beach their angry waves, unceasing in strife and heedless of the havoc made on all around.

Without this moral standard, earth-life would prove a punishment instead of a blessing. The passional of man would run around in horrid recklessness, destroying all of life that is valuable and useful; reaction might appreciate its untold horrors, and raise a power adequate to crush it.

Will not that power be used to break down every league that may be formed to taint that holy principle we are now discussing?

Morality, so pure and holy in thy tendencies, all hail! Thy friendly hand we'd touch and catch thy magic influence to make us what we should be. Time may test thy worth; justice may try thee in the balance, and no lack be found; man may adopt thee as his oracle, and thus become a better, holier being. With such convictions, who can doubt thy potency? The world may often claim thee as its friend and guide; but, O, how little proof it gives of friendship well defined and comprehended. A faithful friend need ne'er be doubted, being ever ready by clearest demonstration to prove that nothing short of death can break the bonds uniting them together.

How long, we ask, would such bonds remain

unsevered, was Morality excluded from your midst? Alas! how short the time would be without that moral cement, binding man to man in bonds so everlasting in their nature, that while unperverted, would remain firm as the adamantine rocks, and preserve intact a well-formed friendship.

But let us once again con o'er our subject—Morality. A furtive thought appears to suit the inquiry, Can man himself, surrounded as he is, conceive a thing while altogether ignorant of what it is like? Can the immoral man imagine what morality can be? Talk to such a man about morality, does he comprehend your meaning? We think it is doubtful; or, if he should, would he lay aside the one, and take the other? Ah, no; the idol of his soul he would cling to with unceasing grasp, till apprehension of its loss had ceased. With fond affection will he hug the accursed thing as if it were to him invaluable, and is it not? 'Tis all he knows, and therefore fears to lose it.

If such affection can be shown for that which but degrades humanity, and sinks it lower and still lower in the murky cesspool of abandoned vice, how strange an effort is not made to extirpate this evil. By such Moral teachings as, perchance, may reach the souls of men, and by contrasting Immorality with its opposite, Morality, discovers a method better suited to remove the blackened stain immoral practices have left upon the soul, making it more holy in its nature, by which a vast amount of crime will be avoided. But, till that is done, Morality and Virtue will be alone in name amongst those who form, perchance, the largest share of all communities. And is not this an awful waste of human life, which must be counted on where Immorality exists? Who would willingly expose a life 'midst pestilential swamps, where filthy miasmatic vapors rise and fill the air with poisonous influences, creating terrors which no power can check, no hand can set aside or drive away? Would such locality be chosen by a man of common sense? We cannot think it would, unless earth's cares had broken every tie which bound the human soul to earth.

Now, let the application here be made. The man who lives within the fetid influences of Immorality encounters equal risks of moral death as the other does of physical departure. But we have somewhat wandered, making of the *Immoral* more a theme than its opposite; for, by contrast, we desire to show the beauties of Morality, which being the brightest jewel we can boast of, we fain would try by contrast to enhance its value; for, as shadow is as essential to a painting as the bright and glowing hues, so is Morality with all her beauties and adornments. Standing side by side with Immorality, its dark and glowing shadows at once destroys attraction, leaving the one unnoticed, while the other stands a beauteous and attractive picture, pleasing to the senses through the avenue of sight.

But should this end our essay? Is sight the only sense attracted by Morality? We feel that every faculty of the human soul is bettered and improved by close acquaintance with Morality, giving off in all directions a sweet aroma suited to the taste of all who are advocates of purity, combined with intellectual endowments such as a soul would ask for and never meet denial, thus acting in accordance with the injunction "Ask, and ye shall receive." A pure and holy spirit cannot have misgivings, but asks with confidence, even as a child would ask a father for what he craved.

A better, holier condition must be seen by all, as consequent upon a close adherence to Morality, keeping the mind in constant exercise as to all things connected with a future state; that being the ultimate of all moral instruction, leads the soul into a state of happiness and contentment the immoral man can never know. His condition is one of constant apprehension lest detection soon may follow some atrocious act, whilst he who is moral must also be a conscientious man; therefore he has no sleepless nights, no harrowing dreams of fancied dangers, but sleeps in quietude and peace, not caring for the morrow other than to perform his duties well as father, citizen, and neighbor, to whom he is always kind and courteous, giving and receiving courtesies, but never stepping beyond the proper line of demarcation; and by such means a tranquil life is his, performing well and zealously his several duties. No misgivings here assail him, looking on his neighbor as his friend and equal, and in grateful accents asks assistance of the angel world, while with reverential mind he aspirates his needs and feels assured they will be supplied. With gratitude unbounded does he lift his face to heaven and ask for blessings needed by his ardent soul. Such is what we call a moral man. AMEN.

THE BIRTH-PLACE OF ANGELS—ARE THERE ANY FREE FROM EARTHLY ORIGIN?

STRANGE questions often arise about matters apparently of little moment to the interests of man, and yet with all the ardor of his nature are they canvassed, as if the welfare of the entire world depended on their being proved as facts of great importance, and this is one of them. First, then, let us define what we conceive to be the meaning of the word Angel. Nothing more or less than a messenger, a spirit, pure and holy in its nature; free from every taint of character; faithful as a servant, and reliable in every feature of its work, being ever ready to perform its duty as becomes a servant of the living God. Such is what we call Angels in the spirit world.

Whence came they? we are asked. To which we answer, Angels come from earth—the birthplace of the good and bad alike; a place more like to yield a larger portion of the latter than the former, being, as it were, a hot-bed of vice and iniquity, seething with sin and wickedness beyond the thought of human power to reconcile. But, ah! says one, from such a source can Angels come? Can Angels be outwrought from such pollution? To this we answer, Yes; and even worse, if search is made. Here, then, the God of mercy stands out in bold relief, as capable of bringing up from chaos all He wills, to make creation what it should be. And who can gainsay such an act? In beauteous grandeur has he made the sun, the moon and stars in such abundance, that light and heat can ne'er be wanting. Then wonder not, my son, that out of crudest matter Angels may be formed with symmetry and beauty, far transcending man's ability to conceive. And if it is, who can make assertion their origin is not of earth, but a higher, holier condition must have been the place from whence they sprang? Shall we for a moment scan this question? Shall we trace the matter far back into the past, and scrutinize most carefully the acts of God, so far as reason will assist us? and do we see a single reason why an Angel's birth-place could be chosen other than that of earth, from whence has emanated man, described as being the master-work of Deity, the crowning glory of creation? who, living here his allotted time, becomes, through sad experience, wiser, better, holier; therefore, better fitted for the condition needed to govern the passional within his own nature, and give to others such as would tend to purify itself and fit it for acceptance of the high and holy position of an Angel.

Can mortal man conceive the reason why an angel seeks a post so full of labor and perplexity that forever keeps its life a busy one? Indeed, a time of rest has oft been promised them, where all the beauties and adornments of celestial life has been tendered them; and yet they murmur not. Celestial life is not theirs at once. No Christ-like sanction will admit them; the record they have kept themselves must be their passport to the Summer Land.

But somewhat we have digressed—of Angels we were speaking. Where, we ask, is proof of Angels advent into Heaven from any other source than earth?

Is not sympathy the best and surest mode of governing? The King who rules through such a means, draws towards him, love, respect and admiration, all combined. Would such a king seek subordinates from elements antagonistic to his government? We think a better course he would pursue, where he could find the sympathetic element more rife with those whose birth-place was the same; who have together breathed the same atmosphere; whose assimilating habits drew them towards each other, in love and friendship, pure and potent. Then, on what hypothesis can a man assert the Angel world was peopled from a source beyond this planet? No proof can they present, but vague uncertain statements are they seeking to establish, illogical and altogether false; therefore, would we reject them as unsound and useless. Such sympathy existing between the governing and governed makes pleasure of the duty; preserving a degree of harmony strengthening to the law required.

To say much more is altogether needless, because, in all things, God-like adaptation will be seen, which could not be, had nature formed a class of beings, calling them Angels, claiming superiority over those of earthly origin; free from all earthly sympathy; thereby proving their utter inadaptation to conciliate the coming myriads, who, agreeably to the laws of nature, are hourly wending their way from earth-life, to that continuous life beyond the grave. And this we conceive to be an obstacle wholly ineffective, in proving the proposition that other than earthly origin is true.

Inharmony must prevail, where antagonistic feelings exist. The unholy influences engendered spread with great rapidity, and that which might have been a state of happiness, is one of untold misery.

My Son, till recognition of this error is commenced, the world will still remain the same; the purest element in nature's boundary may be sustained with sin, unless securely guarded and tainted by protecting spirits, who, having the power, must use it to protect the truthful. And now, my Son, we will close our essay, in the earnest hope that it will be read with care by many. AMEN.

MEDIUMS NEGLECTED.

How many a glorious mind has sunk in misery, lacking some sympathetic friend to take him by the hand and give encouragement to his forlorn condition. To be a good, effective Medium, sensitiveness must form a very important feature in his constitution; consequently, all the finer feelings of his nature, must be active, rendering such a being keenly alive to all opprobrium, direct or indirect, to which he may become exposed; giving a coloring to existence, dark and gloomy in appearance, so that all the aspirations of the soul are rendered useless, and in time become submerged in misery and wretchedness supreme; whereas, a word of kindly import might have raised its sinking nature, and perchance, resucitated one whose wasted genius had become lost and stultified, by the sad neglect of those whose sense of duty should have prompted holier sympathy and care of one who almost lacked power to ask for what he needed. His worldly wants were few, yet unencouraged as he was, a kind of torpor crept around him, shutting out all hope; and thus despair had driven him to seek Death's dark and gloomy curtain to hide him from the gaze of those who might have saved him, but did not.

Whence comes this sad indifference to a class of humans who should have the unqualfied support of every true and genuine Spiritualist? well knowing the outer world will give no aid, guided and governed as they are by blind and wretched bigotry; all who differ from their own religion are viewed and treated as outcasts from society, and deemed unworthy of their sympathy or assistance.

Is it not, then, the more needful, Spiritualists

themselves, should be more heedful of those through whose organisms angels give their utterances of such glorious truths, by which a world of humans may be saved from sin and degradation and thus made cognizant of a better, holier condition, which may be reached by close attention to their teachings, brought down from spheres celestial by the angel messengers continually surrounding them? My Brother, was your world more attentive to those angel teachings, what a change you soon would see. Vice and all its base associates would be rendered harmless, and Virtue being resucitated, would be resplendent in all her loveliness, drawing to her the former votaries of vice; myriads of souls would join her standard, around which humanity would rally and raise a shout of triumph so overwhelming that sin and iniquity could not show themselves; but in some dark corner, hidden, would waste away and be forgotten.

O, glorious epoch, that, when men and women both shall feel within them the honest glow of gratitude unlimited, by which they would soon become alive to everything which shows the untiring care God and His angels take of those who seek assurance so much needed.

God and nature both give ample proof another life exists, containing more of happiness; and, therefore, should be sought as something worth attaining. By close attention to all the laws which govern such a place, when summoned hence, no stranger you will find yourself; for those, who have in earth-life visited you, will crowd around you in numbers far beyond your expectations, and angel hands will lift the veil which hitherto has shut from you scenes of immortal grandeur, dearer to you than all the tinsel trash of earth—the one being transient, the other for eternity, must be to you of greater value. But while you thus are elevated beyond your expectations, think not ye have no duties to perform. Exertion will be there demanded of you. No idle life will then be yours—all nature works and sets a bright example to humanity; by copying her you may make a happy and contented home, and thus enjoy a life supernal: for, here the secret lies; industry and idleness are such opposites but little contact have they; their interests differ; no clashing have they, which so oft occurs where kindred interests interfere and mars all happinesss till better views are taken and harmony again prevails, and whilst this harmony exists we will close our essay, knowing, as we do, some good may emanate from this feeble, but sincere attempt, to give instruction where it is needed. AMEN.

AN ABSTRACT OF A LONG ESSAY.

GIVEN THROUGH MY ORGANISM, BY FRANCIS, DAUPHIN OF FRANCE, CONSORT OF MARY, QUEEN OF SCOTS.

THUS, my Son, you have, perhaps, the longest essay ever given you by spirit promptings, trying your patience, yet giving you a history of things pertaining to the past of time; yet teeming with the events of later years, deducing from them precepts and examples which cannot harm or injure a single human being, but rather would, I hope, prove a useful adjunct to the investigator in his search for living truths.

For this purpose have I left my beauteous spirit-home; in every sense it is such to me—a home I would not barter for a world's renown, or riches great as those of Crœsus.

And now, my Son, and those who perhaps may read this essay, remember a time is coming when this, a seeming fiction, at the present, will assume the form of truth in all its purity. Look back upon the history of the past, some half century since. What then was mystery is now a truth; practically grand in all its bearings; before unknown, and therefore doubted by the savans of the time, is now accepted, after strict analysis, till comprehended by the merest school-boy. Such has been the march of progress in the last half century. Who, then, will dare to set a limit to the power of God, or say to man: "Thus far shalt thou go, and no farther?"

My Son, that day is past. The glorious majesty of God, in all its brilliancy, is seen. The sun, the moon and stars, have limits to their movements, which they tread from age to age, in course undeviating from the right, and thus a round of duty is performed under direction of the Infinite. Then, with all these glories demonstrated, let the outgushing pæns of a Universe sing loud their hallelujahs to their God for evermore. AMEN.

LAW--WHAT IS IT?

THERE are few subjects you could present, affording so wide a field for consideration, as the above. But few there are on earth who can realize its comprehensiveness, not confined to one particular branch of science, but embracing all of the entire universe of action, reaching down into the very depths of creation, and then again to its very highest altitude, soaring far beyond man's utmost stretch of imagination, and losing itself in broadest space. Law, what is it? Let us pause a moment while we endeavor so to concentrate our thoughts as to enable us to define somewhat understandingly the proposition in its broadest and most comprehensive sense. It is a something intended by Almighty Wisdom to preserve that beautiful equilibrium pervading the entire universe, preserving the various planets in their several orbits, controlling matter in its various forms, placing prescribed limits to all in motion, and giving to each element in nature its destined action, thus preserving that beautiful order and regularity pervading all of Nature's works, wherein is shown infinite wisdom so incomprehensible to the finite mind. Few there are who ever direct their attention to the study of Nature's works, which have been, and still are, amenable to Law, governed and directed by it. The tiny blade of grass which springs from earth, patiently awaits the Law of season; thus receiving its growth agreeable to the Law of vegetation. Each flower that buds and blossoms acts in accordance with the law of progress, observing regularity in its advent, only governed by the Law of circumstances.

The Law of vegetation is perhaps more beautiful than aught else in nature; first, the germ being quickened into life, then the blade seen peering into light and sunshine, receiving strength therefrom, and again the leaf so beautifully enfolded, protected from all harm; a cherished thing of God's own care, and worthy of protection such as angels give it, fostering its budding beauties, and perfecting a form so lovely as to create an angel's admiration.

Thus its blossom seeks maturity so complete, that all around it seems to catch the magic influence, engendering gratitude sublime to Him who thus creates and perfects all His works. We could dwell incessantly upon a subject so sublime and beautiful, but Law as seen in other forms, must be our subject.

Is it not surprising that man with all the intelligence given him by his God, pays so little heed to the Law of his own being ?

There is no subject within our ken of such importance, reaching, as it does, through every avenue of man's existence. O, was it more studied and better understood, the world of humanity would not be as it is, almost entirely bereft of honesty of purpose in the various transactions between man and man ; for then each act would be governed by the Law of strict integrity, preserving man from the spoilation of his neighbor, and bringing them into the close embrace of brotherly love.

Here, then, is seen a Law so potent in its character, so world-wide in its value, that when rightly understood and practiced, binds society together with bonds imperishable ; being the work of Law inmutable in its character, and when prized as it should be, becomes indissoluble, giving light and vigor to the possesser, stimulating him to acts of love and kindness, totally unknown to those who posess it not.

The Law of Charity is shown to be most beautiful and divine in its effects upon society. Its deeds oft shine resplendently when properly administered, yet few seem to who comprehend this Law ; some conceive the mere alms-giving makes up a life of charity. O, poor mistaken souls ; thus blinded canst thou comprehend the solace of a word expressing kindly pathos, the utterance of which has cost thee nothing ? yet upon that desponding soul whose lacerated state required a loving word to raise its drooping nature, can you not realize the joyous feeling respondent to thine own from that poor, yet enlivened soul, engendered by thy kindly speech ?

Here, then, is a feature in that Law which should be known to all creation ; for often has one kind word from smiling lips done more to elevate the soul than aught of riches unkindly tendered Much might be said on this interesting Law, which embraces love, kindness, justice, mercy, etc.; indeed, its ramifications are equal to the demands of all. The Law of Justice seems to call for some remarks, being perhaps, as little studied as aught else.

Justice, O, word of majestic import how shall we describe ye ? Finite words are quite inadequate to define thy value, for being infinite, how can we present our thoughts ? Yet something must and should be said. Thou should'st, if properly administered, be the stronghold of the poor, who, when frequently as they are, oppressed by those of wealth, essay to seek thine aid. Alas! how sparingly thou art administered! But let the rich and pampered man of wealth become a votary at thy shrine, thou wert made to bend in deep humility to the fee presented. Then, where is justice? We say, environed by vice; it cannot act with honest freedom; hence, is human justice *nil*. Not so with the infinite justice of our God, who, in all things earthly metes out justice quite impartially, although perfidious mortals strive to thwart its even-handed measure.

What more shall we say of Law? Where can we find a stopping place, while at every step fresh thoughts come crowding in upon us, showing Law to be the grandest institute throughout all nature; which having but briefly touched upon, we may be permitted to say a few words connected with, or applicable to man's or human Law every portion of which should have for its base the higher Law, God's or Nature's Law, each Law being suited to the peculiar condition of man; and those Laws not the concoction of one man, but the entire nation through its delegates should enact them, thereby rendering it impossible for any one becoming the victim of that Law to pronounce it unjust. If such Law, by experiment, becomes obnoxious, let it be repealed by the same power that created it; but so long as unrepealed, let it be enforced, and no one murmer. AMEN.

REGENERATION.

PEOPLE who aspire to much of worldly piety, frequently talk of Regeneration, about which they, perhaps, know as little as the infant, who has never recognized a letter in the alphabet; therefore, are quite inadequate to form a judgment, much less to express an opinion of it.

This, to us, seems somewhat strange when you look abroad upon the wide extended field of humanity and see therein the great necessity of change, for here again is another link in the grand chain of circumstances connected with that most important Law. Man often speaks of Regeneration as a something which can be acquired by purchase or request, at any, or such periods as may seem necessary or conveinent to himself, or a thing which can be picked up, and again laid down at pleasure, available at all times he considers suitable. O, miserable, deluded souls; are ye so obtuse to common sense as to imagine ye can so act and be free from the imputation of neglect? for surely a time must come when all things earthly will appear to you valueless; when the mind becomes convinced there is little of earth's currency (so to speak) that will be successfully circulated in the upper sphere; when the crude notions and sentiments of earth will be found inconsitent and unrecognized in the realms of ether; when the passional proclivities which have been cherished in earth-life will be found altogether useless, and all that has transpired here on earth will be viewed as unhallowed and of no effect in substantiating a claim to happiness in the Summer Land. When all this becomes truly and forcibly impressed upon your finite mind, you will, perhaps, be induced to ask as did the Publican of old, "Lord, what shall I do to be saved?"

Perhaps to this question some agent invisible to you may whisper "Seek the Regeneration of your own soul," a term you are not familiar with, and not comprehending it, ye cannot ask it. What, we would ask, must be the condition of a soul needing it, but not knowing what to ask for; Such is the condition of thousands who outwardly present the appearance of independence, but without them are they deluged with doubts and fear as to a future state. We ask, would not such Regeneration, or change, be a boon to them?

Perhaps we may be asked, What is meant by Regeneration? We would say to such, having by your surroundings been induced to step aside from the path of virtue and holiness, and thus becomes abrogators of God's holy laws, making you amenable to the penalty attached thereto, which penalty having been paid in the several ways designed by Providence, the soul becomes awakened with the sinfulness of disobedience, and thus repentance ensues, accompanied with a determination to reform, and to relinquish these proclivities which have led to a violation of a divine law. It is the departure from, and entire renunciation of all unholy desires of which constitutes a mortal's claim to Regeneration, and until man becomes convinced of its necessity, he cannot possibly partake of its benefits, which are of incalculable value to humanity; yet apparently so little prized and so palpably neglected, that it would seem, as it were, impossible man could comprehend its benefit, and easily and readily grasp the proffered boon. Yet there are thousands and thousands who pass the river of Death and make their advent on the eternal shores who never entertained a thought of its importance, until too late; entering upon the untried future, conscious of their lack of previous foresight, which would have spared them regrets they then must realize. We must say to those who have yet time on earth they can appropriate, let them at once seek this regenerating influence which shall smooth their progress towards the regions of eternal bliss. AMEN.

MAN A MYSTERY.

HEAVEN and earth are full of mysteries, but none so great as man himself, made up of all that constitutes the Universe, or goes to form the smallest insect in existence.

How then can man assume the right to ask his fellow-man to be his slave, and cringe before him as if he held the power of life and death within himself?

Will God, the Omniscient Father of all and every existent creature, tolerate such desire and not control it by some angel interference demanding whence he derived such power to act the tyrant, and disgrace himself?—for such must be the issue. The soul of every living being should be free, and is it not? The body may be imprisoned, each limb and arm enchained and fettered, but the soul is far beyond the reach of cruel man. Yes, it may bid defiance to tyranny in all its horrid forms, the oppressor it may scorn, for being Divine, no earthly power can reach or harm it, but through the intellect; while connected with the earthly form, by sympathy it suffers; but, when enfranchised from the body, all pain and suffering cease, and to the regions of ethereal bliss the immortal portion of the man has soared, seeking, as it should, continuous life, long promised it. No iron heel of tyrant can now tread it under foot; protected as it is by hosts of spirits, no terror need it feel; for, fed and nourished by angel hands, its growth will far exceed its expectations, and heaven become its resting place.

Is not this encourgement to look beyond what earth can give, to cast aside all earthly pomp, and, accepting what your angel friends present you, praise the God directing them? AMEN.

CELIBACY.

IS IT IN CONFORMITY WITH NATURE'S LAWS THAT MAN AND WOMAN SHOULD PRACTICE IT?

PERHAPS there are few questions of greater importance to humanity than the one above propounded, involving as it does so much of individual and collective interest that it should not, and, indeed, cannot, be hastily treated.

Wide as the universe of God, no man can grasp it and give back a satisfactory response to all who feel an interest in the subject. Therefore, in attempting its solution, we feel there are continuous and wondrous changes amongst this world of humans, which seems, as it were, destructive of their recognition; bringing in their train difficulties almost insurmountable, and giving to those who ask for light, but a feeble ray, a mere glimmer, almost tantalizing, and quite unfitted for the darkened vision of the multitude.

But to our subject—Celibacy; a condition seemingly at war with Nature's inculcations; a state discordant with her Laws; which, when practiced, seems to dampen soul fires and dry up the elements of love implanted there for a wise and holy purpose. A soul without this element seems to have lost the brighter side of life, bartering joy for sorrow, companionship for solitude, and existence, even, at an earlier period than Nature meant you should. And if this is so, there must be a reason why such a practice should be adopted. We, ourself, could never deem the purpose a wise one. A love that is never gratified must soon lose its strength, a cold and frigid nature must ensue. The warm endearments of a loving nature must shrink appalled at such a cruel void presented, and ever and anon the blighted hopes of early life would rise in judgment on the ascetic being who would wander thorough the paths of solitude and gloom in preference to the holy, joyous path of wedded life; blessed with a genial partner who would share his joys or soothe the sorrows of a checkered life, ofttimes so fatal to the aspirant for fame or fortune.

Can the miserable advocate of Celibacy, or rather would we say its victim, imagine what he loses?

The mere passional intercourse is but a secondary consideration with those whose souls are pure. The holy element of unpolluted love is broad, expansive in its nature, and ramifies throughout the entire system, invoking all of Nature's admiration, lifting the soul above all sensuality, and seeking higher and holier issues than man's perverted nature can appreciate.

But 'tis not here alone its beauties are evolved; love and purity combined, produce results more grand and beautiful than heated passion can evolve.

Just in proportion as the soul is pure, so will all nature give response to those of mortal birth; yielding to them more pure and holy sympathies than rank or fortune can impart.

Here, then, we pause to think what possible excuse can man and woman make for leading lives of Celibacy, cut off and ostracised from all the social comforts well enjoyed by others? A strange fanaticism morbid as it is, view it from every standpoint you can recognize, transgressing the Law of Procreation, subversive as it is of all that is destined to improve humanity, and trampling down a decree essential to the Law of Reproduction in its equal and God-given form. Who, then, would advocate a system so void of all that reason and common sense would hesitate to recommend as being best adapted to carry out the purpose of a righteous God, in giving to all humanity a means by which no dearth of population need occur, if properly applied? And with all the privileges recorded, need man practice that which is in opposition to God's will? abrogating a law of such importance to humanity on which successors to himself depends? We are not willing to coerce mankind into any measure if their reason dictates other course of action; but upon principle, we protest against the practice. Individuals may act their pleasure, whilst the masses must, and will obey, a law so needed.

And here we drop the subject, knowing that he who enacts the law can compel obedience to it. AMEN.

DEPARTURE OF THE SPIRIT AS SEEN CLAIRVOYANTLY.

CAN you describe the exit of the spirit from the human form at death, as it is so-called? The spirit is altogether invisible to the finite sight, but to the ethereal, is just as manifest as is the natural form to the finite sight. At its departure from the body it may be seen gradually rising by slow and majestic motion from the apex of the brain, partly enveloped in a kind of vapory mist, until the entire figure is seen hovering over its late companion; senseless as it is, yet still attractive to the hovering spirit, looking benignly down upon the clay-cold form, when suddenly the cord of life is broken, and the ethereal portion of that man or woman rises above and beyond the scenes of earth-life, aided in its ascent by its spirit friends. AMEN.

FORMATION OF EVE.

MY HUSBAND, the symbol, I promised you, I am now ready to impart, hoping I shall be able to give you some thoughts, useful to yourself, and to those who may, in coming time peruse this book of record, which is intended to benefit humanity at large; for, when the human mind has become somewhat more enlightened upon the subject of their immortal interest, these essays will be sought after as corroboratives of their own improved conceptions, which at present are too obscure to comprehend what is their future and eternal benefit. The symbol I propose giving you is based upon a circumstance of by-gone occurrence, when man seemed, as it were, but first emerging from his earliest and most crude condition suited to his then surroundings. Indeed, all nature seemed to partake of the same rude elements; hence, it was not strange that man, himself, rude and untutored as he must have been, should partake of the same character, which was altogether in keeping with infinite wisdom — such should be his then condition, in order to preserve that harmony upon which his happiness depended.

Hence, were all things at that period in a state and condition where each and everything had its peculiar and wise adaptation. We might easily enlarge upon these prefatory remarks, but time demands a nearer approach to the purpose we have in view, that of presenting to you a singular and wonderful detail of circumstances connected with the progress of man from that crude period up to the present era of wonderful progress. Man, at the time we commence, could have had but little conception of a hereafter, because his mental development had but just commenced — having been subject to delay whilst the physical was opening and expanding to those proportions of size and beauty designed by his Creator.

In all of Nature's operations, slow as they appear, yet there is displayed a oneness of purpose to complete that which it has commenced; hence, in the construction of the human body, with all its beauty of proportions, its labyrinthal intricacies and beauteous symmetry may be seen the wonderful working power of Almighty God. Who can trace the intricate windings of thought, elaborating man's mortal structure in all its peculiarities, suited to the purpose of its Creator? And if the combination employed in forming the mere house or tabernacle as a mere temporary habitation for the soul and spirit, we would ask can the finite mind come to aught other conclusion than that the ways of his Creator are, indeed, past finding out? Would we could well define to your mind the nature of soul and spirit; but that must remain a sealed mystery until you have become sufficiently etherealized, and then the truth will burst upon your etherealized senses like a mighty avalanche of thought, but for which you will then be fully prepared.

But, my Husband, I have been carried from the subject of my symbol. I was speaking of man's progress mentally and physically. Few, very few persons, can grasp this thought, that man in all conditions of earth-life, has the slightest conception of the untiring care by which he is watched and tutored by those angel teachers constantly surrounding him, waiting to unfold ideas suggested to him, at times best suited to his receptive powers, evolving thoughts elaborative of ideas and principles so profound in their character and meaning, that withont angel help, would prove to him a myth on every hand. Thus from one stage of development to another, is he enabled to pluck from that eternal fount of wisdom to which the spirits have access. Is it possible, I would ask, for man to devise the cause of all this Angel sympathy? Is it because he, himself, has sought it? Oh, no; but that God, who in his infinite wisdom, has created all things, saw through Time's extended vista how much assistance would man require to carry him through the rudimental, or earth existence; beset, as he then would be by passion's lawless efforts to gain the ascendant in his human nature. Therefore, has he been surrounded by these guardian spirits who have sought by every means to assuage the evils arising from man's disobedience of God's holy laws, and thus have measurably saved him from the devastating influences of unbridled passion.

But, my Husband, I percieve a question rising in your mind: why was man gifted with those passions without the ability of controlling them? To this I would answer, that Almighty God gave them in order that man should be endowed with all necessary vigor to carry out the mighty purposes of his creation, but the perversion of their uses has often stultified their results by turning into unintended channels that God-given energy so necessary in all the important ends of earth-life. With this view of the matter, we cannot see that any blame can possibly attach to the Creator, whose intentions, although partially contravened, must, and will be carried out to the letter; for it has been decreed that all, however sinful and degenerate they have been and are, shall all be brought into one common fold of righteousness.

My Husband, could you gain a glimpse of the busy scene of preparation in this world of ether, for the emancipation and improvement of mankind, how readily would you concede the point that the happiness of the human race will be the ultimate of angel efforts acting as the agents of Him who doeth all things well.

This subject offers so wide a field for thought, that I am constantly digressing, leading you as I clairvoyantly perceive, to doubt my intention of giving you the symbol.

As we before said, the time from whence we date was one of peculiar character; rough and unhewn as all of nature seemed to be, but little could be seen that would call forth that refinement, which, at the present period, seems to form the gist of life; yet even in that period of uncouth time love was not unknown, for, man being a faint emblem or representative of Deity, and it being His grandest attribute, in mercy had received a portion of the same, and although so infinitesimal as scarcely to be recognized; yet, being divine in its nature is capable of such expansion and attraction, that even the smallest spark of the divine fire may at once enkindle it, until its blaze lights up the entire system; and thus the human form divine, being heated by its holy fires, seeks to affinitize with some co-existant beings receptive of its holy influences.

Thus it was with man in the earliest stages of earthly existence. The rugged form of nature then surrounding him, seemed little suited to his finer nature; hence, solitude no longer seemed to please his taste, which daily undergoing the refinement consequent upon the workings of divine and holy element of love, created within his soul uneasiness and discontent—the sure result of an unsatisfied craving, for that the soul of man desires.

Thus it was with the being described in the outset of our symbol. A wretched, desolate state of being; discontented and alone, what improvement could possibly be expected under such untoward condition? Complaint he fain would make to some one; but no companion had he there. True, he might moan and groan his miseries to the sterile rocks and deepest glens, from whence an echo might be heard, an apparent mockery of his woes, but no solace could he gain; and still he sighed, and groaned, and wondered whence had come the thought that he alone was there, with no competitor to thwart his sovereign will, or mar a purpose of his soul. Oh, no;

and yet he seemed to feel a need of that companionship he knew not of, yet something whispered he might have. Whence came that whisper, think you? 'Twas not the rocks, or glens, or trees, or flowers, but something not yet tangible to him, and yet, it seemed to comprehend the desires of his needy nature.

Was this a situation to be borne without complaining? Oh, no; poor human nature forgets not to complain, let its fate be what it will. And so it was with him to whom we have referred; e'en unconscious what his want, would he murmur that he had it not.

My Husband, I would stop to ask you, Is not this, your world, made up of such? Is not the human mind continually outstretched in search of something craved by sordid nature, all unsated as they are, forgetting, in their constant search for more, how good and bountiful their God has been to them?

Here, fain would I stop, and leave poor human nature to chew the bitter cud of remorse for such ingratitude, but I find I cannot in common fairness leave my hero of the forest dense and gloomy dale, alone, and sorrowing o'er his griefs. Oh, no; Philanthrophy and common justice cries out, no; therefore, will I return and join him in that wilderness and, perchance, gain some further insight of his progress. His want he has expressed in general terms which seems not understood because it is not complied with.

What, then, shall be his movement? He knows not whom to ask, therefore, bewildered as he is, in agony and total destitution he casts himself upon the earth, and seeks, in sleep, oblivion of his woes. Poor, fallen, abject creature, there he lays apparently of life bereft., so deep his slumber, when, lo!' a form appears; a human, like himself, with knife in hand and expert movement. From the side of that prostrate form a rib he takes, and, forthwith, by some mysterious process, a woman, beautiful in countenance and exquisite in proportion, soon is seen standing in all her loveliness, seemingly expectant. With such attraction near him, could it be expected the longing, wishful being, lying there before such powerful attractions should long remain in lethargy supreme? Oh, no; for soon with head uplifted from the ground, with dim observance did he see a form so potent in her loveliness, that Nature's promptings bade him rise and cautiously approach that long desired being, who responded by a mutual recognition; and here we leave them to solve the mystery which life presented to them.

Now, my Husband, how does this statement read? Are you satisfied there's aught that can meet the views of one who permits Reason her full sway in all the essential points of human existence? And yet this is a version of a transaction upon which has turned the final condition of the human race, showing that the absurd and fabulous creation of woman has brought a curse upon humanity, made God a tyrant, man a fool, and woman a slave!

What shall I say of those who pretend to know the character of their God, and yet profane His holy name with such untruths, on which they have founded an erroneous doctrine, and by which myriads of earth's children are transferred from earth-life to a condition in the spheres worse than the most abject slavery presents. O, infamy unparalleled, that education should be so prostituted, giving authority to baseness to do its cruel unnatural work of poisoning the minds of men and women of this nineteenth century, by teachings which blast the hopes of expectant children of earth, and attempt to defame the character of a good and gracious God. AMEN.

THOUGHTS ON IMMORTALITY.

OUR BROTHER AND MEDIUM: Coming, as we have, with an intention of strengthening your power to respond, under spirit influence, to such questions as your investigator might wish to put, we desire to give some proofs that the doctrine of Immortality is true in all its several bearings; that each man and woman in existence, however skeptical they may now appear, must ultimately yield obedience to that law of intuition by which things although unseen become as lucid to the mortal vision as those which are recognized by mortal sight. With this conviction, how can ignorance and superstition hover round your hearths, imbuing the human soul with doubts of all ethereal things presented in such wise as Nature shows cannot be wrong? Who, we ask, in all creation, doubts the existence of a God? and if he does, can he find a substitute to fill the place of such a being? We answer, no. With all the sapience man can boast of, and all the power accumulated through ages past and gone, no other has been found adequate to rule and govern this vast universe, varied as it is. The grand and mighty power which governs and controls the various atoms forming one integral whole. To Him should every voice proclaim honor and glory for evermore. And now, my Brother, perceiving thy mind is wandering somewhat from the subject, we will close this brief essay, asking thee to be in readiness for our assistance at some not distant day, for we are ready to attach ourselves to thee as aid on such occasions when needed by you, and thus a pure and holy doctrine may be scattered where 'tis needed. AMEN.

ADAM IN RESPONSE TO MY CALL.

AM I in my senses, well and properly prepared to search the records of all time, and with eager scrutiny peer through the ages of the past, and trace back the centuries that have rolled their course, yielding knowledge in such measure as the mind of man becomes developed? thus aiding him in searching for that wisdom more deeply inbedded in his nature than he conceives. You, through impressions given you, are able to transcribe and give them forth to others as truths, not originating in your own brain, but through a means of God's appointment, can transcribe with accuracy the thoughts of angels, bright and glorious, in their acts portraying wonders far transcending all that earth presents, with all its gorgeous decorations of its churches. The like I have never witnessed.

Understanding nothing of this lower world, with all its grand improvements, the aggregation of so many ages, are puzzling to a mind unused to such; therefore, I must pause a while to contemplate them, and ascertain their uses.

And while I am doing so, I pray you laugh not at my seeming ignorance of things pertaining to a world so changed I scarce can recognize it as the same I once was monarch of by the sanction of my God, as says tradition, they call sacred.

And is it not? perchance you will ask; to which I frankly answer No.

A record credited to Moses, so far removed from truth, it seems to make the whole a falsehood, void of truth and open to rejection by the wise and good of earth.

Here, then, we have fairly launched our bark upon the sea of strife and controversy, where shoals and quicksands may be found in all directions; and who can shun them without a chart to guide him through the mazy darkness there exhibited?

But now a light appears; a star of brightest magnitude is seen to sparkle where no light was seen before. In bright effulgence it is seen shedding its lurid blaze on all surroundings, being to your world of darkness, by comparison, wonderful and glorious, universal in its character and grand in all its projection; nothing more or less than light itself, a blessing all should estimate. The veriest worm that crawls from out its dreary cell peers up to see the coming glory and partake the benefit thereof. With such divine impressions given him, can man be ignorant of what his duty is? For Reason, backed by common sense, denounces him as lacking both, and thus, in sad perverted state, forgets his God and leaves undone the many duties due to Him in whom he lives and has his being.

But is this the object of my coming here? In response to thy kindly call, I came, and now would ask the motive of that summons.

To prove the fact that spirits long departed into spirit-life can be induced to leave their spirit-homes to seek communion with embodied spirits here on earth.

My Brother, such a motive is worthy of our best approval; first, because such a call awakens in the enfranchised soul an ambition to retrace its steps; to see the march of progress in the intervening years of deparure and return; giving an impetus to research for those important changes brought about by the united effort of angels, high in Heaven, aided by those you have on earth, for, such you have amongst you, known only by their acts; no trumpet sounds announce them, and, if not recognized on earth, in Heaven they'll be deemed excelsior.

And now, my Brother, we are ready to make known, as best we can, the name we bore, 'till death removed us to a place where names are little known or needed; a place that's free from all that's mystic in its character; where everyone is known for what he is, and not for what he might be; for in that we see uncertainty, a thing unknown in Heaven. Reality, based on truth, is all the current coin that passes there. No counterfeit can pass as genuine; a scrutiny it undergoes by argus eyes no power can contravene.

But to my name, good friends; are you anxious to obtain it? If so, search the first chapter of Genesis; there you will find it, surrounded with a detail such as some clever school-boy might blush to own as his concoction. And yet, a God of wisdom Infinite, is made to talk in manner better suited to an almost idiot child of tender years. We trust no more will such a volume be the Text Book for as many millions of the future as the gloomy past has had experience of.

We think, whatever good it may have done, like all things well intended, calls loudly for our gratitude as good and honest people to avow it, yet would strive to seek some more efficient guide to Heaven.

That Bible, erratic as it is, worn out with age, and power abridged, we fain would let it rest through all the ages yet to come, being well convinced its almost dead remains will never be disturbed by Vandal hands, but in peace remain revered for all the good it may have done.

If so-called Christians murmur at such disposal of it, let them substitute a better! AMEN.

ADDRESS FROM MY DAUGHTER.

WITH joyous tidings I am here, my beloved father, to impart to you some thoughts I wish to ventilate; not of a scientific character, but to tranquilise your mind, by showing you how good your God has been to you, by giving you reasoning powers intact at so advanced an age as yours—a period few men reach, and many who do attain it are but imbeciles, unfit for life on earth, and, *if unchanged*, almost unfit for heaven.

My Father, I say not this to flatter, as if it was a matter you have the power to control, but to encourage you in every effort you may make, to bear with patient fortitude the seeming ills of life on earth you may encounter as you advance towards its terminus, for great will be your reward in heaven. The by-gone acts of former years may be presented to your failing earthly sight, but soon a brighter gleam of light will flit across your almost sightless orbs, a far more glorious, brilliant light, ethereal in its character, giving to you glimpses of that ethereal world whither your steps are tending.

If earthly sight is lost to you, a compensation there awaits you, grand and glorious in its character. No dimness, such as oft on earth you now experience, but a soft and genial light, well suited to your then condition.

With such a light to guide you, need your steps e'er falter? Angels will be there to aid thee; angel eyes will watch around thee; angel tongues will there instruct thee, and angel love will there encompass thee.

Need, then, departure from mundane to ethereal life be dreaded by thee? We think it should not, for in that moment we may call you home. Those angel friends, who have borne thee on to a good old age will assemble round thy bed, and give thee strength equal to thy need to prove the undying interest thou hast felt in Spiritualism. AMEN.

MOSES.

A STRANGE sensation now is spreading o'er me; the light of heaven seems dim to me; strange figures flit across my brain; all things surrounding me seem changed; reversed are all things; the thing of yesterday no longer seems what it was. A truly wondrous change effected by a power beyond my comprehension—a power no one can contravene; transcendant in its force and grandeur being the *ne plus ultra* and climax of all existent things and principles, absorbing all things and directing all things so conglomerate in their nature, as to render all other forces as nothing when compared to it.

My Friend, forgive me if I trespass on your time a little while to contemplate this state of things, and then compare them with the by-gones of the past. And yet comparison becomes impossible; the strides of science and philosophy completely baffle all research, and nothing can I find which bears resemblance to the past. Even man, the crowning effort of his Father, God, as sometimes so expressed, seems changed, but whether improved or not, seems doubtful. Temptations appear abundant, and by him seem readily accepted. No distaste can I perceive, for vice and immorality are seen in all their several phases. The greater sin, the greater credit thrown around the perpetrator. In fact, it seem to me that Virtue and Vice are greater strangers than they ever were—the one a savior, the other a destroyer.

My Brother, does it not seem strange to you, the latter's popularity increases every moment, while Virtue seeks retirement from your crowded streets and sheds tears of sorrow and regret that she had so little influence among the masses? Every time she comes she meets rebuff, although kind and generous in her treatment of them—deserving their love and gratitude. From almost every soul she meets but contumely and abuse, backed by malignity of purpose, based on all the vilest passions man is heir to.

Think you such conduct can continue? Can Justice sleep the sleep of sweet contentment while Injustice stalks through every avenue, obstructing her in every effort to fulfill her several duties? She must be blind to stamp her as impartial. Need man abuse that blindness by taking undue advantage of it, acting in contravention of laws enacted for his safety, bringing down upon himself a retribution often doubted, but sure to come when least expected? Thus are the acts of Deity but little comprehended, unless aided by angelic intuitions; for that purpose do they hover round your earthly dwellings, imparting and receiving knowledge agreeable to the Law of Reciprocity—a law which seems an equipoise needed by all humanity, being almost a speciality, connected with the changes working in your midst; changes that seem as all-essential to man's wellfare here and in the grand hereafter, —not merely transient, but continuous through all the cycles of eternity. Supposing man was left alone without these angel guides, you, and others, are familiar with, could harmony and peace exist untroubled as it used to be? We think it could not. The love of power has grown to such extent that men, adjudged by merit only, would be found so sparse that tyranny and misrule would soon produce the element of discontent, and all the baser passions of the human soul be stirred to action; and war, that cruel scourge of all humanity, be rife, making demons of the men whom God created to be blessings instead of curses to this beauteous land you occupy under sufferance of your God.

My Brother, are not such convictions almost paralyzing in effect upon the being who can realize the goodness and forbearance of his God? But here we will stop, and tender you the opportunity desired to ask such questions of the past as I am able to respond to.

QUESTION. Your name, for centuries past, has stood conspicuous in the Bible, as being high in favor with the Jewish God, hence you were permitted interviews none other had. Is that an actual fact, without embellishment?

ANSWER. My Brother, nothing but exuberant zeal could make you hazard such inquiry as scarce another would risk the asking; as it were, throwing down the gauntlet to a world of bigots whose narrowed souls would search no further than that Book to find the truth they need—that truth which cannot be disputed with success.

Q. To ask a priest are Bible statements true, think you he would answer no—an assimilating influence would give its answer yes?

A. If of me you ask the question, I can readily

respond in the negative, and have no hesitation in so doing.

Q. Is the statement of your receiving the two tables of stone on Mt. Sinai true?

A. Are you prepared to transcribe the thoughts I purpose giving you, free from prejudice? because what I shall give you is not merely hearsay, but facts beyond denial by the good and faithful of this world. It would be unseemly for myself to deviate one iota from the truth in the detail I shall give you. From all that I can feel, you are reliable, and faithful in discharging your various duties as a transcribing medium, governed and directed as you are by angelic beings whose natures can assimilate with you, and run no risk of finding myself deceived. I shall unhesitatingly give you a detail, such as may be viewed as statements totally devoid of truth, having no foundation but in the heated brain of some fanatic priest, more fraught with an imaginary power than common sense or reason would admit. A fact like that described as being performed by me, is but a fable, written to give importance to my character as a ruler over a nation difficult to govern. Gifted as I was with fair abilities for private life, but as governor lacking an element essential to the power of governing; and, being of sickly constitution, but firm in intellect, fired with ambition to carry out the glorious plan conceived, at once I put in practice a plan of deep deception, having no partner in my secret to share with me success, or, if a failure, I should bear the blame.

Going straightway to Sinai's summit I sat me down in solitude to form my plan of action. A sinful act I felt it was, but expediency was the law which governed and directed me. In former times I had acquired the art of lettering on stone, and thus became the engraver of some precepts I had learned as given by sages of the times in which they lived, long antecedent to the time of which I speak. Fearing to descend abruply, I rested a while, and going to the highest peak I saw the outstretched Israelitish camp in much confusion, as I thought. With hasty strides I made my way towards it. Feeling much amazed, I sought to be informed as to what had caused this seeming tumult, when lo! a golden calf attracted my attention, uplifted high, lest, peradventure, the multitude might not discern it. At first I felt some apprehension a revolt had broken out; but, as I conned the matter o'er, my anxious fears subsided, for, during my lengthened absence *ennui* had seized upon the masses — a sure result where idleness existed — hence they resorted to this mode of filling up their time. What might have been the result had I longer tarried, it was hard to tell, neither did I desire experience of it. Suffice it, then, to say, having again resumed authority, I speedily presented the fruits of my indomitable perseverance, telling the ingenious tale I had prepared. If false, who was there to give denial to its truthfulness? My scheme succeeded; my authority was more than trebled; almost God-like were the honors paid me, for, with credit much improved, who dare question a power they could not contravene, but yet were willing to obey implicitly?

You asked for brevity. Such, my Brother, is not to be. A question has been mooted, and, in ungarbled manner I have told my story; whether believed or not it little matters. Deception seems so natural here on earth, and oft preferred to truth, let those who give such preference have it to their heart's content.

Q. Is the passage of the Israelites over the River Jordan a truthful statement?

A. My Brother, are Nature's laws suspended to gratify humanity? And further, would such a privilege have been then accorded to a people acting dishonestly towards their Egyptian neighbors? Would a just and righteous God have sanctioned such an act as the Israelites were then performing?

Q. Have you any idea to whom the world is indebted for such fabricated statements as that work contains?

A. Giving them credit for ingenuity almost unparalleled, for based upon deceit and arrant falsehood have they produced a book which, with all its imperfections, obscurities and falsehoods, has seemed to form a bulwark around the so-called Christian world for many ages past and gone, pertinaciously insisting on its being the veritable and infallible work of God himself. From earliest times the Book has been accepted by a set of men whose wild and vague ideas have bolstered up a claim to sacredness of character, and thousands upon thousands feel assurance of its truthfulness, and profess to make it their guide and ruling principle of life.

My Brother, with such 'tis useless to confer, for prejudice forms a barrier formidable and potent to remove; in fact, 'tis but a loss of time for which no compensation can be had here or in the hereafter.

My Brother, freedom of thought and free expression of it, gives force to every act from which the fervent heat of man's ambition gains a force that is unexpected until it is tested. At times a force so potent is evolved that Nature scarce can bear the tension forced upon it.

Is not this the case when minds of strongest calibre conceive a thought that is new to science? Philosophy, unaided by angelic power, fails to render such assistance as is needed to solve a question thus through thought propounded. The human mind gives way, and all is dark, chaotic vagueness.

But, on the other hand, a tranquil mind, well balanced as it should be, seldom fails to ask assistance from the angel world, and thus escapes calamity most dreadful in its character. Suspended or abrogated reason oft occur, and life becomes a burden. Reason and Prudence both combined, show where the error lies. Too proud or ignorant to ask for what ye need, can ye expect supply? O, no; the ear that's always open to your plaints, if just, is always ready with response. Then, we ask where lies the fault? In man alone, we answer; the hand that gives does so silently to those deserving it. With such assurance shall we close this essay. AMEN.

THE HUMAN SOUL.

ITS DESTINY AFTER IT LEAVES THE BODY AND SPIRIT.

A SUBJECT like the present seems almost impossible to treat understandingly to the finite mind, yet, by trying, we may, to some extent, be enabled to reach a point of receptivity, which, under the law of universal progress, may be developed, though unseen by us. And, first, we shall make soul and its component elements our essay.

The subject we have chosen must be deemed an all-important one, viewed from whatever standpoint you may choose. Its earthly adjuncts present many things of vast importance, which cannot be passed unnoticed. All the better feelings that pervade the human mind are clustered round the soul, and, by Supreme authority, are garnered up for future use, and carefully preserved for distribution; waiting patiently, till preparation by some angel mind has been effected; and thus, in true and holy conservation, are they meted out as purifying influences for a race of beings who, by reckless expenditure of heaven-born vitality and perversion of the good within them, have fallen far below the standard nature designed they should. The soul at once supplies the need, and thus a change takes place, rendering the triune character of man more in accordance with his glorious destiny, if unperverted.

But while this is going forward, can aught be more consistent than to suppose that all should be equally concerned in bringing to a happy climax the co-existent partnership between the soul and spirit, so that, after the purpose of creation has been attained, in thus engendering life and motion in the human form, during a period governed and directed by soul's discretion, till at last the tenement becomes unfitted as a residence for the refined and holy germ of goodness, a separation soon is contemplated, and the God-like essence seeks a resting-place more suited to its ethereal nature, to await in patience the final dissolution of the earthly body, when the enfranchised spirit seeks earnestly to reach its co-partner, and, by a re-union, becomes its co-worker through the endless cycles of eternity; for, during its connection with the earthly form, it acquired strength and growth adequate to make it a fit companion for the ethereal essence soul?

A more beautiful or consoling thought occurs not to the human mind than this, that while the soul claimed precedence, the spirit was advancing step by step under the law of growth, each day and hour becoming better fitted to claim equality with one whose holy greeting yields superiority, and thus the twain becomes, as it were, blended as a perfect unity, never, through the countless ages of eternity, to undergo a separation.

To contemplate a fact like this, under the convictions of ethereal knowledge, must prove to every seeker after truth the "ne plus ultra" of desire, the pearl of great price, that which no priestly effort can make plain to mortals.

But here we leave the subject for the present not an exhausted one, but from a consciousness that we have taxed your receptive powers enough. But at some other time we'll open the book of spiritual knowledge, compiled by Deity for the instruction of those willing to accept its truths; and O! may each angel utterance of them to poor humanity be powerful in destroying the mazy teachings which blind the intellect of man and make him almost feel there is no reality in life. AMEN.

WHAT AND WHERE IS HEAVEN?

A QUESTION often asked and seldom solved so as to meet the wishes of an inquiring mind. Ask the question of an orthodox priest. In solemn tones he'll answer, It is a mystery, and cannot be solved till Death has claimed you for his own; with this exception it is the ultimate of happiness in the eternal future. O, miserable subterfuge on the part of men who claim to be the God-appointed shepherds of their flocks; displaying far more ignorance than those they presume to teach; hence the misleading of the multitude in all that appertains to ethereal life.

We blame them for their assumption, not their inability altogether. Experience they say they cannot have while mortals; nor willing are they to accept the testimony of spirits who return to earth for the avowed purpose of imparting to humanity of what they have *seen*, yet priestcraft says 'tis false and shut their eyes and ears to that which would enlighten them, and make them truthful teachers of their fellow-men, who look to them for truth and cannot find it. Every day's experience shows conclusively they are not the proper guides to heaven humanity demands, being but "blind leaders of the blind." You ask What and Where is Heaven? We answer it is a place, a location, tangible to all, who, by acts of rightousness, are fitted there to enter; for here the Law of adaptation soon is seen, beautiful in operation; thus tranquility and harmony exist in all things. Theology says heaven is the ultimate of happiness; we assert it is not so. 'Tis but a commencement even to those who are prepared for such a change. As well might it be said that he who travels towards a prospective home has realized expected happiness. It is not so; for perhaps, on entering the premises, the atmosphere at once seems quite unsuited; he finds no rest; no congeniality within, and so it is with thousands who transiently make heaven their resting place. They lose no farther time, but seek an atmssphere more suited to their own condition. Could such a Heaven become to them the ultimate of happiness? We opine not. Then what *is* Heaven? We say a place where adaptation fits you to assimulate with all surroundings; where soul can at once affinitize with soul, and in sweet communion blending, rest assured of copious blessings flowing constantly from the eternal and inexhaustible source of all purity and goodness—a lasting confidence that the soul has found a resting place from all inharmony, such as it had experinced in earth-life, in fact, a culmination and realization of all its higher aspirations for etheareal bliss.

My Brother, when the human soul has attained to such condition, it may truly say, within itself this *must* be Heaven. To which the angelic hosts respond Amen, Amen! No farther explanation of an expected Heaven need be given, we think, to one whose reason still remains intact; therefore we shall pass on to the inquiry *Where* is Heaven? Reason must be satisfied by and through its own perceptive powers. No power on earth can make a man or woman believe that which their reason cannot recognize; therefore, an attempt to do so would be folly; but facts presented and corroborated are the means we propose to use. Thousands upon thousands of well-developed spirits continually surround your earth to reach the minds of humanity, to impress upon them the necessity of preparation for a future state. Think you those efforts would be made if no reality existed as to a future life beyond the grave? And if this proposition be a truthful one, there must be a *somewhere* to exist, for by analogy we are taught the fact this beautiful world of yours was formed and fashioned for humanity to dwell upon; suited in every way to man's condition, crude as he might have been, yet was there a complete adaptation. Progression then became a law essential to the growth of man, fitting him for higher and still higher grades of development, which progression will continue through the endless cycles of eternity.

This earth presents a type of future life. Reason says 'tis so, and if it is, locality there surely must be—a place affixed in mighty wisdom and eternal love suited to the design of an infinite Creator, who, in all things, shows his love for man. Think you, my Brother, the grand designer of a universe would leave unfinished a portion of his work, and thus exhibit a partiality for some, and deep neglect of others in this universe of His? No candid mind can come to such conclusion; while Justice holds the balance all things in nature meets with due attention, and the human soul may rest assured that each one will find a Heaven best suited to its own requirements. All nature seems to ask the question—Where is Heaven? The tiny blade of grass looks upward, peering, as it were, through space, seeking a happy terminus to its brief existence, and so it is with all created matter seeking happiness through every avenue of life, knowing no stopping place, but onward and upward, as it were, ever rising, unchecked by aught of opposition from a world of skeptics, who live but on the pestilential thoughts of bigotry and superstition.

But, to conclude our essay, we feel a more minute reply may be expected to your question. We have often told you that in Heaven all things are found in correspondence with all you have on earth, as tangible to us as yours of earth becomes to you; hence, the fair conclusion must be, with such things tangible there must be a spot whereon to place them; hence, locality is all essential to carry on the business of a population vast beyond conception, where progression is the watch-word. Hence, institutions of learning, arts and sciences, indeed, all that appertains to human life, exists within the immortal spheres; therefore, heaven must be a locality. And now the question is: "*Where* does it exist?" And here we pause, wondering how many of those who read this record at the present moment, may accept our theory. To *you* it is such, but to *us* a knowledge experienced, known and enjoyed in full reality. Alas! but few, we fear, while so forgetful are they no friendly mind can grasp it as a truth, but often flounder in an abortive effort to explain the heaven concocted by some brainless advocate of a mystified theology. Not so with angel messengers. They come with what they know, and are ever ready freely to impart it. The heaven they spoke of is no myth; no distant future in the far-off space, but almost within the vicinity of your own homes, within the atmosphere you breathe, enveloped, as it is, in misty vapor, obscuring from the human sight its beauties; yet, ever and anon, a glorious gleam of sunshine passing from behind the blue ether as if announcing where the Eldorado lies!

Yes, my Brother, its highest altitude reaches to the very verge of space, if such there be, and from that high and glorious position come those angel intuitions to govern and direct humanity; yet, passing as they do, from spirit to spirit, lose much of their angelic beauty, but yet are better suited for mortal receptivity. O, wisdom infinite, in all its various presentations whereby purification and holiness may be attained through angel commune, so that after death no further preparation will be needed: thus a ready entrance to the celestial spheres will be accorded, but while we expect to meet with opposition to our statements, we are supported by a consciousness that time alone is needed to convince mankind there is no speculation in the matter, but all is God's own truth, feebly imparted, yet, in sincerity, submitted to the test of candor. AMEN.

ETHEREALITY.

THE subject matter of this transcript will be ethereality and its mysteries, so conceived by the finite mind.

Whenever the human mind is brought to dwell upon subjects with which it is not familiar, it usually imagines a mystery is presented to it, because of the difficulty it experiences in the attempt to comprehend it, which would not be under a changed condition from material to ethereal life. But we feel, before proceeding further, it were better to give you some idea of that condition, (ethereal) which we have just spoken of.

Ethereality implies heavenly, or that condition in which those who have passed through their earthly ordeal and landed on the shores of the spirit world, leaving behind them all gross materiality and thus become fitted for the ethereal regions, free from all that can disturb their mental quietude, which they have zealously sought in earth-life by purity of conduct and holy aspirations, are now reaping their reward. The condition of such may truly be said to be that of pure and unalloyed happiness; the spirit being unemcumbered of the mortal coil, seems now to indulge all its better and more holy proclivities, and thus soars higher and higher in the scale of spirit-life.

We might dilate upon this subject in more glowing language, but deeming the plainest mode best suited to the finite comprehension, we have done so, hoping it may be more readily and accurately received.

This book of record must necessarily fall into

the hands of persons as varied in their mental endowments as they are in their outward forms and countenances. Our aim is, to make ourselves understood, even at the risk of being supposed incompetent to adopt the style of eloquence better suited to the minds of those who prefer display of oratory, to the *plain common-sense* mode of addressing the human intellect.

We shall now proceed with our instructions as to what further constitutes the ethereal state. No individual but has formed within his own mind a vague surmise of what constitutes that which is often termed the Better Land. Therefore, we are anxious to avoid saying aught that would tend to interfere with previously formed opinion, because it *is*, and must be, based upon their highest capabilities of comprehension; hence, all the efforts we could make would but tend to mystify, until they have entered the Promised Land, and by their own experience become convinced of the crude and imperfect ideas they have entertained of a place estimated by them, through false teachings, to be one of eternal rest from all that partakes of labor or employment; satisfied, as they seem, with that which is better suited to their earthly ideas of rest, which is a mere cessation from all labor, subsiding into a state of listless languor, such as in time would rust out all the soul's best energies, making man a mere automatom, incapable of appreciating the teachings of the spirit-world. Thus would they become useless inhabitants of a world where idleness is not tolerated; for there each spirit has its own especial duty to perform, and in which performance lies the secret of heavenly enjoyment, destroying that hideous monotony consequent upon a life of idleness, totally unknown or practiced in the ethereal world.

No sane person would predicate his future happiness upon so wild a theory as is taught within your churches, that singing psalms of praise to God will form a suitable employment for the pure and holy aspirant for immortal truths. Monstrous absurdity, to suppose an intelligent mind could be thus engaged—perchance a mind of deep research in the mundane sphere, unsated with its exploration of Nature's works, and still alive to all its cravings to increase its store of knowledge; can such a mind, with all its energies increased, rest satisfied with such employment, much better suited to the imbecile than those giant minds of men who, in earth-life, stood on the very pinnacle of science? Think you such men, under the ethereal improvement they are making in their perceptive faculties, could realize happiness and contentment there? O, no; to them heaven must seem a desert wild and barren, whither they have gone in anxious search of a place more suited to their souls' ecstatic yearnings for more of God and

His beautiful and Infinite iufluences, leaving those whose pampered souls had become incapable of realizing heaven in aught but luxury and ease.

O, poor, poor specimens of humanity; ye worldlings who have so often bent yourselves in front of Mammon's altar, it may take an eternity to raise thee to that form erect intended by thy Maker, God. AMEN.

WASHINGTON, LINCOLN, BENEDICT ARNOLD AND WILKES BOOTH.

WHAT IS THEIR RELATIVE CONDITION IN THE SPHERES?

IN REVIEWING this subject, we feel there are some obstacles it may be difficult to surmount. The first person named, having existed in times so widely different, needs to be separately discussed, which would immeasurably extend this article; therefore, of necesity, we shall have to be very brief in the expression of our views.

The well known character of the first, justly termed the Father of his Country, can receive no additional honor from aught we might attempt to express; yet, we think it right to observe that the times in which he lived and reigned in the hearts of the people of these United States, was so different, and by comparison so free from the entanglement which surrounded your late President, that it required less of that mental vigor and sound judgment than latter times have demanded at the hands of Abraham Lincoln.

We have thought it right to make these few preliminary remarks, and shall claim the same privilege in regard to the other two individuals, whom we much dislike to have associated (even in detail) with those two exalted specimens of humanity previously named.

As we stated of the immortal Washington, so we say of that arch traitor, Benedict Arnold. The times in which he committed *his* crime, great as it was, still admitted of some palliation, as compared with that which has lately so disgraced your country. Motive is the standpoint from whence all judicial deduction should be drawn. What, then, was the governing motive by which Benedict Arnold was instigated to commit his crime? We answer, personal ambition, the gratification of which seemed the all-absorbing element of his nature, and for which he would have sacrificed all things else.

Now, base as is this feeling, let us compare it with the leading motives of Wilkes Booth.

Can you perceive one redeeming point in that

man's conduct?—anything which seemed allied to nobillity of thought or purpose? Could the interests of humanity be served by his cruel and attrocious act? We cannot, with all the charity we would fain indulge, see one redeeming point, but all of black attrocity, unparalleled in the history of times most barbarous. But in times like these, when mankind is boasting of such enlightening principles to govern them, that such a man, claiming superiority of intellect, surrounded with all of wealth required, but lacking that one great elemeut to make a great man and a good one—Principle.

Here, then, the error lay. We solemnly conjure those who have the care of youth to look well to this; for, wanting it, man's condition becomes unsafe.

With this brief preface, we may now essay to speak of their relative condition in the spheres, asking your indulgence for having to discuss ethereal conditions; to your finite conceptions it may be truly difficult.

Washington, the Father of his country, has before and ever since his exit, been looked up to with a filial feeling of respect; perhaps, such as never, in any age has ruler been esteemed. Courteous and affable to all, yet maintaining a dignity of deportment suited to his high position, respect, almost amounting to adoration, was readily conceded; hence the appellation Father.

Time rolled on, and varied talent filled the governmental chair with ebbs and flows of popularity; yet under its sway your country prospered, each successive year adding greatly to its power and riches. In individual life this condition is seldom viewed as healthy, and such became your country's state. Undue pride, the offspring of wealth, presented the symptoms of disease; insubordination and distrust became the offshoots of rebellion—aye! black rebellion followed. *Then* came the time of difficulty, and who could stay the whirlwind movements of this monster?

No great, gigantic mind was there to govern such unbridled elements as were then let loose. No Washington was there; and even if he had been, constituted as he was, was he suited to the times? We answer no. The entire masses seemed bewildered, for one untried in state intricacies had been chosen by the people, nncertain of the issue.

With modest mien Lincoln assumed the onerous task; reckless of personal safety he threw himself into the breach and sought to stop the tide of anarchy which seemed about to reign triumphant. Self-abnegating on all occasions, his country's good at once became his war-cry and an overruling providence crowned his efforts with success, and sealed, as with his patriot blood, the freedom of his country!

O! hallowed spirit, we hail thee as worthy of the highest eulogy man or angel can bestow upon thy memory, for *thou* hast been, indeed, the savior of thy country, under the direction of thy God.

Need you, then, ask us what is the relative condition of two such spirits in the spheres, as Washington, the Father, and Lincoln, the savior of your land and all its glorious institutions.

Look down deep into thine own heart. What would be its decree? Wert thou a Washington, thy friend a Lincoln, would not the principle of divine love bring you into such close and holy rapport with each other that soul would intertwine with soul? So now, it is with them.

Would we could be permitted to pass unnoticed the other two connected with this interrogatory. But brief response we'll give, so sickening is the task, and with reluctance is the effort made. The first, Arnold, whose crime we view as of some lighter hue, (being of design, only), may have since become repentant under the discipline he may have undergone, whilst Booth is yet and may continue unconscious for ages yet to come, with all progression stayed and no effort made by aught of spirit power to awaken him from that deadened lethargy which admits of no relief, but is in mercy granted to his guilty soul. Yet, a time may come when resuscitation may ensue, and with awakened horrors will be presented to his view the blackened record of his crime. Unhallowed and unblessed will be his then condition, until some spirit may in mercy be permitted to fan the divine spark within his darkened nature. Then will commence progression towards a condition where he will outgrow his cruel nature, and again be permitted to seek such associations as will eventually fit him for a state more suited to his then improved condition. AMEN.

INCARNATION OF LOVE.

LOVE is a principle so divine in its character and functions, and so widely diffused throughout animated nature, that in every direction its influence is felt, and mankind, revelling in its enjoyments, must partake of its beautiful influences, with gratitude ever welling up from his inner soul. The source from whence it springs is so inexhaustible that, with all the universal draughts that are made upon it, there seems no diminution of supply.

To define this beautiful and God-like element we may find it difficult and almost impossible; for, emanating, as it does, from Deity itself, and we but finite, we fear the attempt may fail; hence we leave our definition of infinite Love to those who may approach the nearest to infinity. We shall, therefore, speak of the love of God as being unbounded, limitless, and displayed in all His works which tend to the happiness of the human race. And here we pause, before we undertake to discuss Love, being the divinest element in man's nature, by which its crudities and angularities are modified and softened to a condition more harmonious and acceptable to society, by which the asperities of his nature are removed and the softer element of love introduced as their successor.

The human mind thus becomes changed in all its proclivities, and stands before his fellow-man as a sympathizer in his hours of suffering and distress, never permitting a brother or sister in danger to be neglected or unattended to; but, soothing their tortured minds, alleviating their sorrows, supplying their hungry cravings, and, indeed, fulfilling duties which his own conscience suggests to him as all-essential. This is a very important feature, and comes under the head of Brotherly Love, so beautifully and emphatically enjoined by the Holy Nazarene, and so shamefully neglected by those who presume to class themselves as His disciples.

The next phase of Love we would present is that of the Parent. Imbedded deep down in the

Parent's soul, its out-gushings are sometimes so overwhelming as almost to unseat reason and lay it prostrate at the shrine of parental Love, not so potent in its display with the father, but who can sound the depth of a mother's love? Who can guage its length and breadth? For deep down in that heart is a well-spring of holy and divine love, untiring, devoted, and so holy in its character that naught in Nature can compare with it. Everything in nature fails in competition. Here seems the culmination of the beautiful, universally admitted. For who has not felt that deep-toned sympathy welling up from her most interior being, lavishly bestowed upon her offspring?

Where lives the man or woman who has not, at some period of life, after passing from a mother's special care, keenly felt her absence? and in moments of mental anguish has pronounced the sacred name of Mother; and often have those exclamations of distress been, by attendant spirits, carried to that mother through spirit intuition. 'Tis then a mother's love is stirred within her, and her entire soul tries to burst the bonds which keep her from that child; and, if 'tis sickness, a mother's keenest sympathies are drawn towards the suffering child; or, if it be misfortune or disgrace, when is a mother known to shrink from fostering that erring one? O, never; for that erring soul seems more closely drawn to seek her soothing influences, by which, perchance, the penitent outpourings may be heard, and a hardened sinner is redeemed!

The next, and, perhaps, the most important phase of this beautiful and God-like element, is that which is, and always has been, least understood; that Love which should be the out-pouring of experience and sincerity, not that tinselled exhibition too oft exhibited, a mere dissembling of the feelings, gross, sordid and disgraceful in its character, emanating from causes most disgraceful (when analyzed.) Thus is the happiness of millions wrecked upon the shores of ignorance, with not a chance of safety; for being only passional, having none of the soul-elevating influences of divine and holy Love, is merely evanescent, unabiding, and, indeed, demoralizing; not partaking of that purity of soul's experienced Love, which warms it into acts of mercy and devotion to the interests of all humanity. With such a guiding element as the former, how can society be benefitted? We cannot see the slightest chance of improvement, for all seems merged in the one degrading passional element, Lust; instead of the beautiful and attractive principle of holy Love, drawing together as if by magic, two kindred souls, mutually imbued with feelings of affection totally unknown to those in whom the animal predominates so potently that every act partakes thereof, subversive of all that is pure in human nature, demoralizing society by corrupting the mind and making sensuality the grand point of gratification.

O, that we could see in the future a change of condition, for the happiness of the human race depends upon it. AMEN.

THE UPS AND DOWNS OF HUMAN LIFE

SHALL be our theme. We shall endeavor to show the disproportion is not so great as many oft imagine. To-day the sky may appear so overcast and gloomy that discouragement almost ensues, when on the morrow's dawn the atmosphere is clear and all of gloom has vanished. The oppressive atmosphere no longer presses on the nervous system; all is blithe, and cheerful, and joy seems almost perfect.

Think you, my brother, this condition affects but man alone? Experience tells you nay. A bright and brilliant sunshine gladdens the heart of man, while every atom dancing in the genial breeze feels the invigorating influence, nor seems to lack the power to show its gratitude. All of animated nature appears refulgent with its glory. Who, then, comparing such a day with that we have named before, can be unmoved at nature's goodness to the creature man? who, in the exercise of reasoning thought, stands high upon the plane of all creation here on earth, and even, when tired of such research, through his reasoning faculty, can soar through space in grand conception of the world beyond this planet, where, could he commune with them, he would find intelligence far beyond his own; and, could he look from hence into the far beyond, still unnumbered worlds he would see, till, being exhausted and impressed with wonder and amazement, he would return and sees pictured in his individual nothingness, the immensity of that power by whose fiat he had become an existing entity.

Think you discontent would then assail him? Rather would he exclaim, "Come weal, come woe," gratitude is all that I can show for blessings such as are bestowed on a race of beings formed for happiness eternal." Think you, my Brother, murmuring or complaint would here be heard, upon this mundane sphere, where God's eternal bounties are better comprehended? O, no; from lips unnumbered would come forth a gush of holy gratitude; the sound of great rejoicing would be heard; the knee of reverence would soon be bent; the body placed in reverential posture in token of humility exhibited by every son and daughter of humanity. The sweet, angelic cadence of celestial music, reverberating in a brighter atmosphere, would stir the souls of men to deeds of grandeur and renown, that all of vice would vanish, and the soul that hitherto had sought its company would suddenly eschew it as a thing of bitterness and distaste.

All this must come to pass in the few or many years between the present and the future; the good which now in embryo lies, will then have burst its bonds, and Nature will assert her right to rule. For, then, the purity of truth will tread the path of universal progress in company with the million aspirants for heavenly joys.

Strifes of the past shall act as beacons to the hosts of coming humans, to fill the vacant places of those who have gone before. Thus, as one generation quits the field of action, so another fills its place, with intellect increased, and vital force engendered by coming angels sent from the higher spheres with knowledge before unknown, and such regenerated power changing the current of human thought by the sublimating influence of holy and divine love, making that the glorious standard of universal action; driving away all grossness from the souls of men, bringing them, progressively, nearer and still nearer to the angel world; each day's intercourse giving them more purity of thought, which, having action correspondent with them, would make of man a being better and more fully fitted for an ethereal residence.

But, my brother, these crowding thoughts have almost driven from my mind the given subject—The Ups and Downs of Human Life. A life's experience of them needs no copious essay to define them, if other thoughts were not engendered by the subject. Man's natural skepticism as to things ethereal makes him often discontented here in mundane life; with means quite adequate to his necessities, how oft he murmurs, deeming them but scant; whereas, a better course he would pursue by feeling grateful for that he has, nor ask for angel aid to swell the means supplied him. Does he appropriate that he has to aid some stricken sufferer? If he does, every aspiration sent to angels high above him will be responded to, and like the "Widow's cruse," will e'en be full to overflowing. Is man's condition such, we ask? (whether up or down) controlled by other than a God of mercy, love, compassion and eternal goodness? And if so, has he the right to dictate what shall be the changes of his life on earth? More frequently the Downs of earth-life accrue from ignorance and sad perversion of the moral laws intended for his governance, and then, with unblushing cheek, he'll e'en attribute them to God as strokes of Providence.

Here, then, my Brother, lies the error. The

little knowledge sought by man of his Creator, viewing him as vengeful and malignant. Such are the teachings man has had for centuries past; forgetting all his attributes so beautifully blended in their characters, basing them on a law of universal grandeur far transcending human thought, and casting into dark oblivion everything that tends to mystify the Being we and all humanity must worship as the true and holy God. AMEN.

PROFESSSOR HARE'S RESPONSE TO MY CALL.

As a friend to all humanity I greet you, and as an efficient medium I further greet you; therefore, I am here in cheerfulness to answer such questions as you may like to put concerning Spiritualism.

Q. Then I would ask, are you alone with me?

A. No; myriads of invisibles are now around us, but each enveloped in an atmosphere entirely its own.

Q. If you can describe distances by our rule, what distance are you from me at the present time?

A. About twenty inches, more or less.

Q. In front or behind me?

A. Rather behind you, resting lightly upon your left shoulder, in a reclining position, giving to you vitality equal to the demand I make upon you. With a younger person this would not be needed, nature maintaining the needed equilibrium.

Q. In such a situation as you describe, can we feel entirely removed from spirit observation?

A. Yes, my friend; isolated as you then become, no power can scan your thoughts or hear your speech, other than the unknown power of Almighty God, or those to whom he delegates important trusts, and there your secrets lie inviolable.

Q. In such condition the two atmospheres, while so close in contact, must there not be a kind of blending, making each receptive of the other's nature?

A. Assuredly, it must be so. The blending of which you speak is undefinable to mortal mind. An entire vocabulary would not provide words adequate to do so, and yet, the disembodied spirit feels and knows it; and you, while thus in sympathy with me and others, who so often come in holy rapport with you, can mutually enjoy it. My Brother, is there not a beauty in this law, when understood, that cannot be surpassed, giving to the earthly aspirant for Heaven a foretaste of its joys by actual demonstrations of the life beyond; by coming living entities from yonder blissful land, to tell of wonders man has no conception of?

Q. Are disembodied spirits all around us while communing thus?

A. I have already told you that a room however large, may be almost filled to overflowing, yet, still, there is room for more. The air you breathe will bear compression to such extent as to burst a cask or bottle, and spirit being light as air, is not inconvenienced by such pressure as would kill a human form and drive the spirit from its flesh encasement; yet, the spirit dies not from such event, but in proper time, prescribed by law, unerring, in resurrected state, it comes again to earth and manifests itself a living entity, beyond the power of doubting, by those prepared with spirit vision, to behold the wonders then presented. And yet, this sight so grand and beautifully true, to some is *manifest insanity.* Has God become so powerless he cannot strike with well-directed vengeance the authors of such calumny as oft you have listened to. But, my Brother, we had forgotten; ours is not the Christian God; no vengeance is there in the God we worship; all Love, and compassion, giving to the wicked and the good alike, showing no partiality for the one or other, bestowing happiness and reward when earned by strict obedience to his laws; and to the wicked abrogators of those laws, an eternity of time for that repentence they must evince before they can outwork their self-kept record of a wretched life. This is the God whom Reason seeks and clings to. And does she cling in vain? Oh, no, at every turn is seen God's goodness and benificence.

Q. Why are there so few Dial Mediums?

A. In answering such a question we would state that God and Nature ever uses means best suited to the end designed. The time has not yet arrived for man's capacity to grasp the everything by nature now presented. Improvements made in such quick succession, the human mind becomes almost bewildered, accepting from necessity of that most needed, or so esteemed at least, and rejecting that which seems too complex for their use and comprehension. Was this not clearly shown, when I, with honest purpose and intent, yet in sad delusion, made my efforts (through science) to uproot the truth of Spiritualism, but, through a power I could not stay, became defeated? With me, defeat became a triumph, greater than a Napoleon or a William could enjoy. The voice of omnipotence seemed to say, more will be effected through thy defeat to bless humanity than had victory crowned thy brow in such investigation. Around that brow a never fading halo rests; a mark of tested wisdom imparted to thee from a source that's ever open to the true investigator. Thy work is almost done; thou hast earned thy crown of glory; enter where thoul't find it.

Science like nature, ever works by measure. No chance or guess work in the matter; everything must correspond and everything by law adapted, makes the whole complete. And now, we turn to Dial Mediums. Why, and how are they controlled?

A two-fold influence must work within their natures. A dial medium needs an influence dual in its character, as we have said before. First, the impressional in largest measure; for, a thought, seemingly but whispered, must be grasped with great activity, for being rapidly imparted, the slightest inattention may scatter to the winds some gem-like thought, which, if then imparted as it should be, would benefit the universe of man—transferred through various grades of intellect, might give fresh beauties to this lower sphere; and on, and on, through all the devious windings of this mundane life. But it is not this, alone, we would revert to. Impression seems a needed element in evolving dial mediums; because, without another, it must fail. A mind inert and listless in its character, would be unsuitable. Appreciation of a living truth must be instantaneous, or doubts may soon arise to make a living truth an *almost lie*; the mere shadow of a doubt, would be too readily accepted, and thus, delay retard expression of it, perverting time and talent from the channel where most needed.

To be a dial medium in the truest sense, it follows, much of worldly interest must cease; for, upon a tranquil state of mind, so much depends, that constant intercourse with worldly matters would render sparse the visits of your angel friends, depriving mediums of the instructions they impart in copious measure to their pupils, giving of all they have; asking no recompense, for, free as air is all instruction given.

Q. Will such mediums need an increase?

A. Assuredly they will, and in full accordance with the law of supply and demand, will they be provided.

Q. Which would you prefer, man or woman as Dial Mediums?

A. Why ask such a question, where full equality exists?

Q. Because in the Divine economy, degrees are seen in everything. Each sex being better adapted for one employment than another, is it worth the inquiry? We are told to copy nature to avoid mistakes. Are we swerving from the right in doing so?

A. My Brother, I find no fault with such a question; but, admitting the equality of woman on the intellectual plane, and doing justice to infinity as being impartial, leaving woman a fair competitor for what she is adapted by a good and gracious God, we waive a further answer to your question.

Q. I would ask, have you any means of judging what is the present status of professing spiritualists. Have they a healthy growth on this our earth?

A My Brother, no better opportunity have I of judging than yourself, although clarivoyantly, I see within the human mind a growing hatred to Priestly Rule, discordant feelings rife, a growing dislike of church formulas, rituals, and superstitions of the former dark and gloomy ages. Claiming the right of thought and free expression of it, by which the man or woman is not by the "Thus Saith the Lord" being an imagined authority to rule sacred and important in its character, but now through liberal thought and act, has become almost a cypher, no longer tyranizing over the human intellect, till debased and reckless it has sunk into the slough of superstition and despondency almost without a hope of ultimate retrieval.

Q. Do you recognize obcession as an evil damaging to man?

A. My Brother, sin, in all its phases, is disgusting to the mind that's pure, but in this demoralizing phase so monstrous are its influences, that with trembling hands we contemplate the issue. The passional of human nature, bestirred to action by such a means, makes the cheek grow pale, the heart's blood recede, and stagnant as it then becomes, paralysis ensues, and almost Death itself may close the solemn scene. This is no isolated statement, but a fact that's well attested, and as time rolls on, the growing evil must be recognized and grappled with, in firm determination to uproot the evil or die in the attempt.

Q. What are its causes, and what will be the remedy applied?

A. This, like all things else, must first be traced with all becoming care to its lowest depths within the human soul, for there it will be found imbedded and encrusted with the accumulated filth of ages past and gone, checking the growth of virtue, and giving countenance to Vice in all its base deformity and wretchedness. It now runs riot in your midst, cherished and admired, while Virtue shrinks affrighted and restrained therefrom. This is a truth beyond all doubt, and what shall be the remedy applied? At present may be seen whole multitudes gliding down the stream of time, so totally unconscious of the mælstrom vortex ready to receive them; careless of the certain sequel, they seem to lack all power to resist the influence; but, like the cherished babe at its mother's breast, knowing nothing of the danger, falls and dies a victim of unconsciousness. Such, my brother, is *that* you ask about? Time, indeed, it is the public mind should be awakened to their danger. While seemingly in safety sleeps the unconscious soldier at his post, a mine is sprung with dire effect, spreading death and desolation all around. With vigilance and proper caution this might have been avoided. Are the peoples of the present day one whit more careful? Are they ready to investigate this evil and remove it, if not modify its virulence? May God and His holy angels so impress humanity as to wake them up to scrutinize this matter as it should be, for, sooner or later, it must outburst the boundaries prescribing it.

Q. Are obscessions practiced in the spirit world?

A. My brother, strange it seems, such questions should be asked by you, but seeing your motive, we most readily accord response. Beyond this earth of yours there is a place where much of earth's perplexity is realized. Proclivities of earth are there demonstrable beyond all cavil. The same demoniac feelings are there exhibited as when such spirits dwelt on earth, having the desire, but not the power, to sin, and that desire being potent in their natures, they seek to gratify the same by finding some assimilating spirit in the form on whom they exercise their own *will* power to psychologyse their victim to perpetrate the act desired by them; and thus, by an aggravated sympathy, they seemingly obtain their purpose, leaving their unconscious victim uncared for and suffering from such obcession. Oh! if the accumulated ills of human life could all be heaped together, it would be as nothing in comparison with this astounding curse humanity endures.

Q. Can you see an end to such calamity, so world-wide as it is?

A. How often are we sought for such a purpose, hoping we, as spirits, have the power to look into the future, and foretell events of much importance to the race. Oh how gladly would we use it, was it a privilege possessed by us, yet what credit would the world accord to us—*that* we offer at the present is scarce accepted. What credence does the skeptic give to statements made of spirit-power to return and hold communion with you? But if given under *church authority* they'd hug it as a sacred treasure, but lacking such, they ruthlessly denounce it as insanity.

With such a feeling rampant in society few men are safe. The utterance of a truth, or that esteemed as such, has endangered life and liberty, the latter of greater value oft than life itself. But Oh, the blessed God-sanctioned thought; they may incarcerate the body of the Man, but, the Soul and Spirit, the ethereal portion of the real man, can laugh at such endeavors and taunt authority with baseness.

Q. Will not compensation be required for such outrageous conduct?

A. With justice still intact through all coming time, for each injury inflicted by man upon his fellow, a righteous compensation must be paid; in what way or manner is of little moment; governed by the law of justice, it must be met.

Q. Can God or Nature act outside the law to punish any individual?

A. Law being the limit prescribed by Deity, is equally as binding on himself as man, Justice demanding mutual recognition of it; and here the beauty lies. The wants of man, if unperverted, are God's desires; and farther, the happiness of man is watched and cared for by his angel messengers; and every want supplied, together with assurance of celestial life, if sought in spirit and in truth.

Q. My Brother, with such assurance given, how can so-called Christians reject the glorious doctrine we present?

A. All men are not alike in countenance, form or constitution; and is not this a wise precaution? What dire confusion must ensue, were not this the case! No means of recognition would there be. The man who prides himself upon his individuality, thinks and speaks of it as something priceless to him. One man might have a claim upon another, but, without identity, the chance of being paid would be but small. Thus, diversity becomes a need of man's existence; indeed, without it, monotony would rend society, scattering its fragments far beyond man's recognition.

But here we have digressed. You ask why such indifference as so-called Christians manifest? to which we answer the narrow-minded theologian fears encountering Truth in all its glowing beauty, offering Error in lieu thereof; hence, their indifference to our glorious doctrine, Spiritualism. Why the appellation "*so*-called?" you, perhaps, may ask? Simply because they should be known for what they are, with many exceptions, we must admit. The *so* cuts off their claim of being what they assume to be; but, like the wolf in sheep's clothing, seems to be the thing he is not, professing, but not possessing, the elements which go to form the real Christian. The follower of Jesus, having no fears, no doubts, that by performance of his duties, His promises will be fulfilled, such believer needs no persuasion to endorse such principles as form the basis on which we rest our doctrine, sublime and glorious in its character, requiring no hyperbole of words to recommend it to the attention of a soul prepared by angel intuitions, who, in gratitude and deep humility, becomes the associate of Spirit entities within the immortal spheres. Thus it seems no marvel that Christians of modern date treat with contumely that which bears but slight resemblance to their own erratic creeds and dogmas. Men of better thoughts eschew as deleterious to the happiness of man, sapping the elements of Love and Truthfulness by statements quite absurd, falsely aspersing those who claim to know the promised place of rest beyond this mundane sphere, where hosts of pure and holy spirits are, who, not content with promises, leave their beauteous homes at all convenient periods, to give to men and women such assurances of after life that to reject the proffered boon would seem but black ingratitude, unworthy men of progress.

Q. My friend, was death to you a painful issue?

A. I know on this and other kindred subjects, your information is extensive, but, as investigation knows no limits, I feel bound to answer. Death, or, rather, change, (the latter term is more correct), cannot be generalized othèr than as it may be viewed, by many as a finality. The Atheist may view it in that light, and there we fain would leave him to enjoy his dark and gloomy reverie. With such belief we are at war, because it is not natural; indeed, we know of nothing but the horrible to which it bears affinity, and here we leave it, feeling better satisfied to recognize a change in man's condition; not, as many erroneously suppose, a momentary change of earth-life, but to patiently await the movements of the angel hosts to waft you to the summer land. 'Twere well to end this subject for the present, for many things as yet untold I have to give. AMEN.

JESUS' RESPONSE TO MY INTERROGATIONS.

Q. Is the book called sacred by the Christian World, actually the Word of God? and calculated to guide men through earth-life to a state of happiness in the future?

A. The Bible as a book contains but little that is needed by men engaged in business; nothing that can aid their speculations; nothing that can lead to fame or fortune, unless to those who take the road to Church preferment, and that too oft is slow, and almost motionless, giving to the few, superfluous riches, but adding little to their truthful sanctity.

The Mitred Priest at times may be tempted to step aside from virtue's path, as is the practiced Libertine, who worships at the shrine of Vice in open violation of the sacred laws of God, contained within that Bible. Here let us trace the line of difference between the two. The Libertine unversed in Bible teachings, follows out the course of his perverted nature and lacking the moral bonds, which binds the one to virtue's path, he seeks the haunts of wickedness in open day, and shamelessly he acts the character he has professed to be.

It is sin with him assuredly, but the other, what name is fitted to describe the demoralizing effect of sad hypocrisy? On bended knees, and in solemn tones he asks for blessings from his God and seeks forgiveness of him for all omitted duties, but says nothing of committed sins, and why, because *he* knows there is no forgiveness for them, although, perchance, when called to the bedside of the death-stricken Libertine, redolent as he is of crime and sinfulness, how does he address him? Not in tones of chiding and denouncement No indeed, but in honied tones of softness, tells him his God is good and merciful, that Jesus died for such as him, that God will surely grant him pardon, not for his sake, but for the sake of *Jesus*, through whose sacrifice his sins however deeply damning, may be washed away in the sacrificial blood of *Jesus*.

Is this a religion for men of sense and truthfulness? We wot it is not; and further, we denounce it as damaging in its influence.

Let men be told there is no forgiveness here, or in the world to come, Crime will soon be lessened. The sinner looks not upon his sin as e'en he should, as blots upon his character no Jesus blood could e'er remove the stain, till compensation has been made, through suffering and affliction merited by all who in impassioned state violate the Laws of God and man.

Q. Does such a Priest perform his duty towards his fellow man, by tendering such a doctrine to a dying Brother?

A. Let reason act her part with common sense to aid her, she will answer *No.* The man entrusted with the care of human souls, (if such is true and much we donbt it is,) should possess integrity of purpose in all his several functions, whether in relation to the present or the future. Truth, ungarbled truth, should be his motto. No matter what the expected fee may be, no falsehood should be told, no sophistry should ever enter the sick man's room; a purer atmosphere is needed there, for whether rich or poor it is equally a need and should not be withheld. The Priest that flatters a sinking soul in dying moments commits a crime he ne'er can compensate.

Q. Is the life beyond a great improvement on the present?

A. My Brother, the mind that has a single doubt on this point must be unhappy. Consult the law of progress; is there aught within that law, but means or indicates improvement? In all directions progress shows it, and if it were not so, how could men endure the hardships they encounter in attempts gigantic in their character, was not improvement witnessed as the work progresses?

Q. I would further ask, are the general details in the New Testament based upon truth immutable?

A. To this I answer, not in all their several details. Much of it is fabulous, intended to evoke an enlarged interest in the miraculousness of my parentage and birth, which was one of shame and poverty, aggreeable to the chronicled averment, but was undue publicity a need? Certainly not, unless to serve some sinister design of an ambitious conclave, seeking to lure the unthinking and superstitious multitude, into the performance of acts, subversive of good order and right principle.

Q. The Holy Ghost is spoken of within that so-called sacred book, and in the Christian Ritual as the means used for your paternity. With deference we ask the question. Is that a turth?

A. My Brother, was such a question asked by other than yourself, if aught of anger lingered in my nature, I might feel resentment, but your motive being known to me, I e'en must give reply.

The man or men that wrote such statement, lacked every principle of truthfulness. Liars by nature they must have been; and *was* there an existent hell, it seems they must have dipped their pens in the foulest element within its borders. The brain that could concoct so vile an item, must have sought it in some darkened region where no light could come, hence would we denounce them as wretches unparalleled in history's record.

But as to who my father was, it little matters. I have neither gained or lost by such event; angel messengers have kindly cared for me, as oft they have for others, fostering all of virtue in my nature, letting reason, aided by angelic love, give guidance to my acts, making me a useful member of community, furnishing me with gifts to benefit humanity, even as at present mediums now are gifted to impart ethereal knowledge to the masses, which, for ages baek was practiced yet not recognized as now it is. Such was my condition and with it I felt contented. Free from all undue ambition to be great, I deemed it better to be good, to obey the holy intuition given me at times I needed them. Humility was ever mine and much I valued it as being an inspired action of the soul to obey the laws of Him I felt I had the right to call my father, such as every son and daughter of humanity claims they have the inherent right to do. With this was I content, nor sought a higher honor.

Q. Were you crucified between two criminals?

A. In that particular, the record tells the truth, it was even so. Their priestly fury knew no limit, and by every means within their power the Jewish rabble sought to crush me, hence they placed those victims to the law beside me, but fruitless was the effort. My soul's best aspirations was to aid the sufferers and in kindliest tones I made the effort; with one I was successful, with the other I failed. With hardened heart he scoffed and railed at me.

Q. It is said on the day of thy crucifiction the heavens were darkened as at midnight, and confusion dire seemed to reign; was such the truth?

A. My Brother there is just as much truth in such a statement as in many others made to give effect to some event mysterious as they tried to make it. The element of common sense and truthful judgment must have taken their departure, giving men the opportunity to display their folly in making Nature's movement a seeming miracle to aid them in deception.

Q. Did you raise Lazarus after Death had taken hold upon him?

A. Had Lazarus been dead no power on

earth or in heaven could have done such work. Omnipötence itself must have failed in making such an attempt. No, Lazarus slept the sleep that many of the present day are sleeping. In trance they lie for days, not in sleep exactly, but in a state of consciousness, without the power to speak or move a muscle indicating life or slightest animation. Such was the state of Lazarus. With eagerness his infatutated friends and those surrounding us claimed a miracle for that which was but nature's work. Men of sinister designs were there, seeking for means to beguile the people. I never claimed I had the power to work a miracle or even the desire to endorse them.

Q. Much has been said about your cursing the Fig Tree. Please explain.

A. My Brother, I am glad you named it, because at first sight such an act would he unseemly in one whose soul was seldom if ever stirred to anger that would evoke a Curse; neither is it natural to suppose that I as a teacher among the Jewish Nation would or could commit an act so vile as to curse a thing of God's creation, an act so fraught with injury to myself, by showing the little power I had over the passional, that I, as a teacher, should control? No, my brother; whatever faults I had (and of them I never felt myself exempt) asperity of temper never could be charged against me. Meekness and humility I claimed to be the brightest spots I had to boast of. The charge I claim is false, and but another item chargeable to such detraction.

Q. Is eternal salvation (by you) of the entire human race, as taught by Christians true?

A. Many are the inquiries in this direction, and this shall claim attention. God in every way impresses man to lead a life of purity and holiness; then, we ask, is a Savior needed? Let this be my answer to your questicn.

Q. Was your ascension witnessed by five thousand persons in the form?

A. The atmosphere then, as well as now, was filled with hosts of living witnesses unseen by mortal eyes, for who can see a spirit unaided by clarivoyant power, and then somewhat imperfectly, or who could number such a host; a Universe would fail in computation of their number. Hence we deem the statement doubtful.

Q. Did Satan take you to a high mountain and there tempt you, as described?

A. Are not all mankind sometimes tempted, and why should special note be made of my being iufluenced in the self-same way as other men, the same passions and desires within my nature, perhaps a little better governed and controlled, and yet existent? Exposed as I became at times, need it be deemed a marvel that I, as well as others, should become its victim? Common sense if used would show at once the falsity of such a statement. That Satan, if such a being then existed, should select me out from others to make such offers as Sacred Writ avers he did, seems more like a schoolboy fable or a tale not fitted for adults to name as being real.

Q. Was the descending of the Holy Ghost in shape of a dove, correct or a mere fable?

A. Often will you find figures used instead of words, being more brief and pungent in their meaning. If such a person then or now existed as the Holy Ghost, no better figure could be used. To make this question plainer let us inquire, if by the Holy Ghost is meant the second member of the Christian's God-head who left his high abode in heaven, to visit earth and make selection of a mortal from the unnumbered masses as a special favorite, born from all eternity as such, then and there proclaimed as one in whom the Father took much pleasure. Can such a God be deemed impartial? We think he cannot, and here we take our stand. That such incongruous statements misrepresenting Deity, makes each and every statement doubtful, where truth immutable is not exhibited in form that men may know it. is such. No Holy Ghost or sacred dove was seen by me or others, being the mere concoction of some priestly brain exhibited and well adapted to the superstition of the times gone by, and even to the 19th century, has such trash been given and received as truth. To contravane such statements I am here from yonder blissful home, to show a world of humans better things than have hitherto been dealt out to all humanity.

Q. Is the Bible statement of your walking on the water a truth?

A. My Brother let me ask you, does Nature ever suspend her laws for any special purpose? if such is true and man, reliant on them as he is, what dire confusion must ensue; in all of Deity's arrangements may be seen order and regularity no man can imitate. It far exceeds his calibre of intellect and if used in proper manner, smooths his path and gives him confidence in all that appertains to Spirit Life by such assurance as his angel friends have given him of life beyond the grave. But I have wandered somewhat from my subject, my walking on the water. Can such an act, so far beyond the power of man, be deemed as possible, unaided by some artificial means? It is not the element prepared for man to tread upon. No power that he posesses can supercede the law of gravitation and keep him on the surface safe from drowning. And here we ask again, are Nature's laws suspended, or have they ever been? They being immutable can never change. The man who waits for such a change in times of peril, must surely perish, unless impelled by sense of danger he puts forth the strong right arm to save himself, the means he has within his nature he must use, and doing so may perhaps escape the danger, or perchance a passing stranger impelled by intuition of some guardian spirit, to obey the natural impulse of his manhood, hazards his own to save another's life. Such possibly was the case with me. Complaint I might have heard, and impelled by Nature's bidding, I forgot all self and sprang to rescue one, who lacking moral courage, had lost the power to save himself.

Q. 'Do you speak of this as a remembered fact?

A. No, my Brother, but merely give these reasons to remove the erratic show of miracles which were meant no doubt to make the statement more impressive on the minds of those who advocate the marvellous in preference to more substantial truth. To me it seems but loss of time to say more npon a subject that common sense can test correctly.

Q. Did Thomas place his hand within the wound inflicted in your side, to overcome his unbelief?

A. This is a question based on mere surmise, for who could see the act performed. Has mortal vision ever seen a spirit? Do you not say it is invisible? and here you speak the truth. Was not Thomas an embodied spirit having no clarivoyant powers but simple sight as others, and if so what credence can you give to such a statement? No proof corroborating it, but a mere assertion of the fact. Would reason, if consulted, readily accept the statement? In the superstitious ages of the past, and even now, the marvellous is far more readily accepted than a well authenticated truth. But whether the fact is proved or not it little matters; no important issue can be realized by the imputed act of Thomas, more than any other man, and with this remark we will leave the subject for a world's decision of its truth or falsity.

Q. Did you delegate to Peter the right to act as Apostolic Head of the Church or Pope, as claimed by the Romish Church?

A. My Brother, based as that Church is upon the most egregious falsehoods ever framed by ignorance and sheer assurance, both combined, what right had I to make appointment for a single moment, much more for future times that now have passed away, joined with which, what motive could I have for interfering in a matter altogether foreign to my own desires? Jews and Gentiles all I loved as members of one common family. It was all humanity I came to benefit, no sect or party did I choose, but the one great human family did I claim as being worthy my attention. No superiority of creed I ever recognized, feeling convinced that Charity should be the guiding star of all professing Christians. With such a guide no sect or creed could claim superiority. The general welfare of the race will mark the genuine Christian's conduct. No mother church will claim a Peter for its head, a situation never sought by him, preferring to remain a follower of mine. Humble as the station was yet was it preferred by him. The Roman Church may claim him as their prototype of Popes to strengthen their assumptive claim to primitive superority notwithstanding.

My mission here on earth has nothing worldly in its character, other than man's improvement in ethereal knowledge. Law and Nature are the guides I recognize, and for this special purpose I am here to use thy organism, by inspiring thee to write such thoughts as seem to come intuitively to the many, who from lack of apprehension lose the benefit thereof. In this they are not blameable, while pity oft we feel and fain would strive to raise their comprehension to a higher standard than yet they have exhibited. Surrounded as they are with worldly pomp, they try, but try in vain, to grasp successfully the truth we would present to them. With dull encircled eyes they peer beyond the range of mortal vision to seek the far beyond, of which they may have heard, but could not recognize, and this may terminate their search. Not finding what they have sought they become discouraged and abandon what they deem a useless task; are not millions thus impressed? Therefore need it be deemed a marvel that your halls are empty, your efforts to maintain societies are all abortive. My brother your present status in this city stands a monument of carelessness, the sad result of what we have named. The great and glorious work of man's redemption may be slow, and many years may pass before success may be attained, *notwithstanding the saving power ascribed to me*, but does it follow God has lost his power, or that Nature falters in her course? We wot it cannot be. Man may scoff and call it a delusion, but where's the proof it is so? Spiritualism in all its grandeur still is flourishing; its brightening rays are giving light in all directions, opening the flood gates of investigation, making man a wiser and morally a better creature, more ready to accept of angel teachings,eschewing Vice,and taking into close enbrace the all of Virtue, making this lower world an almost Paradise, better fitted for the growth of Virtue, standing as she is with uplift foot in readiness to crush the incipient growth of Vice in all its varied forms of base depravity.

With such a prospect, who can doubt that Spiritualism, with all its grand and noble principles, will be raised to such a glorious altitude that those who hitherto have deemed it dead, will in astonishment look around to find its compeer. With God to give it sanction, need it fear what man can do? In maddened frenzy he may scoff and threaten but sustained by angel power the Spiritualist can laugh to scorn the superstitious ignorance of a world almost engulfed in the maelstrom vortex of Fanaticisms.

And here we'll close our essay, giving our medium rest, and hastening forward to some other place and people needing our instruction. Adieu. AMEN.

KING DAVID'S RESPONSE AND CONFESSION.

AT last my ardent expectations may be fulfilled, and I released from bondage most revolting to a soul that has so long yearned to leave a place but illy fitted for such aspirations as mine puts forth for that deliverance I often hear of others gaining; yet my especial case seems to be a marvel, and alone in misery I have dwelt, year after year, and century after century, expecting change and yet relief came not to me! With weeping eyes and outstretched hands I have implored forgiveness of my sins, yet no confession could I make; all seemed dark and gloomy to me, and constant silence there continuing, my ambition seemed inert and useless to me; the energy of former ages seemed to leave me, when at times the thoughts of what I once had been would stir me up to action, and with all the efforts I could make I strove to speak, but that had failed me, and every trial proved unsuccessful, leaving me a poor discontented being. Yet hope would sometimes flit across my brain, and once again give courage to my sinking and desponding soul to still hope on. Eternity was mine as well as others. Sinful, perchance, as I had been, yet governed and directed by better and holier impulses, they had sought relief by ventilation of a sinful life on earth, made all the compensation in their power, whilst I, with all my earthly pride unchanged, continued an unyielding advocate of by-gone habits, yet altogether powerless in every attempt I made to practice them.

What would I give to abrogate the recollection of my life on earth, and sink in deep oblivion scenes, the mere remembrance of, has often made me shudder to admit myself their perpetrator. Oh, how often has the blush of shame and terror mantled on my cheek at thinking of the record made of "The God chosen of my race," "The man after God's own heart," and other statements equally untrue.

A lie more foul was never uttered, blasphemous

in its purport, wicked and profane in its utterance, producing a reaction in the minds of men while thinking of their God.

With deep humility I now look back upon those times with feelings more allied to horror than aught else, for the sun of Heaven has never shone upon a greater sinner than he who now is prompting you. I fain would now make full confession of my crimes, yet what compensation can I make, bereft as I, and all of mortal birth must find themselves on entering Spirit Life, with nothing left to compensate, but by penitence and truthful prayer may ask relief, but no forgiveness can I seek, for that I know to be impossible. All the sins committed while on earth must be admitted and repented ere thou cans't become an aspirant for mercy from thy God, who will yield accordance to thy needs, if sought in spirit and in truth.

But to my confession: All my acts have been recorded by a pen unused by other than myself, and that, a record never known or seen by any one of earth, of past or present times, but those unseen by you have looked upon them and know the every item there contained.

To those who doubt, the fact may soon be known, aye, sooner than expected by them, and then with sad regrets like mine, deplore the recklessness they have evinced, when warning after warning has been given them to have their record ready. My

Brother, some may laugh and ridicule such statements as these I now am making. The scrutinizing glance of angel eyes is now upon them. Death may now be in close attendance on them; the dark and dismal grave may now be yawning to receive them, and what have they to comfort them? The icy hand of death perchance has clutched them, producing chills and terrors they had little expectation of.

Little further must I say upon a subject all must yet experience. Death, the grand leveller of all things mundane, making no distinction whether rich or poor, black or white, we are *his*, who by nature's promptings places each where attraction aided by the law of gravitation may direct him. But, my Brother, such delay may lead you to suppose me somewhat reluctant to make the promised confession, therefore in humblest mood I will now present the facts as best I can.

Let me ask you am I a murderer because under law I take another's life in retribution of a sinful act committed? Does that act constitute me a murderer in the sight of God? If avarice be a crime I am not innocent. Can a man who cheats his neighbor claim the badge of honesty? Of this I have been accused, and still must bear the odium. Can lewd obscenity of conduct be deemed other than a crime? I will not deny its earthly practice.

Following out the same idea, for they are all connected, Adultery, Fornication, and all those base concomitants clustering around each other, as kindred sentiments, working towards one common center (*man's almost total-ruin*). If this be true, and overwhelmed as I have been with such, my case must be beyond retrieval.

Anon, methinks I hear an Angel whisper "Thou art not lost, for *thee* there still is mercy flowing from that fount eternal," meandering from its source down through its mazy windings into the receptive soul, that like yourself aspires to gain it.

Cheer up, nor yield one tittle of the ambition now bestirring thee; withhold no portion of the confession thou wouldst make; clear thy breast of all that can disturb thy mind or mar thy holy purpose in becoming an aspirant for that change thy soul so yearns for. With such encouragement I am here, and once again resume confession of the many sins committed by me while on earth.

Fearing I may tire you with too long a detail, I shall endeavor to abbreviate as much as possible my further statements. Fear and dread of public scrutiny prevents the perpetration of crimes of deepest dye, such as would make the blood run cold to think of. From such I am not exempt, and many and many a victim to the basest tyranny has fallen by my hand.

'S hatred to his child forms another

feature in my acts of sinfulness; that Child I once had loved with all a father's tenderness became a thing of hate to me, and the love I once had borne him became as poison to me; everything he said and did was chronicled within my fevered brain as promise of a means by which I might destroy him; if in battle he was seen in rear of others, if present, I would send him to the front, feeling assured his danger was more imminent, and thus his death might save me further trouble.

But still an over-ruling power seemed ever present to protect him. At length a battle being fought, in which my son was conquered, by rapid flight he sought to save himself. In hottest haste he was pursued; to avoid being captured he took refuge in a neighboring wood; the branches hanging low and he being helmetless, his long and flowing hair became entangled in the low hanging branches, and thus suspended in fearful agony, he yielded up the life his God had given him. Thus I became his murderer. Can such a crime as this receive forgiveness? And yet the so-called sacred record accuses God of doing the self-same act. But here the difference lies; God being omniscient does what he pleases, and this cruel and erroneous statement, uttered by men who know the law, denouncing murder as a crime, is as binding on the enactor of the law as upon his creature, man. But does the suppositious crime ascribed to

Deity exonorate me from the crime of premeditated murder? Oh, no, my brother; the canker-worm of guilt is ever gnawing at my vitals, rendering even spirit-life a burthen, preferring annihilation to obliviate the anguished recollection of my crimes. "The man after God's own heart." Can such avowal become accepted by men of common sense and truthfulness? To such it must seem blasphemy, indeed? Oh, that I had the power to expunge that record from the world's remembrance; methinks it would pluck one throb of torture from my anguished soul.

But, in conclusion, the men of God, as they are called, and founders of a faith called "Christianity," professing to be followers of the meek and lowly Jesus, may have the power to assume the name, without the inclination to adopt his principles. Such appears to be the condition of that church at present, but a change must come o'er all things, and in that direction will be seen a renovated Christian Church, free from blighting pride, which now suffuses the majority, with principles at war with Jesus' teachings of humility, so beautifully exemplified by him in every thought and act. And here I close my essay, grateful as I feel to him who has transcribed with strict fidelity my prompted thoughts. AMEN.

JOSEPHUS.

FREE from prejudice and all that appertains thereto, I am here, my Brother, far from my very distant home, in respondence to thy call. Justice to all is the motto I assume, nor crave one moment's credence to aught else but manifest truth.

My Brother, if thou hast any doubts of my being a truthful spirit, give me that so-called sacred Bible, and I'll swear upon its leaves I am all I represent myself. Art thou satisfied 'tis even so? I am, My Brother, thy oath I'll not exact. Heaven bless thee for that mark of generous confidence in one who must be to thee a total stranger. Would it not seem a marvel to give thine invitation to one so distant from thee, and then, by doubting, cast me off as one unworthy of thy credence? History speaks of me in better terms; yet history is not always truthful, therefore, thou art right in asking such a test, which, at this moment I am ready to comply with. Knowing my own truthfulness, and feeling I have thy confidence, I will endeavor to repay it by utterances of facts no one can contradict, for truths I'll give in such ungarbled manner, that your mind and that of others who may read these lines will have no doubt about it.

And here I'll take my stand: whether the world credits me or not it little matters; the truthful soul within me flatters no one to gain applause or popularity. But of this enough ; my path is plain before me ; no side issues shall I seek to make my statement one deserving credence.

Do you require solution of a special subject? My Brother, I answer no, I will not give thee one, but if thou canst divine the one I would have chosen, I shall be gratified: if not, pursue the course most satisfactory to thyself.

My Brother, I would have preferred thy utterance of the subject, for underlying thy remarks, it seems thou still must doubt. Well, be it so; 'tis perhaps, a fair and equitable test indirectly demanded.

The question has often been asked: If Jesus was and is a living, real entity?" because so seldom named in history, called profane. Wherein profanity is shown I cannot see. My own, for instance, often there is placed. God and his angels, too, may scrutinize my works, and no profane expression can they find ; not a word or sentence immoral in its character. Why, then, speak of it in such a manner? Take my work or works in uncorrected form, and place them close beside the *infallible Word of God*, the pride and boast of millions who call themselves its devotees, and ask them which they choose, that Bible soon would carry off the palm of victory, with all its faults, with all its lewd obscenities, its defamation of a good and gracious God, making him a cruel and vindictive being, creating a world of humans unasked by them. Nay, forced by nature's laws into a world of sin and misery apparently without other guide or director but that fabricated book which few can comprehend. Hence, so many sects founding a superstitious creed no one can say is quite correct, for men of sense and learning to waste their time upon, and that of others seeking to become authors, and thereby mystify the thoughts of well-intentioned men, seems a refinement upon cruelty almost amounting to atrocity; for the man who attempts to poison and corrupt the avenues of human thought, does that he never can retrieve. The mind of man in its untutored state often lacks the power to reject the wily snares which priest-craft lays within his path, to catch the unwary sons and daughters of humanity; watching a favorable opportunity of some unguarded moment, they cast before their feeble minds great inducements to become members of their churches. Alas! farewell to liberty of thought, of conscience! within the net they hold them, freedom being a thing unknown to them and seldom practiced by them. No fiction can be seen in what we say; the world has long acknowledged it, therefore denial by any of the several sects would be unseemly, rather injuring than forwarding a cause having no foundation to sustain its superstructure.

Here then we'll end our stricture and commence the subject you have proffered, asking: Was Jesus an actual living entity?

My Brother, little have I ever said upon this subject, and it would have been much better had others been as careful as myself; yet I claim that merit, when exhibited, should have its meed of praise in like proportion as that merit turned in right direction; for, by its proper application, the world at large might be improved. Such result we find eliminating from the teachings of the man called Jesus, of humble parentage, having no peculiar prestige other than his humility of character, evidently wrapped in deep devotion to the cause of all humanity.

The world became attracted to one whose soul's best impulses were ever ready to assist the sufferer in distress, to share his pittance with the needy, to uplift a fallen sister or a brother to a higher standing in society; ever self-abnegating, just and true in all his several dealings with his fellow-man. Unsinister in all he said and did, could one like him remain long unnoticed? and such a man was Jesus, who by virtue of his acts was well entitled to the soubriquet of Christ—the man Christ Jesus, and here you see the name reversed, showing conclusively a man so pure and holy as he was, deserved a higher, holier name than Jesus, Christ being deemed synonymous with every principle of goodness, assimilating him more closely with the nature of his father, God. Why such a man was overlooked and little noticed, we scarce can comprehend, unless the high encomiums passed upon him, led a fanatic priesthood to make avowal of his God-head ; hoping to become more noticed by the masses, they in deep fanaticism feigned to call him Jesus Christ, the Savior of the world, unsanctioned by himself, his deep humility controlling him. Having brought the Jewish mind into or under a wild excitement, reaction eventually took place and he who had been by priestly fervor made an almost God, became the victim of a base and murderous multitude. An event like this in priestly hands became a lever by which to raise themselves to favor and importance with the most cruel-minded of the Jewish nation whose prosperity had ever been baptized in blood. Hence the cry "Crucify him, crucify him," and demanding the release of Barrabas. Can you conceive it possible that a man like Pontius Pilate, high in office as he was, could so boldly have used hypocrisy to please the bloodhounds of the time, by giving them a choice between Barrabas and the meek and humble being who stood in bended attitude awaiting their decision.

O, cruel mockery of justice! thus assumed to cover o'er the coward heart that beat within a breast most foul and noisome, more fit to occupy a place within the bosom of a fiend incarnate or murderous assassin. Every hour of torment then endured by him, (the victim of their treachery,) will need a compensation, which, if paid in full, would make bankrupt of a universe and casting back to chaos the fragments of a world having no parallel, unique in all that appertains to nature's works, the very acme of eternal wisdom.

My Brother such harrowing thoughts as now oppress my brain, while thinking of that cruel and unneeded act, are almost maddening in effect; making me feel almost antagonistic to the God who suffered such a profanation of misguided power. Yet, Reason asks, how know you it was so? Have I or any being the power to scan the acts of Deity? How know we He had sanctioned such an act? Yet He who has the power to prevent and does not use it, seems to give sanction to the act.

Let us scan this subject somewhat closely. God being the source from whence all power proceeds, metes out that power to those who, seemingly, are fitted to dispense to others the needed means of governing those committed to their care, from the highest potentate upon the throne to the lowest specimen of his creation in this vast universe of His. Hence, each and every one possessing it, has given to them instructions how to use it, which being immutable as every law of God must be; yet man by sad perversion abrogates the law and thus makes God appear to sanction or permit such acts as make the blood run cold and humans almost curse their day of advent on your earth.

Oh, my Brother, the present state of things seems so anomalous, giving such evidence of base ingratitude to that God whose forbearance is a marvel to those who know Him as He is and ever has been, the friend of all who seek his aid in spirit and in truth, making the path a pleasant one by the adaptation of each and every soul whatever its condition may be, whether under torture or privation, His loving agents will be there to give of consolation all it needs. If under the painful grip of poverty, food would be supplied by evoking through angel agency some pure and holy being, seeking some worthy object on whom to bestow His charity. Thus are God's bounties sometimes well dispensed. He gives in bounteous measure: not stinting any one designedly; but treating all alike, yet many in this extended universe suffer most severely. Often have the apparently wisest projects failed for want of faithful agents; thus is world-wide suffering and affliction brought about by means the most far-sighted mind had no power to guard against. Perversion may be deemed an element of greatest injury to the entire human family; destroying all of confidence between man and man and making God a doubted benefactor; whilst His every thought is directed to man's happiness here and in the coming future.

Have I not said enough to prove beyond all cavil that Jesus was an actual, living entity? Giving up his natural life to prove his mission was a holy one, as many martyrs of more recent date have done, fearless of the licking flames surrounding them, have uttered words of sheer defiance to their persecutors? Not so that meek and lowly being, whose friends on earth being few, made no parade, but meekly submitted to his fate; a willing victim to a law he had from sense of duty impinged upon. No murmur escaped those truthful lips, till in agony intense, in almost abberated state of mind, he exclaimed: "My God my God! why hast Thou forsaken me?" When almost instantaneously some angel influence called forth an appeal to God, his Father, to forgive his enemies, they not knowing what they did. This, then, may be deemed the crowning period of his chequered life; forgiveness sought for those who had thirsted for his blood; taking from him all he had to lose, translating him from earth even to the highest heavens; not to plead for pardon at the hands of God, not to advocate an unrighteous cause, not to ask a thing impossible, for crime cannot be pardoned or forgiven, but must be compensated; not in a prescribed time, but having an eternity before them they hope redemption may be theirs, for their victim bore no malice, but, in return for their vindictiveness comes back again to earth, teaching the ignorant and superstitious denizens of earth a better, holier doctrine, giving strength and vigor to its advocates who, by angel power implanted in their receptive natures, can impart to others the secrets of ethereal life, before unknown to them, proving, beyond all doubt, the existence of another, better world beyond, typified, to some extent, by this lower world of yours, where spirits live continuously, and, at times, return as I, at present have, to hold communion with and through such organisms as thine own.

My Brother, dost thou ever feel thyself as giving that to mortals which they scarce can comprehend? Does thy confidence in spirit power become diminished? And art thou often disappointed? To this thy answer must be no; and having such proofs of punctuality, the Law of Reciprocity is truly strengthened, making prompter and transcriber mutually satisfied with their work of harmony and love. AMEN.

HOME.

My Beloved Friend: Your theme is beautiful, engendering much of thought; for, present it as you will, it excites the feelings of humanity, and seems to thrill the very soul with ecstacy. Talk of Home to the mariner on the shore of some far off country; note the workings of that man's countenance; every muscle of his face in active motion, with the unbidden tear of sympathy coursing down his sunburnt cheek, emblematic of the deep-seated feelings of affection for the absent loved ones. Oh, could that tear speak the workings of his soul, moved, as it seems, in all its hidden recesses by impulses which nought but the awakened reminiscences of home could possibly evolve, showing that within the breast of that storm tossed mariner there existed a well-spring of the purest affections humanity possesses.

Home seems to be his watchword. During the silent hours of the midnight watch, when all nature seems hushed in quiet slumber, his thoughts are traveling with lightning speed, seeking communion with those who are the objects of his holiest love; so entwined around his heart that although mute, yet an inner spirit-commune is going on between them. And thus those hours of apparent solitude are passed. Shall we call it solitude? Oh, no; for then and there, although unseen by mortal vision, stands the spirits of these loved ones, drawn thither by the attractive principle of divine and holy love, giving to the supposed loved ones those beautiful imaginings of wished-for scenes as intuitions of his mind, producing that calm and tranquil influence which strengthens his faith in spirit commune, and brings him almost in rapport with his God. How many persons speak of Home without being able to define its meaning, or what constitutes a home. Indeed we feel it somewhat difficult, and with us formidable. Perhaps, the best and safest course is to give our own experience of a Home whilst in the form. Home is, and is not a mere locality, in the common usage of the term; for when we speak of Home, we generally refer to the dwelling we either possess or constantly occupy. But, as I view it, every place we use as a domicile where we seek happiness and contentment should be such. It is not the mere house, location, or neighborhood, but the association, the combination, and clusterings of all the affectional in nature. The interchange of loving words, expressing glowing sentiments so exquisite in their character as to elevate the soul, enabling us to impart to others a portion of those joys we are wont to revel in ourselves.

The constant reciprocity of thought in all the circumstances of life, evokes anxiety to be happy, by and through our own impulses; to throw open wide the doors of hospitality, and by our conduct towards our guests, awaken in their souls an affinitizing element, which, when absent, shall remind them of us as dear and valued friends.

But my friend, these are but the *outward* necessities to form a Home. We would speak of that Home on which is predicated our hopes of happiness—the social adaptation of man and woman as husband and wife. What can successfully compete with two individuals whose connubial happiness is based upon mutual respect, which has, and is continually ripening into that love which is of divine origin, being of God, never varying, but ever constant, and undying in its character? Not that evanescent, worthless passion upon which the majority of married persons base their hopes of bliss in that uncertain state. O misery untold! the wreck of happiness from such a cause.

Have they a Home? O, no; in the truest sense they have no Home; 'tis to them a desert, with no green spot upon it—a dreary, miserable waste, from which we turn with joyous feeling to such as have exhibited more wisdom, or who, have fortunately, been guided less by passion, and thus escaped the charybdis of destruction, becoming the approved of men and angels. Here, then, is a nucleus Home. When blessed with those heaven-born pledges of affection, ever greeted as such by the true father and mother, then does the dwelling we have described assume the features of a Home, indeed; increasing the propriety of such appellation as each day develops some improvement mentally and physically, in those beauteous inmates of their happy Home. Thus, then, from day to day the parents look with hope to a period when the expansion of their youthful minds requires much and incessant care in checking the unruly passions and desires of youth, so as to fit them as useful members of that society which draws them, as it were, within its folds by all the allurements suited to satisfy their eager minds; who, if not guided by some loving spirit, may yet be wrecked upon the shoals of dire adversity before they have yet given a single thought to that most important consideration—of a heavenly Home celestially prepared. Here, then, is what we would call a *culminated* Home, tendered to mortality as a boon inestimable, a Home for all, eternal in its duration, no mutation, but one continuous round of happiness unalloyed by aught of suffering. A Home of universal usefulness; where the principle of brotherly love dictates every movement; where holy and divine impulses governs all and everything, making it a place of rest to the weary, a place of progression to the seeker after truth, and a finality to which all mankind should endeavor to attain; being open to all, exclusive to none, who are attracted thither; but to the unrighteous, altogether repulsive so long as they continue disobedient to those laws which govern the disembodied occupants of the Summer Land. AMEN.

SPIRITUALISM OPPOSED BY SKEPTICISM.

NOTHING can be more mortifying to a true Spiritualist than the unmerited sarcasms and revilings of those who oppose the doctrine; being ignorant themselves, conceive all others are the same, and particularly such as are impressed to utter sayings much beyond their comprehension, eliciting severe and unjust criticism of the various promptings given through you and other mediums in the shape of Angel Essays—so condemned almost without a reading, and then pronounced a humbug.

Is there aught of fairness in the matter, oft censuring you as the mere amanuensis of our thoughts; performing your duty faithfully; transcribing to benefit humanity? Is aught of justice here exhibited? Can reason give endorsement to the practice? We opine not; hence all perplexity with you should cease.

Let all the world condemn them ; they still will stand as monuments of truthful promptings from the Spirit World. No effort will be made to persuade a single soul to accept them other than as being messages from the ethereal spheres.

Superstitious bigots and perverters of the truth must lay aside their unmeaning dogmas, and embrace such truths as angels from the brighter realms are willing to present to them as worthy of their best attention.

All hail! we say to modern spiritualism; thy glories (as yet but partially exhibited,) will fill the entire world with great rejoicing, as being the harbinger of bliss unutterable, in realms as yet unknown to mortals,each day and hour comes teeming with intelligence such as but few are prepared to comprehend, but which, in time, by angel guidance must be received as truth, no man can contravene.

Who, then, need falter on the road? With angels to instruct you can ye make mistakes? Oh, no, thy sight will be improved, thy power renewed to overcome the obstacles raised to check thy purpose. Thy angel friends will watch thy progress, and every obstacle being removed as on eaglet's wings, thou wilt seem to travel towards thy eternal destiny, where thou wilt be received with genial smiles, and outstretched hands extended as a welcome to thee. Cans't thou doubt this fact, Oh, Sceptic; can'st thou shut thine eyes and ears to facts so palpably presented to thy senses by coming spirits, seeking those who need assurance of Ethereal Life being theirs? With all the love we bear humanity; with all the angelic energy possessed by us, we would entreat thee to embrace the glorious doctrine, sent to tell thee of the grand hereafter, which thou may'st call thy own; for by seeking thou can'st find it, and, when found, it is thine to hold forever; no power can wrest it from thee, being thine by virtue of obedience to the laws of God and nature.

Oh, that the time had come when Spiritualism, with all its brilliant scintillations of a glorious epoch was arrived, to lead the truthful ambition of the sceptic student to investigate its glorious truth; when the beatifying influences may work within the souls of men and women; when righteousness and truth may so pervade their natures, that vice and crime shall flee your presence, and joy and gladness smile on every countenance.

For this purpose are these essays given, in fullest hope they may prove salutary to those who need them; "for seeking ye shall find." Then we implore ye do so while time and opportunity is yours; lose not the precious moments given you; use them diligently; needful as it is, for, time being uncertain, demands attention to its fleeting movements; a brief delay may produce unheard of difficulties in the way of that improvement needed. Let this conviction fasten on your soul, and soon you'll see its grand importance. The present is the time; delay, short as it may be, may lead to untold misery. Life is quite uncertain; eternity is ever ready to receive you.

With feelings of most kindly import, we would close our essay, hoping the thoughts contained within it may be received as they are given—in holy love and friendship, brought by loving spirits who have but gone before to make preparation for your advent into the Ethereal Realms beyond your present ken, where love and gratitude will rise to God, your Father—in fine, where dwell those kindred spirits once your earthly companions, *now* your angel friends and directors on your journey home. For this purpose are these Essays published. May they under the divine and holy influence of our Father, God, be realized by all mankind. AMEN.

www.ingramcontent.com/pod-product-compliance
Lightning Source LLC
LaVergne TN
LVHW020112110826
845151LV00001B/130

* 9 7 8 1 4 2 5 5 4 3 1 7 4 *